Ethnicity on the Great Plains

Books by Frederick C. Luebke

Immigrants and Politics: The Germans of Nebraska, 1880–1900 (1969)

Ethnic Voters and the Election of Lincoln (1971), edited

Bonds of Loyalty: German Americans in World War I (1974)

The Great Plains: Environment and Culture (1979), edited with Brian W. Blouet

Ethnicity on the Great Plains

EDITED BY
Frederick C. Luebke

Published by the
UNIVERSITY OF NEBRASKA PRESS • LINCOLN AND LONDON
for the
CENTER FOR GREAT PLAINS STUDIES
University of Nebraska–Lincoln

Library of Congress Cataloging in Publication Data
Main entry under title:

Ethnicity on the Great Plains.

    Papers originally presented at a symposium sponsored by the Center for Great Plains Studies, University of Nebraska-Lincoln.
    Includes index.
    1. Minorities—Great Plains—History—Congresses. 2. Great Plains—Civilization—Congresses. I. Luebke, Frederick C., 1927- II. University of Nebraska-Lincoln. Center for Great Plains Studies.
F596.2.E86   978   79-17743
ISBN 0-8032-2855-4

To Norma

Contents

Preface   ix

Introduction, *by Frederick C. Luebke*   xi

Historical Approaches to the Study of Rural Ethnic
    Communities, *by Kathleen Neils Conzen*   1

The Great Plains as a Colonization Zone for
    Eastern Indians, *by Arrell Morgan Gibson*   19

Touching the Pen: Plains Indian Treaty Councils in
    Ethnohistorical Perspective, *by Raymond J. DeMallie*   38

Plainsmen of Three Continents: Volga German
    Adaptation to Steppe, Prairie, and Pampa,
    by Timothy J. Kloberdanz   54

Prairie Bound: Migration Patterns to a Swedish
    Settlement on the Dakota Frontier,
    by Robert C. Ostergren   73

The Old Order Amish on the Great Plains: A Study
    in Cultural Vulnerability, *by John A. Hostetler*   92

A Religious Geography of the Hill Country Germans
    of Texas, *by Terry G. Jordan*   109

Folk Religion as Ideology for Ethnic Survival: The
    Hungarians of Kipling, Saskatchewan, *by Linda Dégh*   129

Czech-American Freethinkers on the Great Plains,
    1871–1914, *by Bruce M. Garver*   147

Agricultural Change among Nebraska Immigrants,
    1880–1900, *by Bradley H. Baltensperger*   170

Land, Labor, and Community in Nueces: Czech
    Farmers and Mexican Laborers in South Texas,
    1880–1930, *by Josef J. Barton*   190

Ethnic Assimilation and Pluralism in Nebraska, *by J.*
    Allen Williams, Jr., David R. Johnson, and
    Miguel A. Carranza   210

The Contributors   231

Index   233

Preface

The essays presented here were originally prepared for presentation at the second annual symposium sponsored by the Center for Great Plains Studies, which is an interdisciplinary agency of the University of Nebraska–Lincoln for the coordination of research, teaching, and service activities contributing to an understanding of the Great Plains. The symposium attracted the participation of anthropologists, folklorists, geographers, historians, linguists, and sociologists, as well as students of literature and architecture. They came from many parts of the United States, Canada, and Europe, including Germany, Norway, Sweden, and the United Kingdom.

The response of scholars to the center's call for papers revealed an unexpected richness of research into ethnicity on the Great Plains. Even though the conference was enlarged to accommodate the presentation of thirty-three papers, many worthy proposals could not be accepted. At the same time, there was a dearth of proposals treating certain topics, such as ethnic political behavior, and important ethnic groups, such as the blacks. Inevitably, therefore, this book cannot provide a comprehensive view of its subject. Instead it samples contemporary research and suggests possibilities for further work.

The essays selected for publication in this volume were chosen on the basis of several criteria. I have sought to maintain a balance among the academic disciplines, the ethnic groups treated, and the subregions within the Great Plains. I also tended to select papers that treat numerically larger rather than smaller groups, studies that relate the characteristics of the physical environment to patterns of either persistence or accommodation of ethnic culture, and, finally, essays that analyze intergroup conflicts or make comparisons between two or more ethnic groups. Several papers treating the ethnic literature of the Great Plains will appear in a future volume to be published by the Center for Great Plains Studies.

Many persons, in addition to the authors whose essays are published here, contributed to the making of this book. I am especially indebted to the members of the symposium committee: Stephen Cox, Dale Gibbs, Elaine Jahner, Paul Olson, Paul Schach, Joseph Svoboda, Ralph Vigil, Allen Williams, Susan Welch, Roger Welsch, and David Wishart. They were unfailingly helpful, wise in counsel, and deliberate in judgment. Max Larsen, dean of the College of Arts and Sciences, Paul Olson, the first director of the Center for Great Plains Studies, and Janet Pieper, administrative assistant, supported the project in every way possible. The Department of History of the University of Nebraska-Lincoln also lent its aid. To all I extend my sincere thanks. Finally, I wish to express my gratitude to the Newberry Library of Chicago for the fellowship that enabled me to use that institution's exceptional resources to complete a major part of my editorial task.

FREDERICK C. LUEBKE

Introduction

Frederick C. Luebke

Immigrants from Europe formed a major element in the population that settled the Great Plains in the nineteenth century; their descendants constitute the majority of persons in many parts of the region today. A century ago, as the agricultural frontier moved across central Nebraska onto what is considered the Great Plains, foreign-born persons consistently formed a much larger proportion of the inhabitants on the western edge of settlement than they did in the state as a whole. Some years later the census of 1890 revealed that in North Dakota, for example, 42.7 percent of the population of that newly admitted state was foreign-born, easily the highest proportion for any state in the Union. According to the census of 1970, immigrants and their children still account for 22.7 percent of North Dakota's population, and in ten of the state's fifty-three counties the proportion exceeds 30 percent.[1]

Although many students of American literature will find such data validated by impressions gathered from the works of Ole Röl-vaag, Willa Cather, Mari Sandoz, and other writers, most scholars seem unfamiliar with the importance of ethnicity for the history of the Great Plains. Through the years, state and local historical journals have published many articles, usually written by amateurs, that recount the settlement of various immigrant groups on the plains, but most professionally trained historians have tended to ignore ethnic history and to concentrate on traditional political and economic issues. Some, no doubt, have been influenced by Walter Prescott Webb, who observed in his widely read book, *The Great Plains* (1931), that European immigrants, as well as blacks and Asians, avoided the Great Plains, especially in the southwest, and left the region to old-stock Americans of English and Scottish ancestry. Carl Kraenzel, a sociologist whose *Great Plains in Transition* was published in 1955, described the racial and ethnic minorities of the region in one brief chapter, but concluded that "factors of race, nationality, and religion" played "only a small part" in accounting for the minority groups of the region. Instead, Kraenzel defined his minorities in economic or occupational terms and emphasized that such groups lacked the techniques needed to control their own economic affairs. Recent journalistic treatments of the Great Plains either ignore ethnicity as a variable in human affairs or treat distinctive groups as curiosities.[2]

The explanation for this failure to incorporate ethnicity into studies of the Great Plains region lies chiefly in the ideas scholars have used to organize their work. Regional studies are naturally conceived in spatial terms; that is, they are founded in the notion that a region has fairly distinct boundaries encompassing uniform physiographic characteristics, such as climate, topography, and soils, that require the inhabitants to act in certain ways or at least within certain limits. Cultural adaptation to the dictates of the physical environment thus becomes tantamount to a successful inhabitation of the region. The scholar may thus be disposed to assume, for example, that all farmers in Rawlins County, which is located in northwestern Kansas and extensively populated by the descendants of German-Hungarian, Swedish, and Czech immigrants, adapted to the environment in much the same way, regardless of ethnocultural origin.[3]

Cultural historians, folklorists, linguists, and other scholars interested in the maintenance of immigrant forms are likely to come to opposite conclusions. They tend to recognize and interpret evidence indicating that newcomers to the plains, either native- or foreign-born, successfully sustained important elements of their culture despite the corrosive effects of the harsh and unyielding environment. Spatial relationships and peculiarities of place are usually not central to their inquiry; instead they attach primary importance to the character and quality of a culture and to the time of its importation into a given area. From this point of view one should expect the patterns of culture on the Great Plains to be mere extensions of what may be found in Minnesota, Wisconsin, and Iowa in the north, and Arkansas, Louisiana, and Tennessee in the south. Thus, North Dakota's 42.7 percent foreign-born in 1890 compares to Minnesota's 35.7 percent, just as the 6.8 percent recorded for Texas is similar to Louisiana's 4.4 percent.[4] In the conceptual framework used by the culturalists, the Great Plains naturally lose significance as a region or even as a viable unit for study. The culturalists have tended to slight the unique physiographic and historical characteristics of the Great Plains in much the same way that environmentalists have tended to ignore the presence of substantial ethnic populations in the region.

Scholars also perceive boundaries in different ways. The environmentalist more than the culturalist is likely to delineate space. This may be seen in exaggerated form in the work of Walter Prescott Webb, who compared the eastern edge of the Great Plains, which he placed in the vicinity of the 98th meridian, to a geological fault line. Few students of ethnicity, however, would see meaningful distinctions based on subtle physiographical differences. The setting of Ole Rölvaag's novel about Norwegian settlers in southeast South Dakota, located east of the 98th meridian, is almost indistinguishable from that described by Willa Cather for the Czechs near Red Cloud, Nebraska, located west of Webb's cultural fault. Popular writers are especially unconcerned by the problem. One merely observes that on the east the Great Plains are bounded by the weather; another expands the region to include Minnesota, Iowa, and Missouri.[5]

The northern and southern boundaries of the Great Plains province are also difficult to define. Some scholars include at the southern end little more than the Texas Panhandle; others extend the region south to the Balcones Escarpment, thereby including the Edwards Plateau and the German Hill Country; still others continue to the Gulf of Mexico and add the semiarid, treeless plains that lie between the Nueces River and the Rio Grande. Similarly, in the north the plains do not halt at the Canadian border, but encompass vast stretches of prairie in Manitoba, Saskatchewan, and Alberta. Some scholars end the Canadian plains where the forests begin, but others extend the physiographic province to the Arctic Ocean.[6]

Because this book treats cultural rather than environmental topics, it follows that a broad definition of the Great Plains region should be adopted. The essays included here therefore range from Linda Dégh's study of Hungarians in Saskatchewan to Robert Ostergren's analysis of Swedish settlement in southeastern South Dakota and to Josef Barton's comparison of Czech and Mexican patterns of culture in Nueces County, Texas. In the case of other essays it is most appropriate to speak, not of the Great Plains *region*, but of the Great Plains *states*, chiefly North Dakota, South Dakota, Nebraska, Kansas, Oklahoma, and Texas, even though significant parts of those states are not included within the limits of the physiographic province.

Given the lack of consensus regarding the extent of the Great

Plains and how the area should be studied, it is understandable that
in the past scholars tended to neglect thinking systematically about
the concepts and methods of analyzing ethnic minorities in such
places as the Great Plains, where cities are few, low population density prevails, and the economy is based on agricultural production.
One essay in this volume is addressed specifically to such problems.

Kathleen Conzen, a historian at the University of Chicago,
reviews the concepts scholars have used in analyzing immigrant
groups in rural environments and outlines a structure for comparative studies based on family and community history. While some
scholars have stressed rapid assimilation as the main characteristic
of ethnic life in rural environments, Conzen notes, others have emphasized that rural conditions offer favorable opportunities for
cultural maintenance. The crucial question, she points out, is whether a given settlement achieved the measure of concentration or
density essential for ethnic community formation. For this reason
systematic study of rural ethnicity must begin with the compilation
of subcounty data on location and residence patterns. It must also
account for variations among different ethnic groups in the density
required for a community to develop. The role of institutions and
agencies in promoting immigrant settlements must be assessed, but
attention must focus on the chain migration of families as the main
instrument of ethnic clustering. Conzen also stresses the importance
of variables such as the availability of land, opportunities for non-
agricultural employment, patterns of land acquisition, family size,
age, and a wide range of cultural variables, all of which influence the
adaptive experience of rural ethnic groups.

Long before the arrival of such white ethnic groups as Conzen
has in mind, the Great Plains were inhabited by a variety of aboriginal people who moved in and out of the region over many millen-
nia. They differed from each other in language and custom in much
the same ways that Latin, Teutonic, Celtic, and Slavic peoples of
Europe were distinguished by widely different linguistic and cultural
traits. Much movement among the many tribes of the Great Plains
occurred in recent centuries. For example, different Caddoan groups
—Arikaras, Pawnees, and Wichitas—migrated to the central plains
from the lower Mississippi River region. A Uto-Aztecan tribe, the
Comanches, drifted out of the northern intermontane region to the
southern plains of Oklahoma and Texas. Various Siouan peoples
were forced westward out of the forest lands of the Great Lakes
region by the Chippewas. The Sioux, in turn, displaced the Cheyennes, an Algonquian tribe, from the Missouri River valley to the

upper branches of the Platte in Nebraska and Colorado. Such inter-tribal pressures and migrations continued well into the nineteenth century, when they were further complicated by the forced removal of eastern Indians to present-day Oklahoma and Kansas by the United States government, beginning in the 1830s. At that time the Great Plains region began to serve as a resettlement zone for eastern tribes, which is the topic treated by Arrell M. Gibson, a historian at the University of Oklahoma.

Gibson places Indian removal, a much discussed topic, into the context of Great Plains settlement and briefly compares the experiences of the Indian exiles to those of later arriving Americans and European immigrants. The eastern tribes, notably the Cherokees, Chickasaws, Choctaws, and Creeks, had moved rapidly toward assimilation with white culture by the 1830s. In an earnest effort to escape displacement, these tribes had adopted an accommodationist strategy of cooperation with the federal government and sought to be acceptable neighbors of the whites by welcoming Christian missionaries, establishing churches, introducing schools, and adopting constitutional government. Such endeavors failed to hinder the policy of relocation undertaken by the Jackson administration. The so-called Five Civilized Tribes, together with various bands of aborigines from the Old Northwest, were forcibly removed to the "permanent Indian reserve" west of Missouri and Arkansas. Thus these involuntary migrants were the first permanent settlers to introduce aspects of Western civilization to the plains region.

The Great Plains as an environment is only peripheral to Gibson's inquiry. To many decision makers in Washington in the 1830s, the Great Plains were the Great American Desert, an inhospitable wasteland, neither suited to nor needed for white habitation. Most eastern Indians also perceived it as an unattractive and undesirable place. Gibson tells us that Indian delegations sent to inspect the colonization area for its suitability as a new home returned with uniformly negative reports. The environment of the plains was radically different from that to which they were accustomed; the scouts predicted ruin for their people if they tried to establish themselves there.

The environment is also incidental to Raymond DeMallie's essay on treaty making between the plains tribes and the United States government. DeMallie, an anthropologist at Indiana University, explores the cultural clash of two idea systems—Indian and white—that symbolize the world, its many parts, and their interrelationships, as observed in the formal proceedings of treaty councils from 1851 to 1892. Both sides attempted to bridge the cultural gap. For Indian leaders, smoking the peace pipe had a significance comparable to that which white men attached to "touching the pen"—signing the treaty document. Each side used strategies to combat the other on its own ground; sometimes the devices used were too subtle for the other side to comprehend. DeMallie analyzes the symbolic significance of rituals practiced by both Indians and whites, the recitals of requests and demands, and the distribution of presents. He demonstrates how each side manipulated kinship metaphors, for example, as tactical devices to gain diplomatic advantage. Throughout his essay, DeMallie seeks especially to understand the full meaning of treaty negotiations from the Indian point of view.

At the same time that the Sioux, Cheyennes, Arapahoes, Kiowas, and other plains tribes were striving to preserve their way of life, an unprecedented wave of immigration from Europe swept across the United States. The great majority of the newcomers emigrated from Germany, the British Isles, the Scandinavian countries, and, beginning in the mid-1870s, Russia. Although most of the immigrants remained in eastern cities, others, especially those who hoped to continue an agricultural livelihood, moved to the frontier of settlement, which was then pushing onto the Great Plains in Kansas, Nebraska, and Dakota Territory.

The settlement of the plains advanced rapidly compared to earlier frontiers. Important technological developments stimulated the process—barbed wire, windmills, the revolver, but above all the railroads. In many parts of the Great Plains, the railroads preceded settlement. Great companies such as the Union Pacific, Northern Pacific, Santa Fe, and Burlington railroads were eager to settle European immigrants on the vast tracts the federal government had granted them as subsidies for railroad construction. Although formal colonization programs were developed for some ethnic groups, especially those with strong religious bonds, most Europeans arrived in family units. Relatives and neighbors often followed soon after until clusters of one ethnic group or another developed here and there.

Table 1 reveals the numerical and proportional distribution of foreign-born inhabitants in the states and territories of the Great Plains region during the latter half of the nineteenth century. The major demographic fact to be derived from these data is that the proportion of ethnic stock decreases substantially as one moves south from the Canadian border. Usually a state has roughly half the proportion of foreign-born persons found in its neighbor to the north.

TABLE 1

Distribution of Foreign-Born Persons in Great Plains States and Territories
by Number and Percentage of Total Population, 1860–1900

State or Territory	1860 N	1860 %	1870 N	1870 %	1880 N	1880 %	1890 N	1890 %	1900 N	1900 %
North Dakota	1,774	36.7	4,815	34.0	51,795	38.3	81,461	42.7	113,091	35.4
South Dakota							91,055	26.1	88,508	22.0
Nebraska	6,351	22.0	30,748	25.0	97,414	21.5	202,542	19.1	177,347	16.6
Kansas	12,691	11.8	48,392	13.3	110,086	11.1	147,838	10.4	126,685	8.6
Oklahoma Territory	—		—		—		2,740	3.5	15,680	3.9
Indian Territory	—		—		—		13	.0	4,858	1.2
Texas	43,422	7.2	62,411	7.6	114,616	7.2	152,956	6.8	179,357	5.9
Montana	—		7,979	38.7	11,521	29.4	43,096	30.2	67,067	27.6
Wyoming	—		3,513	38.5	5,850	28.1	14,913	23.8	17,415	18.8
Colorado	2,666	7.8	6,599	16.6	39,790	20.5	83,990	20.3	91,155	16.9
New Mexico	6,723	7.2	5,620	6.1	8,051	6.7	11,259	7.0	13,625	7.0

Source: "Distribution of Immigrants, 1850–1900," *Reports of the Immigration Commission*, Sen. Doc. no. 756, 61st Cong., 3d sess., 41 vols. (Washington, D.C.: GPO, 1911), 3:444–47.

Thus, in 1900, one of three persons in North Dakota was foreign-born, compared to one in six in Nebraska and nearly one in twelve in Kansas.

The data of table 1 should be qualified in several ways. Virtually all of the persons listed for 1860 resided in humid areas east of the Great Plains proper. Most of the foreign-born persons in Montana, Wyoming, Colorado, and New Mexico lived in the mining areas of the mountains. Not until the end of the century did immigrants inhabit the Great Plains parts of these states and territories. Many of the foreign-born persons in North Dakota, Texas, and New Mexico were Canadians or Mexicans rather than Europeans. Since the central and southern plains were settled first, the numbers of immigrants were greatest there, even though the proportions of the foreign-born were highest in the northern plains. By 1890 the concentrations in Kansas, Nebraska, and the Dakotas attained their fullest development. Thereafter, however, numbers and percentages declined as immigration to the United States from northern and western Europe declined, except in North Dakota, where agricultural development continued, especially in the western part of the state.[7]

Each Great Plains state has its own pattern of ethnic group settlement. Table 2 lists numbers and percentages of foreign-stock persons (first- and second-generation) in 1900 for the eastern tier of states. By that time the pattern of ethnic distribution had been firmly established and the flow of emigrants from northern and western Europe had substantially subsided. The census revealed that in North Dakota 30 percent of all persons in the state were born in the Scandinavian countries, with Norway far in the lead. Germans formed the second most numerous group. Virtually all of the numerous Russian-born persons were also German-speaking. This was likewise true of most Austrians, Swiss, and Hungarians in the state. Canadians also constituted a large group in North Dakota, especially in the northern tier of counties and in the broad plain of the Red River, which flows northward into Canada. Although the percentages of foreign-born persons by counties are distributed fairly evenly across the state, Germans from Russia were exceptionally numerous in the south-central part of the state on both sides of the Missouri River. Numbers of Norwegians were especially heavy in the eastern and northern areas.

In South Dakota the Germans plus the Germans from Russia were only slightly more numerous than Scandinavians combined. Norwegians accounted for about two-thirds of the latter and they resided especially in the eastern counties. German-speaking people

TABLE 2

Number and Percentage of Total Population of Foreign-Born White Persons
plus Native-Born White Persons of Foreign Parentage in Selected Great Plains States by Country of Origin, 1900

Country of Origin (Total Population)	North Dakota (319,146)	%	South Dakota (401,570)	%	Nebraska (1,066,300)	%	Kansas (1,470,495)	%	Oklahoma Terr. (398,331)	%	Indian Terr. (392,060)	%	Texas (3,048,710)	%
Austria	2,014	.6	1,692	.4	8,085	.8	6,329	.4	1,032	.3	356	.1	15,114	.5
Bohemia	3,654	1.1	6,361	1.6	38,471	3.6	7,788	.5	2,698	.7	50	—	22,713	.7
Canada (English)	31,086	9.7	13,058	3.3	19,304	1.8	18,939	1.3	3,600	.9	819	.2	5,446	.2
Canada (French)	6,512	2.0	3,516	.9	3,003	.3	5,547	.4	702	.2	173	—	1,004	—
Denmark	7,139	2.2	10,450	2.6	26,418	2.5	6,687	.5	582	.1	71	—	2,361	.1
England	7,710	2.4	12,402	3.1	33,586	3.1	45,633	3.1	5,540	1.4	2,586	.7	23,722	.8
France	582	.2	835	.2	2,897	.2	5,813	.4	1,048	.3	568	.1	6,304	.2
Germany	32,393	10.1	55,860	13.9	191,928	18.0	131,563	8.9	18,117	4.5	3,446	.9	157,214	5.2
Hungary	1,797	.6	881	.2	882	.1	935	.1	280	.1	40	—	979	—
Ireland	11,552	3.6	16,017	4.0	45,535	4.3	48,525	3.3	5,534	1.4	2,233	.6	25,373	.8
Italy	731	.2	566	.1	1,278	.1	1,543	.1	74	—	734	.2	7,086	.2
Norway	71,998	22.6	51,191	12.7	7,228	.7	3,726	.3	350	.1	98	—	3,405	.1
Poland	2,112	.7	1,146	.3	7,328	.7	1,478	.1	298	.1	357	.1	8,148	.3
Russia	23,909	7.5	25,689	6.4	14,537	1.4	25,048	1.7	5,536	1.4	398	.1	4,048	.1
Scotland	5,664	1.8	3,943	1.0	9,818	.9	14,186	1.0	1,596	.4	1,008	.3	6,839	.2
Sweden	14,598	4.6	17,163	4.3	54,301	5.1	35,219	2.4	1,290	.3	215	.1	9,297	.3
Switzerland	845	.3	1,638	.4	5,852	.5	9,204	.6	1,108	.3	187	—	3,776	.1
Wales	452	.1	1,889	.5	3,098	.3	5,748	.4	439	.1	392	.1	871	—
Other	2,942	.9	7,065	1.8	5,073	.5	6,050	.5	744	.2	410	.1	146,643	4.8
TOTAL	227,690	71.3	231,362	57.6	478,622	44.9	379,961	25.8	50,568	12.7	14,141	3.6	450,343	14.8

Source: U.S. Bureau of the Census, *Census Reports*, vol. 1, *Twelfth Census of the United States, 1900*, pt. 1 (Washington, D.C.: GPO, 1901), pp. cxcvi-cxcvii; for division into first and second generations, see *Reports of the Immigration Commission*, Sen. Doc. no. 756, 61st Cong., 3d sess., 41 vols. (Washington, D.C.: GPO, 1911), 3:512-21.

settled most frequently in the east-central and southeastern parts of the state. As in most other states, English-speaking immigrants tended to be evenly distributed. Because of the large Indian reservations in the western half of the state and the wasteland character of much of the terrain, fewer Europeans settled there, with the exception of the Black Hills country. The northwestern corner of South Dakota received large numbers of immigrants later when much agricultural land in that area was homesteaded early in the twentieth century.

In Nebraska the Germans were by far the largest ethnic group. They settled throughout the state but especially in the northeastern quarter. Nebraska's contingent of Germans from Russia (mostly Protestants from the Volga River valley) was smaller than the colonies of Black Sea Germans that predominated in the Dakotas or the Volga German settlements in Kansas. But more Swedes, Danes, and Czechs settled in Nebraska than in any other Great Plains state and strong concentrations of each group developed in the eastern half. Immigrants tended to avoid the sparsely populated Sandhills, a vast area in north-central Nebraska, but farther west, in Nebraska's Panhandle, first- and second-generation immigrants were nearly as numerous proportionately as in the eastern section.

Ethnic-group settlement in Kansas forms a mosaic much like that in Nebraska, though the number of immigrants was only half as large in proportion to the total population. A major concentration of Swedes developed at Lindsborg, Germans west of Marysville, German-Russian Mennonites north of Newton, German-Russian Catholics near Hays, French Canadians at Concordia, and Czechs west of Ellsworth. But in many parts of Kansas, notably in the southern third of the state, comparatively few Europeans settled. Germans were easily the largest single category in Kansas, but English-speaking immigrants collectively were also numerous, English and Irish especially. Welshmen and Scots settled in Kansas more often than in any other plains state.

Few European immigrants chose Oklahoma as their new home in America. This was partly due to its special history as a reserve for Indians relocated there by the government from other parts of the country. Oklahoma did not become a state until 1907, when Indian Territory in the east and Oklahoma Territory in the west were merged to form the state. The heaviest concentrations of foreign stock, which never exceeded 25 percent on a county basis, occurred in the counties north and northwest of Oklahoma City. The Germans were much the largest group, with German Russians next in size, followed by the English. No other group of immigrants formed more than 1 percent of the total population in 1900. Later, other newcomers from Europe settled in the southeastern, non–Great Plains portion of the state.

Most counties in north and east Texas had even fewer foreign-born inhabitants than Oklahoma. But the proportion rose sharply in the coastal cities of Galveston and Houston and continued in a westward direction to San Antonio and to the German Hill Country west of Austin. This region received large numbers of German immigrants as early as the 1830s. Later smaller numbers of Czechs and Poles entered the area. Farther south, Mexican immigrants formed large proportions of the population of the Rio Grande Valley from El Paso to Brownsville. By 1910 European and Mexican immigrants and their children together constituted more than half the population in south and south-central Texas.

The ethnic populations in the western tier of Great Plains states—Montana, Wyoming, Colorado, and New Mexico—followed eastern settlement patterns, although English-speaking immigrants were proportionately more numerous in the west. In general, the Great Plains counties of these states attracted fewer immigrants than the mountainous areas; the proportion of foreign-born persons was highest in the north and decreased steadily toward the south. Near the border, however, Mexican populations were predominant. In the eastern counties of Montana, especially in the Missouri River valley, immigrants averaged between 15 and 25 percent of the population by 1910. In Wyoming the proportion was typically 10–15 percent in the plains counties. The high plains of Colorado averaged between 5 and 10 percent, with the South Platte Valley in the northeast higher and the southeastern corner lower. In New Mexico, the foreign-born rarely exceeded 5 percent of the population in the eastern counties. In the mountainous southwestern counties, which border on Mexico, the percentage rose to 35 percent by 1910.

In New Mexico, as in Texas and Colorado, the substantial native Hispanic population is naturally not included in the census category of the foreign-born. An ethnic group resulting from the intermarriage of Indians and Spanish since 1600, the Hispanos spread eastward from the Santa Fe area onto the Great Plains. This movement began in the nineteenth century, and today Hispanos form a major element in the several Great Plains counties of northeastern New Mexico and southeastern Colorado. Hispanos are thus to be distinguished from Mexican immigrants. The movement of the latter onto the central and northern plains is a phenomenon of only the past fifty years.

Extensively employed in agricultural field work, railroad maintenance, and meat packing, they now form substantial enclaves in plains
cities such as Garden City, Kansas, and Scottsbluff, Nebraska.

Blacks, like the Hispanos, have lived on the Great Plains since
the time of the earliest settlements. Their numbers, however, have
never constituted a large element in the population except in Oklahoma and Texas, where they have lived in areas not usually considered part of the Great Plains. Following the Civil War blacks were
often employed as cowboys or cooks on cattle ranches. Moreover,
they formed a major part of the United States Army—the Ninth
and Tenth Cavalry and the Twenty-fourth and Twenty-fifth Infantry
divisions—that was stationed in the Great Plains region during the
last quarter of the nineteenth century. Later blacks found work as
porters on passenger trains and as house servants. The circumstances
of their employment generally tended to discourage family life and
permanent residence.

Blacks made their first substantial efforts at permanent residence
in 1879, when many thousands of former slaves migrated from the
South to Kansas. Most settled in cities in the eastern part of the
state, but some homesteaded as farmers on the western plains. By
1900 the black population exceeded 50,000 in Kansas and 6,000 in
Nebraska. But in the northern plains they constituted less than .1
percent of the population. After Oklahoma was opened to settlement it also attracted many blacks, most of whom lived in a cluster
of counties stretching west from Muskogee. By 1900 the number of
blacks in Oklahoma increased to 56,000, of whom few resided on the
Great Plains proper. Texas, as a slave state before the Civil War, had
many blacks in its eastern counties and along the Gulf Coast, but
few ever moved into areas considered to be part of the Great Plains.
(See table 3.)

The experiences of blacks, Mexicans, Hispanos, and Indians in
migration and settlement on the Great Plains were substantially
different from those of European immigrant groups because of
deeply ingrained habits of racial discrimination in American society.
But while the former groups usually moved relatively short distances,
the migrations of the latter were often on a world-wide scale and
involved careful and deliberate choices. Such movement and its
implications for cultural adaptation is illustrated by Timothy Kloberdanz, an anthropologist at North Dakota State University, in his
review of German-Russian experiences on three continents.

Kloberdanz's purpose is to study the adaptations made by Volga
German settlers in three of the world's major grasslands—the Russian

TABLE 3

Number and Percentage of Total Population in Selected Great Plains States by Racial Groups, 1900

Racial Group (Total Population)	North Dakota (319,146)	%	South Dakota (401,570)	%	Nebraska (1,066,300)	%	Kansas (1,470,495)	%	Oklahoma Terr. (398,331)	%	Indian Terr. (392,060)	%	Texas (3,048,710)	%
White	311,712	97.7	380,714	94.8	1,056,526	99.1	1,416,319	96.3	367,524	92.3	302,680	77.2	2,426,669	79.6
Black	286	.1	465	.1	6,269	.6	52,003	3.6	18,831	4.7	36,853	9.4	620,722	20.4
American Indian	6,968	2.1	20,225	5.0	3,322	.3	2,130	.1	11,945	3.0	52,500	13.4	470	—
Chinese and Japanese	180	—	166	—	183	—	43	—	31	—	27	—	849	—
Mexican[a]	1	—	13	—	27	—	71	—	70	—	64	—	71,062	2.3

Source: U.S. Bureau of the Census, *Abstract of the Twelfth Census of the United States 1900*, 3d ed. (Washington, D.C.: GPO, 1904), pp. 40, 61.

[a]Includes first-generation immigrants only; data for Spanish-speaking native-born not available. Mexican immigrants were included in the "white" category.

steppes, the North American Great Plains, and the pampas of Argentina. His focus is on the ways an immigrant people altered its culture in relation to a physical and social environment. He reviews the emigration of Germans to the Volga region in the eighteenth century and the many changes they made in agricultural practice, housing, clothing, diet, and social organization in accommodation to the dry, continental climate and flat terrain. Volga German adaptation to social and political forces, Kloberdanz shows, was much less flexible and led to their reemigration beginning in the 1870s to North and South America, where they deliberately sought physical environments similar to what they had known in Russia. Kloberdanz then summarizes Volga German adaptations in America and, more briefly, in Argentina, and relates them to the culture they had evolved in Russia.

The next essay shifts the analysis of migration and settlement from the continental scale to the microcosmic. Robert C. Ostergren, a geographer at the University of Wisconsin–Madison, analyzes the movement of Swedish immigrants to the Dalesburg settlement in Clay County, South Dakota, in the late 1860s and early 1870s. In its own way, his work is an example of the kind of research called for by Kathleen Conzen earlier in this volume. By systematically organizing and mapping data concerning 206 heads of families, Ostergren reveals in detail the migration experience in relation to settlement patterns. Most of the Dalesburg immigrants came from three distinct districts within Sweden. Sharp variations existed among the three groups with respect to the mode of migration— direct or indirect. Further differences were found in the length of time that elapsed between emigration and settlement in Clay County. Ostergren also relates place of origin in Sweden to the spatial distribution of immigrants within the Dalesburg settlement and suggests, finally, that both impinge on the boundaries of church administrative districts.

A third paper treating migration and settlement is by John A. Hostetler, an anthropologist at Temple University. Hostetler's essay, a study of Old Order Amish colonization efforts on the Great Plains, describes experiences that contrast sharply with those of Kloberdanz's Volga Germans. The latter, with their prior life in a grassland environment, adapted easily and successfully, but the Old Order Amish, a German-culture religious group found chiefly in Pennsylvania, Ohio, and Indiana, were reluctant to modify their ways and therefore failed. Hostetler's purpose is to identify those aspects of Amish culture that rendered them vulnerable to the adversities of the Great Plains climate. He finds them in the religiously rooted adherence to intensive farming on a small scale, with horse-drawn implements, in an environment that calls for large-scale, heavily mechanized operations. Unable to adapt without violating their religious raison d'être, most Old Order Amish abandoned their farms and returned to familiar surroundings in eastern states. Of the many Amish settlements attempted on the Great Plains, only three colonies near Hutchinson, Kansas, survived. In these instances, Hostetler reports, prohibitions were relaxed and modern technologies adopted, thereby permitting agriculture on a larger scale, all to the disapproval of eastern church leaders.

Religious belief and custom did not ordinarily inhibit ethnic group settlement, as it did among the Old Order Amish. Instead, church-related institutions usually adjusted to the circumstances of the new environment and often dominated rural and small-town ethnic communities, as Terry Jordan, a geographer at North Texas State University, illustrates in his religious geography of the German Hill Country of Texas. Jordan reviews the history of the several denominations in the area—Lutherans, Evangelicals, Methodists, Catholics, and freethinkers—maps their locations, and reveals varying patterns of residential segregation and spatial organization. He also studies the distinctive architecture of German church buildings erected before 1910, but notes that in burial practice, radical departures from European custom have occurred. Jordan's investigation shows that despite varying degrees of acculturation, much evidence of German ethnicity survives in the Hill Country today.

In the article by Linda Dégh, a folklorist at Indiana University, religion as an aspect of folk culture is shown to have evolved in the plains setting as the central integrative element in a community of Hungarian-Canadians. Dégh, herself an immigrant from Hungary, illustrates the concepts and methods a folklorist may use in the study of religion among immigrants on the local level. She examines spontaneous expressions of ethnicity to reveal the role religion plays in Kipling, Saskatchewan, which is the largest and oldest rural settlement of Magyars in North America. The newcomers, who began to arrive early in the twentieth century, called their settlement Békevár (Bastion of Peace). But religious life was seldom peaceful in this community; strife between two groups of Hungarians of different provincial origins has continued throughout the history of the settlement. The original founders of Békevár were highlanders who through the years formulated an intensely pietistic folk religion that rests on myths about the settlement's founding and fosters the display of ethnicity. They were joined later by more rapidly assimilating low-landers who dismiss highlander religiosity as superstition and heresy. Rivalry between the two groups results in much petty jealousy, mistrust, hostility, and the abandonment of joint action. Dégh concludes that in this way religion continues to dominate community life and perpetuates an ethnic identity that would otherwise have disappeared over the years.

The relationships of the Great Plains environment to ethnoreligious experience are remarkably varied. In Hostetler's interpretation of the Old Order Amish, environmental forces are basic. In Jordan's study of the Texas Germans, spatial relationships are important but they are not explicitly connected to the character of the Hill Country environment. For Dégh, the Canadian prairie, an area of low population density, is merely the place where the Hungarian immigrants of her study settled. In the last contribution in this book that treats a religious topic, the physical environment is regarded by its author to have been without significant influence on ethnic-group religious experience in comparison with the impact of men, institutions, and ideas. Bruce Garver, a historian at the University of Nebraska at Omaha, describes the history of Czech freethinkers, the "believing unbelievers" of the Great Plains states.

Garver surveys the ideas, activities, and organizations of Czech freethinkers from the beginning of mass immigration in 1871 to the advent of World War I. The only immigrant group in which the majority had deliberately abandoned all formal ties with organized religion, the Czechs are the most important Slavic people in the Great Plains region. Garver summarizes the numerical strength and distribution of the freethought movement and describes its leaders and publications, and guiding principles. He characterizes freethinker institutions as resolutely secular and dedicated to the maintenance of Czech language and culture. Among them were educational societies to supplement public school instruction, gymnastic organizations, fraternal and benevolent associations, and cemeteries. The most militant of Czech freethinkers organized themselves into Free Congregations. By the time of World War I, Garver reveals, the movement began to decline, a victim of the acculturation process.

The final group of contributions to this volume are conceptualized in ways intended to permit comparisons among different ethnic groups of the Great Plains and with native-born persons. Bradley Baltensperger, a geographer at Michigan Technological University, examines ways in which immigrant farmers in Nebraska adopted American crops and practices. By using census manuscripts and county assessment records as sources, Baltensperger compares the agricultural behavior of German, German-Russian, and Swedish farmers with that of the American-born from 1880 to 1900 in three counties located near the 98th meridian. In some respects, most notably in corn production, the immigrants rapidly adopted American cropping and livestock practices, but other habits were less subject to modification. He also observes differences among the three immigrant groups. Swedish farmers, for example, tended to conform to the American mode rapidly, while Germans and German Russians retained distinctive cropping systems for a longer time. In some cases crops traditionally preferred by immigrants, such as rye and flax, were dropped shortly after settlement, only to reappear later. By 1900 most of the distinctive aspects of immigrant agriculture in Baltensperger's sample had faded.

The discovery of similarities and contrasts between Czech farmers and Mexican laborers in a modernizing society is the purpose of the essay by Josef J. Barton, a historian at Northwestern University. Barton examines relationships of land and family in Nueces County, Texas, early in the twentieth century. He finds that both groups were highly transient, but each was united by bonds of common origin and kinship. Whereas Czechs were linked by generational lines, Mexicans were united by lateral ties among kinfolk. Among the Czechs landownership quickly became the mode, but Mexican tenant farmers were reduced to a migrant, landless rural proletariat. Both groups, however, attempted to use familiar forms as they faced new and altered circumstances in Nueces County. Out of such confrontations, Barton observes, emerged ethnic cultures that shaped and sustained their lives. Religion became the bond of community in both groups, as cooperative efforts were transformed into institutions and ritual associations into resources for collective action.

The final contribution to this anthology is an analysis of ethnic assimilation in contemporary Nebraska by J. Allen Williams, David R. Johnson, and Miguel A. Carranza, sociologists at the University of Nebraska–Lincoln. The study offers measurements of cultural, social, and psychological assimilation among seventeen different ethnic groups by analyzing the responses of 1,867 randomly selected adult Nebraskans. The results of the survey are compared with similar findings for a national sample and show that the ability of Nebraskans to identify their ethnic origin is above the average for the United States. Nebraskans also tend to attach more importance to ethnic origin than do persons in the nation-wide sample. Generally, the findings of the study indicate that the earlier an ethnic group settled in Nebraska, the higher its socioeconomic status is, and the lower the social distance is between the ethnic group and society at large, then the greater its assimilation will be. Although assimilation in Nebraska has been extensive, it is far from complete.

Although Williams, Johnson, and Carranza do not directly treat the Great Plains environment as impinging on assimilation, they consider the matter implicitly in their ecological variables of the degree of dispersion of ethnic-group population across the state and the degree of population density. Their data support the hypothesis that a high dispersion rate and a low density are positively associated with rapid assimilation; their findings conform to Kathleen Conzen's observation that a given ethnic group seems to require a certain degree of concentration or density for community formation to occur. Thus, in places where low population density generally prevails, the great distances between neighbors tend to limit the ability of immigrants and their children to support the organizations and institutions necessary for an ethnic community to emerge, unless they constitute an unusually large proportion of the population in a limited area.

Collectively the essays of this volume show that the Great Plains region has been marked strongly by the various ethnic groups that settled there. Among the earliest to arrive were eastern Indians who had been removed to the plains by the United States government. Confrontation between Indians and whites has been a major theme in the history of the area. The immigration of Europeans, chiefly Germans, Scandinavians, and English-speaking persons from the British Isles and Canada, as well as Czechs, has been of transcendant importance for Great Plains states, particularly in the North. They arrived in America as the wave of agricultural settlement swept across the Great Plains in the last decades of the nineteenth century. A large proportion of these newcomers sought to establish themselves as farmers and they arrived at a time when technological advances in transportation, communication, and farm machinery enabled them to persist in an environment that often seemed threatening and unattractive. In more recent times, immigrants from Mexico, together with native Hispanos, have imprinted portions of the southern plains with their form of Latin culture.

Assimilation has not been uniform among the several groups studied here, and it has been more rapid in some areas of life than in others. Except for exclusive ethnoreligious groups, ethnic differentiation in economic activities, such as agricultural practice, has been less apparent than in cultural and religious affairs. Ethnicity as manifested through religious culture is shown to have been a strong integrating force for certain groups of Mexicans, Czechs, Germans, Swedes, and Hungarians, but it is not clear that this was the case for those groups generally.

Evidence concerning the effect of the Great Plains environment on ethnicity is inconsistent and seems to be related to the nature of the question asked. The spatial distribution or concentration of specific groups in a given area has been influenced by environmental factors, but social and cultural variables—especially kinship and religion—seem generally to have been more important. Moreover, essayists who consider the semiarid, treeless environment with its low population density to have been significant generally interpret its effect as having accelerated the process of assimilation. Paradoxically, however, ethnic identification continues in the Great Plains at a rate apparently higher than in the United States as a whole. This is partly due, one suspects, to the recency of settlement in the region in comparison with other parts of the nation. In this sense the Great Plains area is still a new country, as the world measures time. Even though ethnic institutions are rapidly fading and immigrant languages rarely function as they once did, group memories remain strong, especially among persons who retain traditional attachments to the now thoroughly Americanized immigrant churches, such as the Catholic, Lutheran, and Mennonite.

The census of 1970 suggests the present-day number and distribution of racial and ethnic groups in the Great Plains states (see table 4). American Indians continue to be important minorities in North Dakota, South Dakota, and Oklahoma. Blacks are especially numerous in Texas and Oklahoma, but relatively few of them reside in the Great Plains portions of those states. Chicanos are exceptionally strong in south Texas. They constitute a majority of the population in the area between the Nueces and the Rio Grande.[8]

In most parts of the Great Plains, however, the pattern of ethnic-group distribution established during the settlement period of the nineteenth century remains today, even though the second generation of European immigrant groups outnumbers the first by a ratio of ten to one. Taken together, the two generations still constitute more than a fifth of the total population of North Dakota; the proportion in other states decreases steadily to about 3 percent as one moves south to Texas. The continuing importance of European ethnicity on the northern plains is suggested by the fact that in 1970 nearly a sixth of the population of North Dakota still identified German as their mother tongue. At the same time, another sixth

TABLE 4

Racial Groups, Selected Mother-Tongue Groups, and Foreign-Born Persons plus Native-Born Persons of Foreign Parentage by Country of Origin in Great Plains States, by Number and Percentage of Total Population, 1970

Race, Country of Origin, of Mother Tongue (Total Population)	North Dakota (617,761)	%	South Dakota (665,507)	%	Nebraska (1,483,493)	%	Kansas (2,246,578)	%	Oklahoma (2,559,229)	%	Texas (11,196,730)	%
American Indian	14,369	2.3	32,365	4.9	6,624	.4	8,672	.4	98,468	3.9	17,957	.2
Black	2,494	.4	1,629	.2	39,911	2.7	106,977	4.8	171,892	6.7	1,399,005	12.5
Spanish mother tongue (foreign- and native-born)	1,139	.2	1,488	.2	13,289	.9	31,577	1.4	21,843	.9	1,793,462	16.0
Mexico	276	—	472	.1	5,552	.4	13,728	.6	6,071	.2	711,058	6.4
Other races (mostly Chinese and Japanese)	1,413	.2	1,182	.2	4,091	.3	8,861	.4	8,507	.3	62,640	.6
Subtotal (omit Mexico)	19,415	3.1	36,664	5.5	63,915	4.3	156,087	6.9	300,710	11.8	2,190,660	19.6
Canada	15,630	2.5	6,617	1.0	8,247	.6	10,425	.5	7,811	.3	35,900	.3
United Kingdom	3,537	.6	4,562	.7	11,083	.7	15,986	.7	9,812	.4	49,185	.4
Eire	1,248	.2	1,980	.3	4,846	.3	4,853	.3	2,386	.1	12,143	.1
Norway	38,722	6.3	18,898	2.8	3,183	.2	1,920	.1	901	—	5,442	—
Sweden	8,434	1.7	7,790	1.2	17,099	1.2	9,622	.4	1,962	.1	10,873	.1
Denmark	3,443	.6	6,584	1.0	13,202	.9	3,200	.1	1,396	.1	4,801	.1
Netherlands	1,120	.2	5,126	.8	1,754	.1	1,692	.1	1,101	—	4,722	—
Germany	21,004	3.4	26,792	4.0	62,726	4.2	43,252	1.9	21,475	.8	104,726	.9
German mother tongue (foreign- and native-born)	*94,036*	*15.2*	*68,900*	*10.4*	*107,608*	*7.3*	*106,040*	*4.7*	*37,428*	*1.5*	*237,572*	*2.1*

TABLE 4 (Continued)

Race, Country of Origin, of Mother Tongue (Total Population)	North Dakota (617,761)	%	South Dakota (665,507)	%	Nebraska (1,483,493)	%	Kansas (2,246,578)	%	Oklahoma (2,559,229)	%	Texas (11,196,730)	%
Poland	1,952	.3	1,047	.2	8,333	.6	4,046	.2	2,670	.1	15,328	.1
Czechoslovakia	2,473	.4	3,507	.5	19,551	1.3	4,978	.2	3,411	.1	29,536	.3
Austria	2,254	.4	1,305	.2	3,612	.2	5,581	.2	1,893	.1	13,397	.1
USSR	33,177	5.4	14,041	2.1	14,160	1.0	17,664	.8	5,463	.2	16,149	.1
Italy	485	.1	616	.1	6,414	.4	4,552	.2	3,431	.1	26,886	.2
Other Europe	6,973	1.1	5,215	.8	12,119	.8	16,066	.7	7,882	.3	45,100	.4
Subtotal, Europe and Canada (omits German mother tongue)	140,452	22.7	104,080	15.6	186,329	12.6	143,837	6.4	71,594	2.8	374,188	3.3
All other	3,533	.6	3,020	.5	8,623	.6	9,458	.4	5,623	.2	75,094	.7
Grand total (omits Mexico and German mother tongue)	163,400	26.5	143,764	21.6	258,867	17.4	309,382	13.8	377,927	14.8	2,639,942	23.6

Source: U.S. Bureau of the Census, Census of Population, 1970, vol. 1, Characteristics of the Population, pt. 1, United States Summary, sec. 1 (Washington, D.C.: GPO, 1973), pp. 293, 472–80.

claimed some other language—chiefly Norwegian or Swedish—as their mother tongue. South Dakota, Nebraska, and Kansas display similar though lower proportions. Obviously, the mother-tongue groups in these states include many more persons than those included in the first- and second-generation immigrant categories. Since the ranks of the Germans, Scandinavians, German Russians, and others who settled the plains have not been replenished by many new immigrants in recent decades, this remarkable retention of ethnic language will soon fade. But other characteristics rooted in ethnicity—values, attitudes, behaviors of various kinds—are likely to continue for many years and to influence the social and political affairs of the region in subtle ways, as they have in the past.

Notes

1. I have attempted to give a systematic introduction to this topic in "Ethnic Group Settlement on the Great Plains," *Western Historical Quarterly* 8 (October 1977): 405–30. U.S. Bureau of the Census, *Census of Population, 1970*, vol. 1, *Characteristics of the Population*, pt. 1, *United States Summary*, sec. 1 (Washington, D.C.: GPO, 1973), p. 472. In addition to the published data in the decennial census reports, see *Reports of the Immigration Commission*, Senate Doc. no. 756, 61st Cong. 3d sess., 41 vols. (Washington, D.C.: GPO, 1911), 3:444–47.

2. Walter Prescott Webb, *The Great Plains* (Boston: Ginn, 1931), p. 509; Carl F. Kraenzel, *The Great Plains in Transition* (Norman: University of Oklahoma Press, 1955), pp. 235, 238–49; Neal R. Peirce, *The Great Plains States of America* (New York: Norton, 1973); and Russell McKee, *The Last West: A History of the Great Plains of North America* (New York: Crowell, 1974). The most recent treatment of the region, Alexander B. Adams, *Sunlight and Storm: The Great American Plains* (New York: Putnam, 1977) omits all ethnic groups save the Indians and only summarizes briefly the period since 1870.

3. J. Neale Carman, *Foreign-Language Units of Kansas*, vol. 1, *Historical Atlas and Statistics* (Lawrence: University of Kansas Press, 1962), pp. 240 f. Cf. Terry G. Jordan, *German Seed in Texas Soil: Immigrant Farmers in Nineteenth-Century Texas* (Austin: University of Texas Press, 1966), and Russell W. Lynch, *Czech Farmers in Oklahoma*, Oklahoma Agricultural and Mechanical College Bulletin no. 39 (Stillwater, 1942).

4. *Reports of the Immigration Commission*, 3:444–47.

5. O. E. Rölvaag, *Giants in the Earth* (New York: Harper, 1927); Willa Cather, *My Ántonia* (Boston: Houghton Mifflin, 1918); McKee, *Last West*; Peirce, *Great Plains States*.

6. See A. K. Lobeck, *Physiographic Diagram of the United States* (New York: Geographical Press, Columbia University, 1922 and later editions); Nevin M. Fenneman, *Physiography of the Western United States* (New York: McGraw-

Hill, 1931); Webb, *Great Plains*, p. 8 and passim; Great Plains Committee, *The Future of the Great Plains* (Washington, D.C.: GPO, 1936), p. 24; E. Cotton Mather, "The American Great Plains," *Annals of the Association of American Geographers* 62 (June 1972): 237-39; and Elwyn B. Robinson, "An Interpretation of the History of the Great Plains," *North Dakota History* 41 (Spring 1974): 5-18. See also the discussion by Richard A. Bartlett in *The Great Plains Experience: Readings in the History of a Region*, ed. James E. Wright and Sarah Rosenberg (Lincoln, Nebr.: University of Mid-America, 1978), pp. 15-22.

7. Maps showing the spatial distribution of racial and ethnic groups in the United States vary greatly in quality. Among the best for historical purposes are those found in the decennial census reports; they formerly included extensive and detailed maps showing in color the distribution, density, and concentration of the various racial and ethnic groups. For example, see U.S. Bureau of the Census, *Statistical Atlas, Twelfth Census of the United States, 1900* (Washington, D.C.: GPO, 1903), plates 55-75. Richard Hartshorne, "Racial Maps of the United States," *Geographical Review* 28 (April 1938): 276-88 is a useful introduction. On the state level there is nothing comparable to Carman's extraordinary work, *Foreign-Language Units of Kansas*, vol. 1, *Historical Atlas and Statistics*, but see Terry G. Jordan, "*Annals* Map Supplement Number Thirteen: Population Origin Groups in Rural Texas," *Annals of the Association of American Geographers* 60 (June 1970): 404-5. For individual racial groups, the Bureau of the Census has produced useful maps for Negroes and American Indians with data mapped on the county level. For European ethnic groups, only the Germans have been adequately treated. See Heinz Kloss, *Atlas of Nineteenth and Early Twentieth Century German American Settlements* (Marburg, West Germany: N. G. Elwert, 1974). For a review of other efforts, see Karl B. Raitz, "Ethnic Maps of North America," *Geographical Review* 68 (July 1978): 335-50.

8. See Donald W. Meinig, *Imperial Texas: An Interpretive Essay in Cultural Geography* (Austin: University of Texas Press, 1969), pp. 87, 90-101.

Historical Approaches to the Study of Rural Ethnic Communities

Kathleen Neils Conzen

America in the past decade has awakened to the fact that, a half century after the end of mass immigration from Europe, it is still haunted by the ghosts, friendly and unfriendly, of its immigrant past. The nation has come to recognize, somewhat belatedly, that ethnicity still continues to influence everything from religious orientation to residential choice to behavior in the voting booth. Scholars too have renewed their concern for ethnicity—for the sources of this sense of shared identity based upon assumptions of common origin, for the factors that have sustained or diluted its relevance for individuals and for larger groups, and for its changing content and significance within American society.

Their explanatory models of the American ethnic experience have been largely urban. They have sought for the roots of ethnic identity, community formation, acculturation, and assimilation or ethnic continuity in the adaptive responses of European peasants attempting to cope with the hostile world of the industrial metropolis. But did rural immigrant settlement result in a similar emergence of ethnic cultures? Did ethnicity itself leave a mark on rural America in any way comparable to its urban impact? Scholars have seldom addressed such issues directly. Some fifty years ago, Edmund deS. Brunner noted that "in all the immense volume of literature dealing with the question of immigration hardly any consideration has been paid to those of the foreign-born that live in rural America." By and large that still remains the case.[1]

One searches in vain in recent surveys of immigration history for anything approaching the depth of historical treatment given the urban experience, nor does the immigrant fare any better in most western or agricultural history texts. Their authors seldom venture beyond description of immigrant settlement patterns to consideration of the resulting adaptive process or its consequences either for immigrants or for rural society. The same charge can be leveled against most rural sociology texts. In their concern for rural-urban differences and for the changing character of rural society in the course of economic change, they pay little attention either to ethnicity as a variable or to rural society as a setting for a parallel process of ethnic cultural change.[2]

Surveys, of course, merely reflect the state of the monographic literature. Despite occasional flurries of interest in rural ethnicity in the sociological journals, Brunner's 1929 study, *Immigrant Farmers and Their Children*, and the earlier Carnegie Commission-sponsored *A Stake in the Land* by Peter Speek remain the major synthetic treatments. It is difficult to find even their parallel in the historical literature. There are important studies of immigrant life in rural settings, and ethnicity has frequently been introduced as an independent variable both in works reflecting a Turnerian concern for frontier egalitarianism and in the recent intensive work on social mobility, but there has been little focus on either the emergence of ethnic identity or the process of immigrant adaptation per se. Rural counterparts of the urban ethnic community studies which have appeared in such profusion in recent years are lacking. Monographs in agricultural history have likewise concentrated on the influence of ethnic variation on patterns of farming rather than on the roots of the ethnic identity itself.[3]

Yet a significant minority of all immigrants, and majorities of some national groups, made their adaptation to American life in rural and small-town settings. In the latter decades of the nineteenth century, a fifth to a quarter of all employed foreign-born males reported agricultural occupations. Even in 1920, when that proportion was less than one-seventh, 21 percent of second-generation immigrants were still employed in agriculture, and about a quarter of all the foreign-born and just under a third of the second generation resided outside of cities. The rural and small-town component within individual groups of European background ranged from over half of the Norwegian first generation and almost two-thirds of the second generation to slightly over 10 percent of the Russian-born. Rural proportions should not be exaggerated: even the other Scandinavians, Dutch, Luxembourgers, and Swiss, who like the Norwegians were to be found at the rural end of the immigrant spectrum, were no less urbanized than the nation as a whole, and most foreign-born groups clustered at the other extreme. Nevertheless, as late as 1910 more than 10 percent of all farm operators were foreign-born, a proportion that rose to over 24 percent in the west-north-central region and 29 percent in the Pacific states.[4]

Immigrants and their children thus were an important element in significant parts of rural America. For several groups, ethnic identity evolved within a predominantly rural context; even where country dwellers formed a minority of the total immigrant group, rural settlements sometimes endured longer than urban as pockets of ethnic culture. Clearly, the same variation in experience from group to group and individual to individual that characterized urban adaptation was registered in rural settings. Just as clearly, the same structural and cultural variables that influenced immigrant life in the cities were at work in the countryside. There were enormous differences in demographic patterns, dates of arrival, areas of settlement and agricultural potential, financial resources, and cultural norms. Such wide variations make specificity in any model of rural ethnic cultural formation and adaptation an elusive goal.

Nevertheless, two distinct and superficially contradictory interpretations emerge from the existing literature that confronts directly the question of the nature and pace of rural adaptive processes. Frederick Jackson Turner sounded the first note: "In the crucible of the frontier the immigrants were Americanized, liberated, and fused into a mixed race, English in neither nationality nor characteristics"—free land eased absorption by promoting equality. As Joseph Schafer, good Turnerian that he was, explained, "European peasants in the new environment . . . quickly became transformed into independent American farmers." For Schafer, the nature of the process of land disposal and settlement generally precluded ethnic concentration. Moreover, "except in the massed centers, foreign agricultural settlers offered but slight resistance to the process of Americanization. And in such centers the schools gradually overcame such resistance as the inertia of habit created."[5]

Americanization could be a painful process, as Oscar Handlin stressed. "For those whose habits of life were developed in the peasant village, the emptiness of the prairie farm was in its own way as troublesome as the crowding of the city slum." Loneliness, debt, and a new kind of market-oriented agriculture all promised a painful, individualistic adaptation to American life. Each family had to depend upon its own resources. "The peasants found nowhere an equivalent of the village," wrote Handlin, "nowhere the basis for reestablishing the solidarity of the old communal life." Such emphasis on the physical and psychological costs of the adaptive process among rural immigrants has received wide acceptance, though some have disagreed. Andrew Rolle, for example, argued that "too much has been made of the 'inner struggle' of the immigrant for security and status in an unfriendly New World." Echoing other frontier historians, he pointed instead to "the fluidity of a western frontier" which "broke down past attitudes"; to the "accommodation and acquiescence to the environment" suggested by "the rapidity with which most nationalities were assimilated." Merle Curti's measured assessment of the immigrant experience in Trempealeau County concluded that despite some "evidence of tension," the democracy of the frontier assured that "the foreign-born were increasingly assimilated into the common community."[6]

In contrast to this assimilationist interpretation, others have emphasized the opportunity for cultural maintenance offered by rural conditions. Despite Joseph Schafer's insistence on the difficulty and infrequency of concentrated settlement, his own work constitutes an extended documentation of the importance of immigrant colonies and ethnic cultural survival in his home state of Wisconsin. Speek agreed: "What is not popularly known is the fact that there are foreign provinces in the agricultural sections of the country. . . . Such provinces have become self-sufficient: they have their own towns, their own schools, churches, industries, stores, select local public offcials of their own nationality, speak their own tongue, and live according to the traditions and spirit of their home country. . . . The larger the rural immigrant colony, the less it showed evidence of American influences."[7]

Adapting Robert Park's urban model to a rural setting, other sociologists similarly argued that "rural life tends to conserve and continue immigrant heritages. . . . In the rural immigrant community there are fewer disorganizing contacts than in the city." Assimilation proceeds more slowly, if "nevertheless surely," as the isolated colony ensures "a certain sense of security and freedom," interprets American culture, and prepares the immigrant for participation in it. "Where the family remained intact in the comparative isolation of a prairie homestead and all the social habits of the family were at first maintained," agreed Marcus Lee Hansen, change "came slowly and the inevitable adjustments were made without strain." As Frederick Luebke summarized the case of the Nebraska Germans, "in general, it seems that immigrant institutions operative in the rural and small town environment were fairly successful in easing the process whereby the newcomer was assimilated, mostly, perhaps, by slowing it down."[8]

These apparently conflicting interpretations lend themselves to a simple resolution: in the country as in the city, the presence or absence of an ethnic community was crucial for the endurance of ethnically distinctive traits. And in the country, clustered settlement was essential for community formation. Rural life can be distinguished from urban life by the difficulties of communication arising from the isolation of distance and low density; by its narrower range of social differentiation; by the more frequent identity of family and productive units; by less division of labor and higher role congruence; by simpler, more undifferentiated institutions and higher levels of self-sufficiency and primary relationships.[9] Without community reinforcement of culturally distinctive behavior, immigrants in such a setting would find it difficult to resist assimilation; and without clustered settlement, country distances would discourage ethnic community life while neighbors of different ethnicity offered alternative cultural models. Thus German farmers, for example, have been found to live up to their reputation for greater stability when settled in colonies, but were apparently as mobile as the next man when left without the support of fellow countrymen.[10]

But to hypothesize that clustered settlement was necessary to maintain ethnicity immediately raises other issues. For practical purposes what constituted a minimal cluster? What accounted for variation in degrees of clustering within and among groups? Did all clustered settlements necessarily support ethnic communities capable of fostering ethnically distinctive behavior? Did such communities remain essentially unself-conscious natural groupings, or did they evolve toward the urban pattern of organizational focus and ideological definition, representing something more than the sum of the behavior of their members? These are the kinds of questions that must be explored if the role of the rural ethnic community in the adaptive process is ever to be understood with the same clarity as its urban counterpart. What follows, then, is a discussion of a set of related research issues that arise in determining the existence of settlement concentrations; the reasons for their appearance, persistence, and character; and the process of cultural change within them.

Settlement patterns are the obvious place to begin. Simple documentation presents the first problem. Adequate data on the extent of local clustering have been compiled for only a few states and a few groups. Where the data on local settlement patterns exist, they can be difficult to interpret. For one thing, distributions are often mapped for a single point in time and may give a false sense of locational stability. Although some groups, like the Texas Germans of the Adelsverein or the Dutch Reformed in Michigan, settled as colonies on land purchased in a unit, longitudinal studies of

land taking more often suggest a slow process of sifting and succession before the ethnic stamp of an area became clear, after which it
could again disappear.[11]

Another problem lies in attempting to summarize and compare
the settlement patterns of different groups or areas. Indices capable
of communicating the ethnic mix of an area or of summarizing the
clustering tendencies of a group would seem useful. Even to be able
to state that a given proportion of a group lived in clustered settlements and to compare it with the proportion for a different group
would represent an improvement over the impressionistic comparison
of mapped patterns. One possible solution is suggested by D. Aiden
McQuillan's use of the crop combinations index to summarize
ethnic mix in a particular geographic area. The conceptual problem
of devising an index for the clustering propensity of a given group is
simpler, and some variant of the commonly used indices of concentration and segregation could be applied.[12]

But what constitutes significant clustering? The degree of concentration required to support group life presumably varied by
group, place, and time. A level of concentration sufficiently high
to support an institutional rallying point—in most instances probably
a church—may well have been critical. Geographers John Rice,
Robert Ostergren, and Robert H. Brown have demonstrated for areas
of Minnesota both the relationship of church membership to other
community variables, and some techniques for community delimita-
tion, that offer possible models for the empirical definition of significant clustering.[13]

Differentiating open-country ethnic neighborhoods from those
oriented toward a nucleated settlement presents a final set of data
problems. A rural community oriented toward a neighboring town
would be subjected to greater pressures for cultural change, although
it might also enjoy stronger leadership and organizational focus for
ethnic life than might otherwise be the case. But with existing census
and other data, it is often difficult to locate lower-level nucleations,
let alone determine their functional specialization or relationship
with the surrounding countryside.[14]

But to document the settlement pattern is not to explain it. That
concentrations emerged as rural immigrant families sought the com-
panionship of others speaking the same language, sharing similar
customs, and experiencing the same accommodation pressures would
appear self-evident. But it does not explain why, for some, like the
British farmers analyzed by Charlotte Erickson, the presence of only
a few other English families was sufficient for mutual cultural

support while other groups spread across entire counties. Nor does it explain why persons of the same ethnic background might be concentrated in one area, dispersed in another.[15]

Clearly, chance and personal choice played major roles, but several more systematic forces were also involved. For frontier settlement—probably more common than Hansen's insistence on the immigrant role as fillers-in has sometimes been taken to imply—part of the answer obviously lies in the availability of land or agricultural employment and in the pace of frontier expansion. Schafer argued that the refusal of Congress to make large-scale land grants to groups ensured that competition at land sales would prevent extensive concentration, but nevertheless clustering almost inevitably occurred when the opening of a new agricultural frontier coincided with massive immigration by a particular group, as in the case of the Germans in Wisconsin in the 1840s or the later Russian-German settlements in Dakota. Moreover, the land disposal system itself was sufficiently flexible and subject to manipulation that it was in fact possible for a group to purchase large tracts of land, from a railroad company, for example, should it so desire. While the existence of interspersed blocks of railroad, state, or speculator-held land kept off the market might interfere with local clustering, it could equally function as a reservoir for later community expansion from an initial settlement nucleus. Where immigrants were indeed fillers-in, purchasing from earlier settlers, constraints against clustering may have been more significant.[16]

Also to be taken into account is the role of various types of agents and institutions in promoting clustered settlement. Agents for railroads and timber companies, and state promotional efforts, have received a fair amount of attention, but equally in need of systematic assessment are the numerous land companies organized among potential farmers in both Europe and America. Religion too played a role in encouraging concentration, not only directly through group emigration for religious reasons or via church-sponsored colonization projects like those of St. Paul's Bishop John Ireland, but also less officially. Numerous rural German-Catholic clusters in the Midwest owe their origin to the private promotional efforts of individual priests, who often located settlements carefully in areas where they would have room to expand. In Minnesota, as Hildegard Binder Johnson has shown, religious affiliation played a primary role in rural German neighborhood coalescence.[17]

But as Hansen early noted, it was patterns of chain migration— the influence of early comers on the later locational decisions of relatives, friends, and fellow townsmen—that were the main instruments in the emergence of settlement clustering. Migration chains linked European villages with specific American settlements and stretched across America, as John Hudson has documented for North Dakota, joining urban staging points with country destinations, older farm areas with newer. The prevalence of migration chains meant that often the first pioneers in an area were not fresh off the boat, but rather brought with them experience from farming elsewhere in America that could be shared with later comers. It also meant greater local homogeneity of background and orientation, as well as personal ties spanning the distance from one cluster to another that diminished isolation and opened channels through which aid, information, and perhaps a common sense of ethnic experience and identity could flow.[18]

But the propensity for chain migration itself must have varied. Ties of family and friendship presumably promoted clustering regardless of the presence or absence of such other encouraging factors as religious commitment or a high level of ethnic consciousness. Thus the selectivity of emigration and the consequent structure of the immigrant group were critical. Where emigration fever raged through entire villages, where the forces propelling it swept up entire families and not just young single persons, where intermarriage was thus not forced upon many of the first generation, where resources were sufficient for large numbers to move directly into farming without acquiring the multiple sources of information (and therefore knowledge of alternative settlement possibilities) that a period of prefarming residence in America would encourage—in such circumstances one could anticipate stronger links in the migration chain. Likewise, the stronger the ethnic infrastructure in America— the press, churches, voluntary associations—the more readily available was shared information on settlements newly pioneered by other group members.[19]

The availability of land also mediated the effectiveness of the migration chain. It presented fewest problems on the edge of the frontier where government or other land was plentiful. But even in older areas, the normal process of high population turnover of which the migration chains were themselves a part meant that as farms came on the market they could be purchased by relatives and friends of those already on the spot. The restlessness endemic in the native-born farming population worked to the advantage of the immigrants, as did the withholding of land from the early market by speculators and others, and the widespread availability of leased farms even in frontier areas. Rural tipping points may have existed, so that when ethnic concentration began to reach a certain level, other groups departed with greater dispatch than might otherwise have been the case. Even where early settlers remained, retirement or death could open up opportunities for newcomers. Although there is little firm information on patterns of interfamily land transmission among native-born American farmers, standard practice often involved leasing the farm upon its owner's retirement from active farming, and its sale or continued leasing after his death to provide an equal inheritance for all his children. Where no child wished to take over the home place, it became available to newcomers for purchase or tenancy. The movement of Poles into Connecticut Valley agriculture is only an extreme case of what occurred in numerous areas much closer to the frontier as rural ethnic concentrations slowly built up over time with the departure of earlier settlers.[20]

Cultural backgrounds and more tangible resources inevitably filtered the responsiveness of different groups or individuals to some combination of these and other stimuli to clustering. Religion would play little role for the indifferent, nor opportunity of purchase for the impoverished. The family values that were so critical to the forging of migration chains were themselves variable. Rather than assuming that conditions of American agriculture—particularly its market orientation and pattern of settlement in isolated farmsteads—made irrelevant or impossible much transfer of rural peasant culture, it seems more reasonable to postulate a process of adaptation in which personal goals changed only slowly and those aspects of Old World culture most suited to their achievement in the new environment were adapted, neutral ones like food preferences retained, and the inappropriate abandoned. The goal of providing better for all family members was a central motive for the emigration of countless European peasants who regarded farming as a joint enterprise involving mutual obligations of family members to one another, to future generations, and to the land. Where those values were present, they would encourage settlement clustering, and the resulting ethnic community in turn would encourage their survival to a greater extent than might otherwise be the case.[21]

Family values as transplanted and adapted would appear equally central to the longevity of ethnic concentrations once established. Ethnic community survival is frequently assessed in terms of the persistence or fading of ethnically distinctive traits and behavior, but such assessment presupposes a simple continuity of settlement that in high turnover situations cannot always be taken for granted.

Minnesota's Upsala community, for example, declined not so much because of local acculturation and assimilation as through the physical departure of ethnic group members.[22] Community survival in this elementary sense was assured either by the long-term persistence on the land of first-generation settlers in turn succeeded by their children, or by the replacement of out-migrants with persons of similar ethnic background. But the latter case presupposes the existence of a vital community capable of attracting others desiring a similar way of life. As mass immigration waned and cities increasingly drained the countryside, there were fewer suitable outsiders to attract. Community continuity must have become ever more dependent upon the prevalence within the community of family values that in one way or another encouraged the successful transfer of family land from first to second and later generations.

Rural sociologists in the 1930s, reflecting European scholarship, noted the importance of the family cycle in rural life. In communities characterized by family farms, the stages of family life—from the initial formation of the conjugal unit, to the appearance of small children, to their maturation as part of the family work force, to their departure and the aging and death of the original pair—vitally affected the productive capacity of the agricultural unit, and thus the needs of the farm in turn helped shape the family. Family labor deficits in the early stages could be made up to some extent by hired labor and consumption problems solved by more intensive labor input per worker, but the greatest earnings were always possible at the stage when a maximum number of children were working the farm with the parents.[23] Aging presented special problems; as the farmer's declining strength made some kind of withdrawal or retirement a virtual necessity, its financing and the transmittal of the farm as inheritance to the next generation were inextricably linked.[24] To the extent that frontier communities were frequently settled by cohorts of roughly the same age and family-cycle stage, the family cycle must have been paralleled by a kind of community cycle, as farms—and with them community leadership and the curatorship of community culture—began to pass one by one to the next generation or to newcomers.

Cultural values obviously influenced the way in which immigrant families reacted to the imperatives of the family cycle. Some might place greater value on family self-sufficiency than others, reinforcing large family size. Some might be able to retain children on the farm longer than others, placing high priority on assisting them in the acquisition of their own farms and on their support in turn of the parents. Some might emphasize the equal provision of land for all the children (or sons) in the parents' lifetime, while others might wait until after the parents' death for distribution. Some might place higher priority on keeping the home place intact in the hands of a single child, while others might place little value at all upon retaining children in agriculture or in the community. To the extent that such values varied systematically with ethnicity, they could directly influence the community cycle and ethnic survival. Thus, to return again to a German example, numerous studies for various parts of the country have documented a strong tendency for German rural clustered settlements, once established, to endure and expand as families spread through the area at the expense of their neighbors with each succeeding generation, a visible consequence of attitudes toward family and farm transplanted and adapted. Conversely, some Scandinavian settlements proved less imperialistic and less enduring, placing greater emphasis on the education of children and the achievement of urban opportunity than on farming as a family tradition.[25]

Increasing knowledge of the history of European peasant family life should illuminate the origins of such variation, but the cultural content of family values was also influenced by the selectivity of emigration, and by such factors related to the American settlement process as location, type of farming, degree of cultural difference, nature of group leadership, etc., in ways that remain to be delineated. Family in turn further promoted persistence simply by multiplying the emotional and assistance bonds that made departure a potentially wrenching experience, as studies of rural communities in Michigan and Nebraska have demonstrated.[26] However, in the absense of research on nineteenth- and early-twentieth-century rural family values and relationships to the land in any way comparable to current work on colonial communities, not only degrees of ethnic variation in community stability but relationships between family values and family size, the role of family in mobility, and even the extent to which changing farm size over the life cycle represents a valid index of economic success all remain subject to a good deal of unfounded speculation.[27]

But what about the nature of the ethnic identity presumably nurtured in the clustered rural communities? Informal ties of family, friendship, common roots, and shared adaptation must have quickly created natural patterns of neighboring, though it would be naive to assume that conflict was not also present, indeed heightened by contempt bred of familiarity.[28] Likewise, there is sufficient evidence of the adaptation of more formal community associations imported from Europe—cooperatives, work groups, fraternal orders. American conditions inevitably called forth other manifestations of communal activity. Lay initiative was often central in the creation of the rural church; the school district and local government offered chances for formal participation where the clustered settlement was large enough to give its members majority status.[29] In time, other voluntary associations might follow. The isolation of the farmstead may have limited the frequency of interaction, but its reality for any given community can be charted in marriage alliances, baptismal sponsors and wedding witnesses, and mortgage lending arrangements as well as through more formal organizational cooperation. It would seem, however, that such community activity should be demonstrated empirically rather than simply assumed from propinquity, since it could well vary with values, internal homogeneity, type of farming, and other circumstances of the community.

It is often assumed that the more highly structured the ethnic community, the stronger its hold on its members. But the strength of the rural ethnic community, in terms of preserving ethnically distinctive life-styles, may well have derived more from the very fact of shared culture than from the proliferation of organizational ties. Comparison with persons of other backgrounds certainly would have created a more self-conscious sense of distinctiveness, which would have been enhanced by the realization of commonalities with other communities of similar background. The organizational stage of national ethnic consciousness impinged upon rural communities and lent shape to their sense of ethnic identity through such local representatives as the pastor, the politician, and the school teacher; through the widely circulated ethnic press; and through membership in national benefit associations, lodges, cooperatives, and other organizations. But primary identity probably remained within the community rather than with a more abstractly perceived ethnic group, permitting gradual cultural change as the surrounding environment itself changed without provoking an acute sense of disloyalty to the old culture.

Even the most ethnically self-conscious community could not and usually would not try to prevent its children from learning English, nor were many farmers unwilling to adopt nonethnic agricultural practices where advantageous. Much would depend upon the size of the area dominated by a group. Paved roads, new means of communication, consolidated education, the out-migration of children, and all the other forces that lessened isolation and altered the basis of rural life in the twentieth century helped to ensure that even where ethnic communities survived, their sense of communal identity often redefined itself in terms that were more frequently religious, regional, or rural-occupational than specifically ethnic in content, despite the persistence of behavioral traits of ethnic derivation. Even the rural family has grown toward national norms.[30] Consequently, the extent to which ethnically derived traits constitute any real basis for the crystallization of interest groups in much of rural America today seems questionable, although the degree of ethnic orientation among the numerous offspring of rural ethnic communities now in the cities merits careful inquiry. The ethnic stamp that was preserved for many groups in rural enclaves long after it was diluted under urban conditions perhaps had greater significance for rural society itself than it has had for the perceived reality of pluralism in the American public arena.[31]

But such speculation is premature. I have in this paper suggested that studying the communal basis of rural ethnicity is a necessary prelude to studies of ethnic variation in rural settings. I have emphasized settlement patterns and family norms in the formation and perpetuation of rural ethnic identities. Such a research approach, if applied in comparative fashion to different groups and areas, is likely to produce a typology of adaptive processes, since there is little reason to expect that rural immigrants will prove any more susceptible to analysis via a single assimilation model than their urban brethren have been. Inquiry so structured certainly will not begin to address all the issues posed by rural immigrant settlement, but it seems central for the resolution of the questions raised by the existing generalizations found in the literature concerning the rural immigrant experience. Ultimately, only when rural social history begins to receive the same careful attention directed to its urban counterpart will the rural immigrant be placed within proper historical perspective.

Notes

I wish to acknowledge the assistance of the American Council of Learned Societies, the Charles Warren Center for Studies in American History, and Wellesley College for the research project on rural ethnicity which underlies this paper.

1. Edmund deS. Brunner, *Immigrant Farmers and Their Children* (Garden City, N.Y.: Doubleday, Doran & Co., 1929), xvi. For similar observations, see Andrew F. Rolle, *The Immigrant Upraised: Italian Adventurers and Colonists in an Expanding America* (Norman: University of Oklahoma Press, 1968), pp.

11-13, and Theodore Saloutos, "The Immigrant Contribution to American Agriculture," *Agricultural History* 50 (January 1976): 45-67. Discussion of the specifically rural dimension of immigrant history is conspicuous by its absence, for example, from Rudolph J. Vecoli's lengthy historiographical essay, "European Americans: From Immigrants to Ethnics," in *The Reinterpretation of American History and Culture*, ed. William H. Cartwright and Richard L. Watson, Jr. (Washington, D.C.: National Council for the Social Studies, 1973), pp. 81-111.

2. John L. Shover's *First Majority—Last Minority: The Transforming of Rural Life in America* (DeKalb: Northern Illinois University Press, 1976) and Richard A. Bartlett, *The New Country: A Social History of the American Frontier, 1776-1890* (New York: Oxford University Press, 1974) take special note of the ethnic component in the rural population but pay no real attention to the consequences of that presence. An exception to the lack of attention to immigrants among rural sociologists is Lowry Nelson, *Rural Sociology* (New York: American Book Co., 1948), whose attempt to interpret rural society in terms of a Park-Burgess ecological model includes genuine sensitivity to the ethnic component of rural society.

3. Brunner, *Immigrant Farmers*; Peter A. Speek, *A Stake in the Land* (New York: Harper & Brothers, 1921). Examples of urban studies include Josef J. Barton, *Peasants and Strangers: Italians, Rumanians, and Slovaks in an American City, 1890-1950* (Cambridge, Mass.: Harvard University Press, 1975); Humbert Nelli, *Italians in Chicago, 1880-1930: A Study in Ethnic Mobility* (New York: Oxford University Press, 1970); Ulf Beijbom, *Swedes in Chicago: A Demographic and Social Study of the 1846-1880 Immigration* (Stockholm: Läromedels Förlaget, 1971); Kathleen Neils Conzen, *Immigrant Milwaukee, 1836-1860: Accommodation and Community in a Frontier City* (Cambridge, Mass.: Harvard University Press, 1976). Examples of works dealing with ethnic variations in patterns of farming are Seddie Cogswell, Jr., *Tenure, Nativity, and Age as Factors in Iowa Agriculture, 1850-1880* (Ames: Iowa State University Press, 1975); Allan G. Bogue, *From Prairie to Cornbelt* (Chicago: University of Chicago Press, 1963); Michael P. Conzen, *Frontier Farming in an Urban Shadow* (Madison: State Historical Society of Wisconsin for the Department of History, University of Wisconsin, 1971).

4. E. P. Hutchinson, *Immigrants and Their Children, 1850-1950* (New York: Wiley, 1956); Niles Carpenter, *Immigrants and Their Children, 1920* (Washington, D.C.: GPO, 1927); Saloutos, "Immigrant Contribution."

5. Frederick Jackson Turner, *Frontier and Section: Selected Essays* (Englewood Cliffs, N.J.: Prentice-Hall, 1961); Edward N. Saveth, *American Historians and European Immigrants, 1875-1925* (New York: Russell and Russell, 1965), pp. 122-37; Joseph Schafer, *The Social History of American Agriculture* (New York: Macmillan, 1936), pp. 209, 216.

6. Oscar Handlin, *The Uprooted* (New York: Grosset and Dunlap, 1951), pp. 165, 83-88, 105; Rolle, *Immigrant Upraised*, pp. 335, 299, 335; Merle Curti et al., *The Making of an American Community: A Case Study of Democracy in a Frontier County* (Stanford, Calif.: Stanford University Press, 1959), p. 138;

see also Thomas D. Clark, *Frontier America*, 2d ed. (New York: Scribner, 1969), p. 20; Bartlett, *New Country*, p. 155, for similar interpretations.

7. Joseph Schafer, *Four Wisconsin Counties: Prairie and Forest* (Madison: State Historical Society of Wisconsin, 1927); idem, *The Winnebago-Horicon Basin: A Type Study in Western History* (Madison: State Historical Society of Wisconsin, 1937); idem, "The Yankee and the Teuton in Wisconsin," *Wisconsin Magazine of History* 6 (December-June 1922-23): 125-45, 261-79, 386-402; 7 (September 1923): 3-19; Speek, *Stake in the Land*, pp. 130-31; see also Brunner, *Immigrant Farmers*, pp. 75-115, who concludes that despite such concentration, more than two-thirds of seventy sample communities studied were on a "well-chartered course" to complete assimilation (p. 115).

8. William Carlson Smith, *Americans in the Making: The Natural History of the Assimilation of Immigrants* (New York: D. Appleton-Century Co., 1939), pp. 211-14, 179-86; Marcus Lee Hansen, "Immigration and American Culture," in Hansen, *The Immigrant in American History* (New York: Harper and Row, 1964), p. 151; Frederick C. Luebke, *Immigrants and Politics: The Germans of Nebraska, 1880-1900* (Lincoln: University of Nebraska Press, 1969), p. 35. See also Nelson, *Rural Sociology*, pp. 159-203.

9. Charles J. Galpin, *Rural Life* (New York: Century Co., 1923), pp. 3-30; John H. Kolb and Edmund deS. Brunner, *Rural Social Trends* (New York: McGraw-Hill, 1933), p. 8; Carl C. Taylor et al., *Rural Life in the United States* (New York: Alfred A. Knopf, 1949), pp. 8-10.

10. John Hawgood, *The Tragedy of German-America* (New York: G. P. Putnam's Sons, 1940), pp. 26-33; Russell L. Gerlach, *Immigrants in the Ozarks* (Columbia: University of Missouri Press, 1977); Schafer, *Winnebago-Horicon*; Conzen, *Frontier Farming*; Bogue, *Prairie to Cornbelt*; Curti, *American Community*.

11. Rudolph L. Biesele, *The History of the German Settlements in Texas 1831-1861* (Austin, Tex.: Press of Von Boeckmann-Jones Co., 1930); Elaine M. Bjorklund, "Ideology and Culture Exemplified in Southwestern Michigan," *Annals of the Association of American Geographers* 54 (June 1964): 227-41; Kathleen Neils Conzen, "Farm and Family: A German Settlement on the Minnesota Frontier," paper presented at meeting of the American Historical Association, Washington, D.C., December 1976.

12. D. Aidan McQuillan, "Adaptation of Three Immigrant Groups to Farming in Central Kansas, 1875-1925" (Ph.D. diss., University of Wisconsin, 1975); Hutchinson, *Immigrants and Their Children*; Karl E. and Alma Taeuber, *Negroes in Cities* (Chicago: Aldine, 1965), pp. 203-4, 223-38.

13. Galpin, *Rural Life*, pp. 287-314; Conzen, "Farm and Family"; John G. Rice, *Patterns of Ethnicity in a Minnesota County, 1880-1905*, Geographical Reports 4 (Department of Geography, University of Umeå [Sweden], 1973; Robert C. Ostergren, "Cultural Homogeneity and Population Stability among Swedish Immigrants in Chisago County," *Minnesota History* 43 (Fall 1973): 255-69; Robert H. Brown, "The Upsala, Minnesota, Community: A Case Study in Rural Dynamics," *Annals of the Association of American Geographers* 57 (June 1967): 267-300.

14. Conzen, *Frontier Farming*; Rice, *Patterns of Ethnicity*; for a British approach to this problem, see Brian K. Roberts, *Rural Settlement in Britain* (Hamden, Conn.: Shoe String Press, 1977).

15. Charlotte Erickson, *Invisible Immigrants* (Coral Gables, Fl.: University of Miami Press, 1972).

16. Marcus Lee Hansen, "Immigration and Expansion," in idem, *Immigrant*, p. 76; Schafer, *Four Counties*; John C. Hudson, "Migration to an American Frontier," *Annals of the Association of American Geographers* 66 (June 1976): 245–47; John A. Hostetler, *Hutterite Society* (Baltimore: Johns Hopkins University Press, 1974), pp. 119–33; Emory Kempton Lindquist, *Smoky Valley People: A History of Lindsborg, Kansas* (Lindsborg, Kans: Bethany College, 1953), p. 37; Conzen, "Farm and Family."

17. Paul W. Gates, *The Illinois Central Railroad and Its Colonization Work* (Cambridge, Mass.: Harvard University Press, 1934); Speek, *Stake in the Land*; Theodore C. Blegen, "The Competition of the Northwestern States for Immigrants," *Wisconsin Magazine of History* 3 (September 1919): 3–29; Lindquist, *Smoky Valley*, pp. 169–79; Noel Iverson, *Germania U.S.A.: Social Change in New Ulm, Minnesota* (Minneapolis: University of Minnesota Press, 1966); James P. Shannon, *Catholic Colonization on the Western Frontier* (New Haven, Conn.: Yale University Press, 1957); Sister Mary Gilbert Kelly, *Catholic Immigrant Colonization Projects in the United States, 1815-1860* (New York: United States Catholic Historical Society, 1939); Hildegard Binder Johnson, "Factors Influencing the Distribution of the German Pioneer Population in Minnesota," *Agricultural History* 19 (January 1945): 39–57.

18. Hansen, "Immigration and Expansion," pp. 68–90; Ostergren, "Cultural Homogeneity"; Hudson, "Migration"; Kenneth D. Bjork, *West of the Great Divide: Norwegian Migration to the Pacific Coast, 1847-1893* (Northfield, Minn.: Norwegian-American Historical Association, 1958); Joseph Scheben, *Untersuchungen zur Methode und Technik der deutsch-amerikanischen Wanderungsforschung* (Bonn: Ludwig Röhrscheid Verlag, 1939).

19. Cf. the discussion concerning the contrast between Danish and Norwegian patterns in Torben Krontoft, "Factors in Assimilation: A Comparative Study," *Norwegian-American Studies* 26 (1974): 184–205.

20. Conzen, "Farm and Family," summarizes this argument and literature; see also Brunner, *Immigrant Farmers*, pp. 213–43; Schafer, *Winnebago-Horicon Basin*; A.B. Hollingshead, "Changes in Land Ownership as an Index of Succession in Rural Communities," *American Journal of Sociology* 43 (March 1938): 764–77; Kenneth H. Parsons and Eliot O. Waples, *Keeping the Farm in the Family: A Study of Ownership Processes in a Low Tenancy Area of Eastern Wisconsin*, Wisconsin Agricultural Experiment Station Research Bulletin 157 (1945); Gerlach, *Immigrants in the Ozarks*; McQuillan, "Adaptation."

21. Conzen, "Farm and Family."

22. Brown, "Upsala."

23. Charles P. Loomis, "The Study of the Life Cycle of Families," *Rural Sociology* 1 (June 1936): 180–99; P. A. Sorokin et al., *A Systematic Source*

Book in Rural Sociology, 3 vols. (Minneapolis: University of Minnesota Press, 1931), 2:41ff; E. L. Kirkpatrick, *The Life Cycle of the Farm Family,* Wisconsin Agricultural Experiment Station Research Bulletin 121 (1934); for use of the life cycle concept in social history more generally, see Tamara K. Hareven, "The Family as Process: The Historical Study of the Family Cycle," *Journal of Social History* 7 (Spring 1974): 322-29.

24. Erven J. Long and Kenneth H. Parsons, *How Family Labor Affects Wisconsin Farming,* Wisconsin Agricultural Experiment Station Bulletin 167 (1950), pp. 6-10; Richard J. Ely and Charles J. Galpin, "Tenancy in an Ideal System of Landownership," *American Economic Review* 9, Supplement (March 1919): 180-212; see also Dan Kanel, "The Land Tenure Process in American Agriculture: The Competitive Status of Family Farms and Their Adjustment to the Life Cycle of Farm Families" (Ph.D. diss., University of Wisconsin, 1953).

25. In addition to the Schafer, K. Conzen, and Hollingshead studies cited above, see also Walter L. Slocum, "Ethnic Stocks as Cultural Types in Rural Wisconsin" (Ph.D. diss., University of Wisconsin, 1940); Gerlach, *Immigrants in the Ozarks;* Terry G. Jordan, *German Seed in Texas Soil* (Austin: University of Texas Press, 1966). It was Germans who moved into the Upsala community when the Swedes departed; Brown, "Upsala." Slocum, "Ethnic Stocks"; Peter A. Munch, "Social Adjustment among Wisconsin Norwegians," *American Sociological Review* 14 (December 1949): 780-87; Marian McNeil Deininger, "Some Differential Characteristics of Minnesota's Major Ethnic Groups in Selected Rural Townships" (Ph.D. diss., University of Minnesota, 1958).

26. Robert E. Bieder, "Kinship as a Factor in Migration," *Journal of Marriage and the Family* 35 (August 1973): 429-39; Hollingshead, "Land Succession."

27. Cf. Richard A. Easterlin, "Population Change and Farm Settlement in the Northern United States," *Journal of Economic History* 36 (March 1976): 126-41. On the European background, see Lutz K. Berkner, "Rural Family Organization in Europe: A Problem in Comparative History," *Peasant Studies Newsletter* 1 (October 1972): 149-56.

28. Any set of immigrant letters or immigrant autobiography will document the kinds of petty quarrels that could rend a community and make harmony a poor measure for the existence of community sentiment; e.g., "George Kulzer, 1831-1912: A Continuing Story of a Stearns County Pioneer," a particularly candid account reprinted serially in the *Albany* (Minnesota) *Enterprise,* summer 1976. See also Robert R. Dykstra, *The Cattle Towns* (New York: Knopf, 1968) on the role of conflict in community formation.

29. But the immigrant majority could also find itself impotent to control local institutions; see J. Olson Anders, "Educational Beginnings in a Typical Prairie County," *Rural Sociology* 7 (December 1942): 423-31.

30. Douglas G. Marshall, "The Decline in Farm Family Fertility and Its Relationship to Nationality and Religious Background," *Rural Sociology* 15 (March 1950): 42-49.

31. Compare with Nathan Glazer and Daniel P. Moynihan, Introduction, in *Ethnicity: Theory and Experience*, ed. Nathan Glazer and Daniel P. Moynihan (Cambridge, Mass.: Harvard University Press, 1975); John Higham, *Send These to Me* (New York: Atheneum, 1975).

The Great Plains as a Colonization Zone for Eastern Indians

Arrell Morgan Gibson

Anglo-American and European homeseekers were not the first people to colonize the Great Plains in recent centuries, as is commonly believed. Rather, this distinction belongs to the Indians. They came onto the plains in two great ethnic migrations. The first, occurring around 1700, was a voluntary exodus; the second, extending over the period 1816–45, was a forced exile.

The early aboriginal colonization of the Great Plains consisted of thirty tribes and included Sioux and Cheyenne farmers from the upper Mississippi Valley, Blackfeet agrarians from north of the Yellowstone, and Comanche and Kiowa hunter-gatherers from the Rocky Mountains. They were joined by woodland-dwelling Osages, Poncas, Otos, Missouris, and other Siouian-speaking peoples from the east. Their new homeland, a vast grassland occupying the continental heartland from Canada to the Rio Grande, was the principal habitat for the bison, huge hairy beasts that ranged in primal herds. The emigrating tribesmen adopted the horse, reintroduced into North America by the European imperial nations; it became the grand catalyst which revolutionized their life-style. The horse, with the bison, comprised the economic foundation for the emerging plains Indian culture that these aboriginal colonists formulated.

The plains tribes remained largely free of imperial dominion because the interior situation and awesome isolation of their new habitat made it less attractive for the European imperial establishment than the accessible littoral of North America. Thus they escaped any appreciable sustained attention and exploitation by explorers, traders, and missionaries, and provide a striking contrast to the general trend of tribal degradation, depopulation, and cultural deprivation endured by those tribes more conveniently situated to the intruders. Left largely to themselves, these pioneer Great Plains dwellers forged a strong culture that increased their martial power, extended their ethnic longevity, and enabled them to form the most

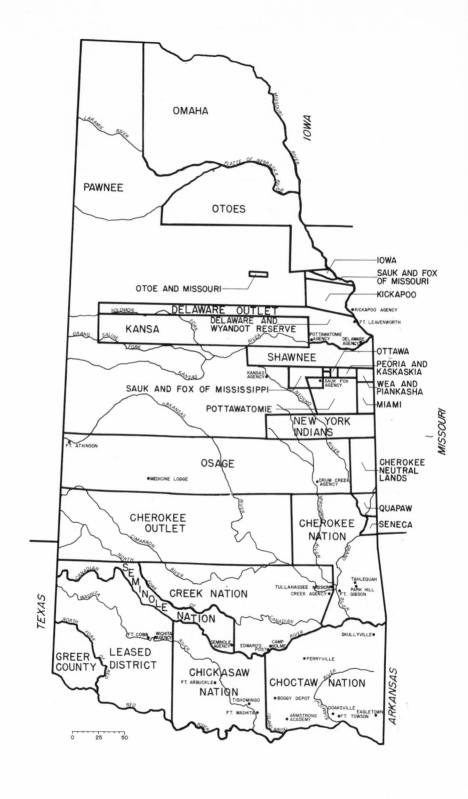

OMAHA

PAWNEE

OTOES

IOWA

LARAMIE RIVER

PLATTE OF NEBRASKA RIVER

MISSOURI RIVER

IOWA

SAUK AND FOX
OF MISSOURI

KICKAPOO

●KICKAPOO AGENCY

●FT. LEAVENWORTH

OTOE AND MISSOURI

DELAWARE OUTLET

SOLOMON

KANSA

GRAND *SALINE* *FORK*

FORK

DELAWARE AND
WYANDOT RESERVE

POTTAWATOMIE
AGENCY

DELAWARE
AGENCY

OTTAWA

SHAWNEE

KANSAS

KANSAS
AGENCY●

SAUK FOX
AGENCY

PEORIA AND
KASKASKIA

WEA AND
PIANKASHA

SAUK AND FOX OF MISSISSIPPI

NEOSHO

MIAMI

POTTAWATOMIE

ARKANSAS

NEW YORK
INDIANS

●FT. ATKINSON

OSAGE

RIVER

CHEROKEE
NEUTRAL
LANDS

●MEDICINE LODGE

●DRUM CREEK
AGENCY

VERDIGRIS RIVER

QUAPAW

SENECA

CHEROKEE
OUTLET

CIMARRON

NORTH

RIVER

CHEROKEE
NATION

GRAND RIVER

SEMINOLE

CREEK NATION

TAHLEQUAH
●PARK HILL

TULLAHASSEE MISSION●
CREEK AGENCY●

●FT. GIBSON

TEXAS

CANADIAN

WASHITA

NATION

FORK OF RIVER

CANADIAN RIVER

FT. COBB●

WICHITA
AGENCY

SEMINOLE
AGENCY

EDWARD'S
POST

CAMP
HOLMES

SKULLYVILLE

GREER
COUNTY

LEASED
DISTRICT

NORTH FORK

RED RIVER

●PERRYVILLE

CHICKASAW

NATION

FT. ARBUCKLE●

TISHOMINGO

●BOGGY DEPOT

CHOCTAW NATION

KIAMICHI RIVER

DOAKSVILLE
●FT. TOWSON

EAGLETOWN

ARKANSAS

FT. WASHITA●

ARMSTRONG
ACADEMY

BLUE RIVER

RED RIVER

MISSOURI

0   25   50

resistive barrier posed by any Indian community to the transcontinental expansion of the latter-day Anglo-American nation.

The second wave of Indian colonists entered the Great Plains region beginning about 1816. They shared several characteristics with the Anglo-American and European immigrant settlers who arrived later in the century. Both groups were ethnically heterogeneous. Just as the later immigrant communities on the Great Plains contained not only the familiar Anglo-American stock and European elements including Scandinavian, German, and Czech, but also a scattering of blacks—freedmen and their descendants—the precursor Indian immigrants were likewise diverse. Chickasaw and Seminole immigrants differed from Ottawa and Wyandot immigrants in language and culture, even physical characteristics, as conspicuously as Czech immigrants differed from English immigrants.

In addition, the second wave of Indian immigrants, like many European settlers of later years, fled oppressive conditions in their homelands. The former were refugees from the callous cruelty of Anglo-American neighbors lusting for tribal lands and from coercive state and national policies; the latter were refugees from economic disaster and political tyranny. Moreover, both groups in varying degrees were carriers of Western civilization, of Anglo-American culture, onto the plains. Northern tribal immigrants, including Wyandots, and southern tribal immigrants, including Cherokees, introduced schools, churches, constitutional government, commercial agriculture and stock raising, and slaveholding into the western wilderness fifty years before the process of cultural transformation was taken up by Anglo-American and European immigrant settlers.

Both Indian and European settler groups were subjected to intense promotion, much of it misleading, concerning the "grand promise" of a new life on the plains in an attempt to offset their reluctance to migrate to this land. Early explorer accounts had depicted the vast trans-Missouri territory as sterile wasteland, the Great American Desert. Thus it was held in low public esteem. The intensive promotion applied to this region by publicists employed by railway companies and immigration bureaus of the Great Plains states and territories during the latter nineteenth century to offset the Great American Desert image is a familiar phenomenon. However, eastern Indians fifty years before were subjected to similar assurances that the region was a "fair land," "the garden of the world," in an attempt to overcome their objections to settling the plains region.[1]

A continuing dilemma facing the national government in its role

as a manager of western development was, on the one hand, satisfying pioneers' insatiable demand for more land and, on the other,
fulfilling its constitutionally assigned duty of protecting the interests
of resident Indian tribes. The seemingly irresistible flow of American
settlement across the trans-Appalachian West and the cession treaties
negotiated between federal commissioners and tribal leaders had
substantially reduced the territory of the resident tribes. Government
leaders, aware of the destructive effect of white contact on the
tribes, knew that successive waves of settlement pushing across the
frontier would soon pose a threat to the remaining Indian lands.

President Thomas Jefferson particularly considered two policies
as a solution to the "Indian problem." One policy was assimilation—a
government-subsidized program of education and vocational instruction to transform resident tribesmen so that eventually they could
be absorbed genetically and culturally into the Anglo-American
community. His other policy was to offer tribes the alternative of
removal. For some time he had considered resettling eastern Indians
in the trans-Mississippi West. He hoped to create in a portion of the
Louisiana Purchase area, which included a substantial portion of the
Great Plains, an Indian colonization zone. An act of Congress in
1804 authorized the president to begin removal negotiations with the
various eastern tribes, and by 1808 portions of several Indian nations
from both north and south of the Ohio River began emigrating to
the west, mostly to the area that would become Missouri and Arkansas.[2]

The period of the War of 1812 was a crucial time in the Indian-
settler contest for land. Tribes in the Old Northwest, battered and
angered at territorial losses, coalesced into the pan-Indian confed-
eration formed by Tecumseh and Tenskwatawa, the Prophet. They
supported the British cause in the War of 1812 as a tactical step to
thwart American expansion into their remaining tribal domains.
The Old Northwest Indians were successively defeated by American
armies led by General William Henry Harrison. Americans demanded
that their government punish those tribes for their treasonable association with the enemy, Great Britain, the punishment to consist of
cession of all their lands in the Old Northwest and their removal west
of the Mississippi River.

William Clark, superintendent of Indian affairs at St. Louis, provided the rhetorical foundations for exiling the eastern tribes in a
statement to Secretary of War James Barbour: "The relative condition of the United States on the one side, and the Indian tribes on
the other," had drastically changed. Before the War of 1812, he

declared, "the tribes nearest our settlements were a formidable and terrible enemy; since then, their power has been broken, their war-like spirit subdued, and themselves sunk into objects of pity and commiseration." He added that "while strong and hostile, it has been our obvious policy to weaken them; now that they are weak and harmless, and most of their lands fallen into our hands, justice and humanity require us to cherish and befriend them." Clark urged that "the tribes now within the limits of the States and Territories should be removed" to the trans-Mississippi country "where they could rest in peace." Thus it was that removal became a certain and continuing policy of the national government as the solution to the problem of clearing the path for American settler expansion.[3]

In the aftermath of the War of 1812, Delawares, Kickapoos, Wyandots, Sacs and Foxes, Potawatomis, and various other Old Northwest tribes began emigrating to the trans-Mississippi West. Bands of these tribesmen—Kickapoos, Winnebagos, Sacs and Foxes—determined to retain their ancestral lands and resisted efforts by federal officials to relocate them. And attempts by relocated Sac and Fox tribesmen to return to their homeland in western Illinois led to the Black Hawk War. Bands of Cherokees and Choctaws also migrated to the trans-Mississippi West between 1817 and 1820.

The western Indian colonization zone initially was an amorphous territory; belatedly it evolved into a legally defined area, much of it situated on the Great Plains, reserved exclusively for aboriginal settlement. In the early years of colonizing eastern Indians in the trans-Mississippi West, the program was complicated by federal officials settling tribes from the Old Northwest and Old Southwest on treaty-assigned reservations in the lower Mississippi Valley, mostly in the future states of Arkansas and Missouri. At first it appeared that this would be the principal use the national government would make of the area. In order to provide space for the emigrating eastern tribesmen, the resident tribes had to be induced to surrender title to vast tracts in the Missouri and Arkansas portions of the Louisiana Territory and to accept reduced domains. Thus in 1808 the Osages ceded claim to lands in Missouri and to the northern half of Arkansas and in 1818 the Quapaws ceded their claim to lands in Arkansas between the Red and Arkansas rivers.

The intent of some officials in the national government to use a goodly portion of the Mississippi Valley as an Indian colonization zone for the eastern tribes manifested a lag in communications and a lack of coordination among government leaders, because at the very time that officials of the War Department were negotiating treaties of removal with certain eastern tribes and assigning them permanent reservations in the Mississippi Valley, the processes of American frontier expansion were at work in exactly the same region. Moreover, the extension of the settler frontier was abetted by leaders in the Congress. The treaties negotiated with the Kickapoos and other tribes of the Old Northwest illustrate this conflict in national purpose, policy, and action. In 1819, when tribal leaders surrendered their lands in the Old Northwest and accepted permanent reservations in Missouri Territory, that region was already passing through the familiar American frontier metamorphosis and was only two years from statehood.

Other cases illustrating this dichotomy in national purpose include the Cherokee and Choctaw treaties, which assigned these Indian nations vast tracts in the Arkansas Territory. In 1817 Cherokee leaders signed the first of several treaties surrendering substantial portions of their eastern lands in exchange for a vast domain in what became northwestern Arkansas. Three years later Choctaw chiefs exchanged much of their eastern territory in Mississippi for a new western home that included the southwestern quadrant of the Arkansas Territory. A portion of each of these two tribes emigrated to those lands under the terms of the treaties.

Two streams of development were thus occurring in this region contemporaneously, and the national government was a party to both. New territories were being created to accommodate pioneer-settler demands, and these political entities were being prepared for admission to the Union. And western Arkansas and western Missouri were becoming a checkerboard of reservations settled by tribes from the Old Northwest and the Old Southwest. The immigrant Indians constituted a formidable barrier to the expansive American settlers, and they effectively arrested the seemingly irrevocable developmental pattern common to the other portions of the Old West. The self-governing Indian communities were states within emerging states. Inevitably, Anglo-American settlers coveted the rich, fertile lands of the reservations and engaged the Indians in a bitter contest for them.

However, it was as always an unequal contest, for the truism of Indian-settler relations was that when interests were in conflict, the settlers always triumphed. The settlers' victories were due to the fact that they were voters while the Indians were not. By his exercise of the ballot, the pioneer could choose the territorial delegate to Congress, through whom he had a voice in the formulation of the law and policy to serve his personal and public interests. A cause promoted obsessively by the Missouri and Arkansas congressional delegates was the clearing from their territories of those obstacles to settlement and orderly development—the Indian communities. Once the Indians were gone, they could achieve the ultimate for their territories—statehood in the American Union.

While their spokesmen in Washington were doing their bidding by making legal the appropriation of the Indian land they so ardently coveted and arranging to relocate the resident tribes farther west in the wilderness, the Mississippi Valley settlers copied the tactics of harrassment being used so successfully by citizens of Alabama and Mississippi against resident native Americans. Bands of settlers regularly terrorized the Indian communities of western Missouri and Arkansas, deliberately making life so miserable for the aborigines that they would surrender their reservations and move west to escape the torment. The raiders burned Indian towns, violated Indian households, and ran off tribal livestock with impunity. Local courts and friendly juries protected presumptive settler rights in any contest over livestock and other property seized in these raids. And if the Indians resisted and drove the intruders off, it was called an "Indian war" and justified calling federal troops from Fort Smith and other frontier posts to quell the "uprising."

In 1825, Secretary of War John C. Calhoun determined to end for all time this periodic tribal relocation. He described to President Monroe the tragedy of the constant uprooting of the tribes to open land for American settlers. He added: "One of the greatest evils to which they are subject is that incessant pressure of our population, which forces them from seat to seat. To guard against this evil . . . there ought to be the strongest and most solemn assurance that the country given them should be theirs, as a permanent home for themselves and their posterity."[4]

National leaders had been accustomed to regard the land between the Atlantic Ocean and the Mississippi River as more than adequate for the settlement needs of the American people. It was surprising, therefore, to many that American expansion had thrust beyond the Mississippi River. Even so, the vast empty regions of the Mississippi Valley, for the most part north of Missouri, contained such attractive lands that it was inconceivable to most government leaders that the needs of the American people would ever extend beyond this westernmost settlement area.

Calhoun therefore recommended that President Monroe set aside the region west of Missouri and Arkansas as a permanent reserve; there the federal government could colonize the tribes remaining in the eastern United States as well as those then residing in Arkansas

and Missouri. President Monroe and his successors followed Calhoun's recommendation. With the support of Congress, a vast tract
situated between the western borders of Missouri and Arkansas and
the 100th meridian, extending from 43°30′ south to the Red River,
and embracing a considerable portion of the Great Plains, was reserved for the exclusive colonization of aboriginal peoples. At first
designated the Indian Country, it was by 1830 called the Indian
Territory, a name its southeastern portion retained until 1907.

The first aborigines to be resettled in Indian Territory and thus
the first pioneers to approach the Great Plains were those tribesmen
already colonized in the Mississippi Valley. In 1825 the Choctaws
ceded their lands in southwestern Arkansas Territory, three years
later the Cherokees ceded their lands in northwestern Arkansas
Territory, and these aboriginal pioneers made their final move into
Indian Territory. The immigrant tribes residing in the new state of
Missouri, including the Kickapoos, were relocated in the northern
portion of Indian Territory, which in 1854 became Kansas Territory.

Granted that creation of the Indian Territory as a permanent
refuge for transplanted eastern Indians on the western margin of the
United States, in some respects, was an act of humanity on the part
of certain federal officials, it was also an expression of self-serving
national purpose. By the early 1820s, many public leaders were in-
fatuated with what could be called the doctrine of "national completeness," the view that, with the national territory from the
Atlantic Seaboard to the western border of Missouri populated,
organized politically, and integrated into the national life, and with a
suitable land reserve here and there in the Old Northwest, the Old
Southwest, and particularly in the upper Mississippi Valley, the
United States had reached the westernmost limit of its development.
Because the organized national territory was regarded as adequate for
the foreseeable needs of the nation, the land west of Missouri was
surplus. Moreover, the region designated the Indian Territory had
become fixed in the public mind as a vast inhospitable waste, an
image formed and reinforced by published accounts of public and
private exploring expeditions which had reconnoitered portions of it.

The public attitude that because the region west of Missouri—
designated the Great American Desert—was unfit for Anglo-American
pursuits, it was a suitable homeland for displaced eastern Indians was
derived from the ethnocentric conclusion held by many Anglo-
Americans that Indian land needs were much simpler than those of
the more advanced white agrarian settlers. They analyzed aborigines in

an evolutionary context. Eastern Indians were rated as more advanced than western Indians; yet, they had evolved only to the stockraising level of economy and thus they needed mainly grassland, which dominated the topography west of Missouri. This in part explains the generous gesture of national leaders in setting aside a substantial portion of the trans-Missouri region as a resettlement zone for the eastern tribes. They clearly believed that the low public esteem for the region would protect the uprooted aborigines from ever again being placed in competition with Anglo-American settlers.

Public discussions of the feasibility of establishing a permanent Indian colonization zone west of Missouri reinforced the "national completeness" view. Congressmen alluded to the Indian colonization zone west of Missouri as a "permanent" aboriginal reserve where the tribes "are outside of us, and in a place which will ever remain on the outside." At that time the Department of War was responsible for maintaining relations with the Indian nations; thus declarations by the secretary of war regarding tribes were of the utmost moment. During 1826, Secretary of War James Barbour stated that "the future residence of these people will forever be undisturbed; that there, at least, they will find a home and a resting place; and being exclusively under the control of the United States, and, consequently, free from the rival claims of any of the States, the former may plight its most solemn faith that it shall be theirs forever; and this guaranty is therefore given."[5]

Thus by the 1820s the national government had abandoned its policy of assimilation in favor of segregation and isolation for eastern tribesmen, exiling them to the Indian Territory. Most natives from the Old Northwest had been relocated and fragments of tribes from the Old Southwest likewise had migrated to Indian Territory. But the populous Indian communities residing south of the Ohio River, the so-called Five Civilized Tribes—the Creeks, Seminoles, Choctaws, Cherokees, and Chickasaws—preferred to remain in their ancestral territories.

To strengthen the cause for their remaining in the East, leaders of the southern tribes developed various strategies to protect their lands and their right to reside where they chose. One tactic was cooperation with federal officials. Thus, they reluctantly ceded to the United States by successive treaties large tracts of tribal land to accommodate settler demands, retaining in each case a cherished homeland core of territory. The Cherokees by 1820 had surrendered most of their lands in western North Carolina, South Carolina, and Tennessee, and retained a domain in northwestern Georgia centering on their tribal capital at New Echota. The Creeks had surrendered their lands in southern Georgia and retained a homeland core in Alabama. The Seminoles, having only recently come under United States jurisdiction, were in the process of accepting reduced territory in Florida. The Choctaws had ceded much of their territory in central and southern Mississippi and were on the verge of agreeing to another large cession. And the Chickasaws, once lords over much of Tennessee, Kentucky, northern Alabama, and northern Mississippi, had retreated through successive land cession treaties to a small domain in northern Mississippi and northwestern Alabama. It was on these reduced domains that the Five Civilized Tribes made their last stand to preserve the land of their ancestors from the onslaught of settlers and to thwart exile to the Great Plains.

Another tribal strategy was coexistence—the hope held by leaders of the southern tribes that they could so order their lives that Anglo-Americans would accept them as worthy neighbors. To accomplish this, they studiously supported the United States in its international goals. Thus during the War of 1812 these tribes remained loyal to the United States. They politely rejected Tecumseh's plea for Indian brotherhood and war on the Americans. The Cherokee, Choctaw, Creek, and Chickasaw nations each formed a regiment of fighting men which joined General Andrew Jackson's army to guard the southwestern frontier against British invasion. One Creek faction, the Red Sticks, accepted Tecumseh's gospel and made war on the American settlements in the Southwest; however, loyal Creek, Cherokee, Chickasaw, and Choctaw regiments in Jackson's army smashed the Creek Red Sticks at the Battle of Horseshoe Bend.

In their attempts to prove to Anglo-American pioneers that they were worthy neighbors, southern tribal leaders urged great changes among their people. Adopting white ways in dress and industry, the Indians established successful farms, plantations, and businesses in their nations—many became prosperous slave owners. In addition, they changed their political systems from traditional tribal governments to governments based on written constitutions with elective officials, courts, and other elements of enlightened polity.

Tribal leaders welcomed missionaries to their nations. The missionaries established schools, which allowed many Indian youths to complete basic studies in local mission schools and then continue their education in colleges situated in the Northeast. Soon in each Indian nation there was formed a corps of elitist leaders, most of whom were better educated than whites in the neighboring settlements and able to cope with their white counterparts in the professions, industry, business, and politics.

Leaders of the southern tribes could not comprehend, in their hope to coexist and to keep up with the fast changes swirling about their nations, that their success in altering tribal ways in education, business, and polity only precipitated envy and antagonism among their Anglo-American neighbors. Indian progress was regarded as a threat. Leaders of the southern tribes did not understand that nineteenth-century Anglo-American society was obsessively ethnocentric—it feared, scorned, and rejected people unlike themselves in culture and physical appearance.

Anglo-American settlers in Georgia, Alabama, and Mississippi regarded resident Indians as barriers to the consummation of their material goals. Indians occupied rich agricultural lands that they coveted. Their wishes were translated into policy and law by their representatives and senators in the United States Congress, and by a chief executive elected in 1828. The exile of the southern tribes to the Great American Desert was profoundly affected by Andrew Jackson's accession to the presidency. Jackson had spent much of his early life on the Tennessee frontier; he therefore held the typical frontiersman's attitude toward any Indian tribes that constituted a barrier to white settlements. So obsessed was the president with driving the Indian tribes to the Great American Desert that he gave his personal attention to the matter. It is significant that most of the southern tribes were removed during his administration and that those removals not completed before he left office had been set in motion.

Jackson's leadership in exiling the eastern tribesmen to the Indian Territory extended to blatant disregard of Supreme Court decisions sustaining the immunity of Indian nations from state action and of the obligation of the national government to provide special protection for them from state and private trespass. And he pressed Congress for an Indian colonization statute which evolved as the Indian Removal Act of 1830.

Federal officials had to take several preliminary steps before the removal program could be effectuated. First, the land west of Missouri and Arkansas set aside for the colonization of eastern Indians was occupied by several tribes. To make room for the emigrating tribesmen the local Indians had to agree to accept reduced tribal territories, and, in some cases, relocation. Much of the work of negotiating treaties and relocating the local tribes was accomplished by William Clark, superintendent of Indian affairs at St. Louis. His negotiations with the Kansas, Osages, Quapaws, and other resident tribes opened the land west of Missouri and Arkansas for the eastern Indians.

Also federal officials had to persuade eastern tribesmen to surrender the surviving homeland cores of their once vast tribal territories and migrate to the West—something virtually all of the eastern
Indians were understandably reluctant to do. Pressed by federal
officials, tribal leaders for a decade had been sending delegations to
inspect the colonization zone for suitable homes. Their reports on
the "fair land" were universally negative. The common statement by
Indians in reports of these western reconnaissances to federal officials was "we cannot consent to remove to a country destitute of
a single corresponding feature to the one in which we at present
reside."[6]

Choctaw leaders exploring the Indian Territory were disap-
pointed in the "new promised land," which was reported to flow
"with milk and honey. Instead, they found a mountainous country,
with soil vastly inferior to that in [their] Mississippi home." They
observed that the western portion of the Choctaw land in Indian
Territory "lacked two vital resources, water and wood, both of
which were abundant in Mississippi." A Cherokee petition submitted
to Congress in 1830 stated that these tribesmen were determined to
retain their eastern homeland: "We cannot consent to abandon it
for another far inferior, and which holds out to us no inducements."
And a Wyandot delegation from Ohio, after visiting the northern
portion of the Indian Territory, expressed in 1831 their reluctance
to remove from Ohio—they found the new land inferior in soil,
timber, climate, and certainly not "as good a corn country . . . as
the country we now occupy." An added deterrent was anticipated
difficulty from the neighboring state. Missouri was "a slave-holding
State," observed the Wyandots, and "slave-holders are seldom very
friendly to Indians. . . . At least they have, whenever they have got
Indians in their power, proved themselves to be the greatest and most
merciless oppressors they ever met with among all the American
population."[7]

A majority in Congress and certainly President Jackson single-
mindedly ignored imperatives of nature and the Indians' sound opposition to migrating to the Great American Desert. Tribal leaders
urged Jackson to fulfill his constitutional duties and protect them
from harrassment by state governments and to enforce recent Supreme Court decisions that favored their cause. Jackson answered
incorrectly that he was powerless in the matter and that the only
hope for the Indians was to accept their fate and move to Indian
Territory. The president's failure to fulfill his constitutional duty
destroyed the will of many Indians to attempt to protect their

right to remain in the East; they capitulated and began to move to Indian Territory.

Factions in the Cherokee, Creek, and Seminole nations refused to emigrate. In contradiction of the president's recent pledge to Congress that their emigration "should be voluntary for it would be as cruel as unjust to compel the aborigines to abandon the graves of their fathers, and seek a home in a distant land," federal and state troops rounded up the recalcitrants and conducted them under military guard to Indian Territory. The United States waged a bloody, destructive war against the Seminole nation in an attempt to force that tribe to submit to removal. So determined were Seminoles not to become colonists on the western frontier that aboriginal insurgents under Osceola and his successors Wildcat, Micanopy, and Jumper carried on a bitter and surprisingly successful resistance that lasted until 1842.

The epic of the national government's merciless uprooting and forcible relocation of Indians in the trans-Mississippi wilderness ranks with the tragedies of the ages. Although federal officials were pledged to supervise the emigration, they assigned to private contractors the job of supplying rations and transportation to the Indian colonists. The result was needless but intense suffering due to poor planning by government agents and the grossest exploitation by callous removal contractors. Far too many Indian emigrants were caught on the overland trail in midwinter and had to endure freezing temperatures, deep snow, treacherous ice, and sudden thaws that mired the removal columns in deep mud. Cholera and smallpox also devastated the parties. Conditions were made all the more deplorable by the rations of spoiled meat, corn, and flour supplied by the contractors. It is said that the emigrant routes to Indian Territory were marked by the gravestones of Indians who perished on the long march. The suffering and hardship endured by the southern Indians on their "Trail of Tears" reduced the population of every nation by at least one-fourth.

Many of the colonists settled in the eastern portion of their territory within a thin band of forest and prairie abutting the prairie-plains and the Great Plains, which successively comprised the central and western portions of their domains. The Chickasaw and Seminole nations were situated within the Great Plains region, the Creek nation extended to its eastern edge, the Choctaws held a joint interest in the land west of the 98th meridian, and the Cherokees owned a hunting range, the Cherokee Outlet, which extended between 36° 30' and 37° north latitude to the 100th meridian. However, the extremes of the Great Plains climate regularly intruded into the eastern Indian Territory settlements, bringing sporadic blizzards, blue northers, death-dealing tornadoes, crop-destroying cloudbursts, and periodic drought.

The national government could do nothing about the drastic forces of nature, but at times it did seriously attempt to assuage certain concerns of the transplanted aborigines. It permitted each of the Indian nations to establish a self-governing commonwealth, and the aboriginal citizens of several of the colonized groups, after recovering from the ordeal of removal, organized constitutional governments, school systems, transportation and communication facilities, towns, newspapers, and prospering economies in the new land.

In most respects the national government managed the aboriginal settlement zone as a colonial territory. Because Indian affairs at that time were under the Department of War, military officers played the major role in its general governance. During the 1830s Secretary of War Lewis Cass conceived a frontier defense plan which was integrated with the federal government's Indian colonization program. Cass explained the primary goal of the plan in a letter to Senator Thomas Benton of Missouri: "The system of Indian emigration will soon concentrate upon our western frontier the powerful force already described . . . common prudence requires the adoption of a plan of defense adequate to any exigency which will probably arise. . . . The great object is to make such arrangements as will distribute along this line a sufficient force to overawe the Indians, and to intercept any parties who might be disposed to make irruptions upon our settlements; and also to facilitate the necessary communication, and to allow a speedy concentration of troops upon these points where it may be required."[8]

The Cass frontier protection plan called for an eight-hundred-mile-long defense line extending south from Fort Snelling in the upper Mississippi Valley to Fort Towson on the Red River, the southwestern boundary of the United States. A chain of posts constructed on this line, linked by military highways, were to be garrisoned with dragoons, the new frontier cavalry force, and infantry.

Troops from these posts seriously attempted to check the traffic in liquor and arms in the Indian colonization zone and to expel intruders. In addition, military officers at Fort Gibson, Fort Leavenworth, and other posts in the system served as United States diplomatic agents, conducting councils with emigrant and resident tribesmen and concluding treaties with aboriginal leaders. Troops stationed in the colonization zone maintained order and protected the emigrants from attack by the buffalo-hunting tribes ranging the Plains on the western margins of the aboriginal colonists' settlements.

The continuing role of the military in this Indian colonization zone is illustrated by the dragoon expedition to the Wichita Mountains of southwestern Indian Territory in 1834 to conclude treaties with the Comanches, Kiowas, and Wichitas guaranteeing peace between them and the emigrating tribesmen. The military establishment in Indian Territory also sponsored the three-member Stokes Commission to supervise the settlement of immigrating tribesmen and to mediate boundary disputes among the newcomers. And troops from the military frontier on the eastern edge of the Great Plains campaigned regularly against the tribes of western Indian Territory to check their raids on the expanding settlements of the transplanted tribesmen.[9]

War Department management of the Indian colonization zone included an investigation of alleged removal abuses. As indicated, federal officials for the most part had let the business of provisioning and transporting aboriginal emigrants to Indian Territory to private contractors, and those Indians who survived the "Trail of Tears" claimed that much of their suffering and high death rate was due to the callousness of contractors who enriched themselves at the Indians' expense. Critics charged that "at so much per head it was entirely a business proposition with the contractors." In their hands "the removal of the Indian was no great philanthropy, but was carried out with the same business considerations that would characterize the transportation of commodities of commerce from one point to another." Vast sums of tribal money were paid to contracting firms, newly formed to render this service for the government, and it was later revealed that most of the contractors were friends and relatives of high government officials.[10]

Angry protests and charges of profiteering and fraud raised by tribal leaders caused federal officials to investigate the removal contractors. Major Ethan Allen Hitchcock was directed by the secretary of war to look into the complaints. Concerning his appointment, John R. Swanton, eminent investigator for the Smithsonian Institution's Bureau of American Ethnology, has said: "Since . . . the national administration was willing to look the other way while this criminal operation [the removal] was in progress, it made a curious blunder in permitting the injection into such a situation of an investigator as little disposed to whitewash iniquity as was Ethan Allen Hitchcock."[11]

Major Hitchcock began his investigation of removal abuses during

November 1841. A highly perceptive investigator, he confided to his journal that news of his mission had preceded him and there was much curiosity about his business in Indian Territory. He added that one of the contractors who had settled on the border "came here so poor that a man with a $400 claim against him was glad to settle for $100. Now he owns a considerable number of Negroes and has offered $17,500 for a plantation." Hitchcock's exhaustive investigation yielded evidence that "bribery, perjury and forgery, short weights, issues of spoiled meat and grain, and every conceivable subterfuge was employed by designing white men on ignorant Indians."[12]

Hitchcock took his findings to Washington; there he prepared a report with one hundred exhibits and filed the heavy document with the secretary of war. "Committees of Congress tried vainly to have it submitted to them so that appropriate action could be taken; but it was stated that too many friends of the administration were involved to permit the report to become public. It disappeared from the files and no trace of it is to be found." Swanton's comment on the fate of the Hitchcock report was "The fact that it did not allow the report to be made public and its mysterious disappearance from all official files proves at one and the same time the honesty of the report and the dishonesty of the national administration of the period."[13]

The comforting belief in "national completeness" was shattered during the 1830s by a renewed burst of American expansion. Beginning in Texas, the virus of territorial acquisition spread across the West to the Pacific shore. Before it spent itself, it had completely marked out the geographic perimeter of the American nation. The Indian colonization zone on the Great Plains no longer was the vanguard of Anglo-American occupation of the trans-Mississippi region. Increasingly it served as geographic connective tissue linking the East and the Far West, its interior a grid of immigrant trails. As growing familiarity with the Indian Territory led to a change in public attitude toward the region west of Missouri, the predominant image became less that of the Great American Desert and more that of a tract worthy of Anglo-American settlement. Thus increasingly after 1850 the status of the Indian Territory as a permanent Indian colonization zone off limits to white settlement was challenged by the expanding tide of western settlement. Pioneers began to agitate for the opening of the entire Indian Territory. Their demands were articulated in a number of bills introduced into Congress providing for the extinguishment of tribal titles and the opening of Indian Territory to settlement.

The tribes of the northern part of Indian Territory—Wyandots,

Potawatomis, Kickapoos, and others, vestiges of once great tribes from the Old Northwest—were weak, disorganized, and poorly led. Thus they were easy marks for federal officials who pressured tribal leaders to sign treaties surrendering their communally owned reservations for individual allotments and opening vast tracts to white settlement. In 1853, Commissioner of Indian Affairs George W. Manypenny was directed to begin negotiations with the tribes occupying the northern half of Indian Territory. He was required to persuade tribal leaders to abrogate treaties containing solemn pledges that "forbade the creation of any organized territory." The commissioner stated that he was serving a "political demand . . . to remove the obstacle to railroad building." Feeling regret and some shame for what he had accomplished so successfully, Manypenny wrote: "By alternative persuasion and force some of these tribes have been removed, step by step, from mountain to valley, and from river to plain, until they have been pushed halfway across the continent. They can go no further; on the ground they now occupy the crisis must be met, and their future determined." During 1854 the United States Congress approved the Kansas-Nebraska Act, which created two new territories, open for settlement, north of 37° north latitude. Thereby the northern portion of the Indian colonization zone, much of it situated on the Great Plains, became a settlement prize for the Anglo-American pioneer.[14]

The portion of Indian Territory between 37° north latitude and the Red River, and west of Fort Smith to the 100th meridian, was the domain of the transplanted southern tribes. It too was coveted by settlers. At the same time that the Kansas-Nebraska Act was approved by Congress, that body was considering a bill, introduced by Senator Robert W. Johnson of Arkansas, to organize three territories in the southern half of Indian Territory and to open the region to settlement. As soon as the mixed Indian-settler population of the three territories had made satisfactory progress in self-government, the three territories were to be fused into the state of Neosho. Johnson's bill failed and the southern half of Indian Territory was spared, at least momentarily. The defeat of the proposal was due primarily to the intense opposition of articulate southern Indian leaders who had spent much time in Washington working against its adoption. Unfortunately, the subsequent folly of these same men in signing alliances with the Confederate States of America provided the federal government with sufficient diplomatic leverage in 1866 to begin the process of appropriating the much coveted Indian Territory lands of the southern tribes.

By the Reconstruction treaties, in 1866, the federal government took from these vanquished Indian nations the western half of Indian Territory, most of it situated in the Great Plains region. Then by conquest, treaty, and executive agreement, federal officials concentrated many western tribes (including Kiowas, Comanches, Cheyennes, and Arapahoes) upon this plains territory. After 1887, under authority of the General Allotment Act, their reservation lands were partitioned, the tribal residents assigned allotments in severalty, the surplus lands opened to homesteading under the land laws of the United States. In 1890, Congress created Oklahoma Territory and progressively extended its jurisdiction over that portion of the Indian colonization zone on the Great Plains. These actions concluded a federal experiment in ethnic segregation through geographic isolation; the rejected Jeffersonian assimilation became the nation's single alternative.

After appropriating the Indians' reservations and national domains and concentrating them on individual farmsteads, the national government opened vast tracts on the Great Plains for settlement by the familiar Anglo-American pioneers, freedmen, and European immigrants. Each of the non-Anglo-American elements has faced some prejudice and ostracism, black immigrants the most. And ironically, although eastern Indian exiles were the first colonists in modern times to occupy the scorned Great American Desert, many of their descendants must pause at the threshold of the dominant society, their full acceptance and assimilation still held in abeyance.

Notes

1. See Francis Paul Prucha, "Indian Removal and the Great American Desert," *Indiana Magazine of History* 59 (December 1963): 299-322, for a discussion of this question.

2. *United States Statutes at Large*, 2:289.

3. Clark to Barbour, March 1, 1825, *American State Papers, Indian Affairs*, 2:653-54.

4. Calhoun to Monroe, January 24, 1825, in ibid., p. 544.

5. Report of the Secretary of War, 1826, ibid., pp. 646-49.

6. *Register of Debates in Congress*, vol. 6, pt. 2, p. 1048.

7. Arthur H. DeRosier, *The Removal of the Choctaw Indians* (Knoxville: University of Tennessee Press, 1970), p. 98; *Niles Register*, March 13, 1830; Report of the Chiefs of the Wyandot Nation, December 15, 1831, *House Document* no. 2, 23d Cong., 1st sess., p. 512.

8. Cass to Benton, February 19, 1836, *American State Papers, Military Affairs*, vol. 5, pt. 5, pp. 150-52.

9. For a discussion of the preliminary concepts of an aboriginal colony on the Great American Desert, see Thomas L. McKenney to Peter B. Porter,

January 13, 1829, Letters Sent File, Office of Indian Affairs, Record Group 75, National Archives.

10. Arrell Morgan Gibson, *Oklahoma: A History of Five Centuries* (Norman: University of Oklahoma Press, 1965), p. 188.

11. Quoted in Grant Foreman, ed., *A Traveller in Indian Territory: The Journal of Ethan Allen Hitchcock* (Cedar Rapids, Iowa: Torch Press, 1930), pp. 7–12.

12. Ibid.

13. Ibid.

14. Frederick L. Paxson, *History of the American Frontier, 1763-1893* (New York: Houghton Mifflin, 1924), pp. 431–32.

Touching the Pen: Plains Indian Treaty Councils in Ethnohistorical Perspective

Raymond J. DeMallie

When Europeans met American Indians in the New World, the clash of human populations resulted in epidemics of disease; social, economic, and political pressures; religious conflict; and sometimes war. All such intercultural conflict takes place in two very different contexts, that of each of the cultures involved. Each culture constitutes a separate and distinctive idea system symbolizing the world, everything in it, and the relationship of all the parts. Culture as a symbol system provides the framework in which human behavior is motivated, perceived, and understood. Abstractly, the clash of two peoples may be viewed as the clash of two idea systems.

But culture contact is not abstract; it is in reality acted out through individual human beings. The historical record documents their behavior and motives and draws out of the accumulation of many individuals' actions a general understanding of larger events. It is rarely possible to separate human behavior from the motivating ideas of the cultures in which the behavior occurs. The clash of ideas cannot be observed as easily or in the same manner as conflict between individuals. However, an understanding of the fundamental conflicting ideas is essential to illuminate historians' accounts of the past by placing individual action within the ideological context out of which it arose.

The large body of transcripts of formal council proceedings between representatives of the United States government and representatives of American Indian tribes provides a unique opportunity to observe the clash of idea systems.[1] Reduced to rhetoric, physical weapons laid aside, the opponents faced each other as representatives of their own societies and cultures and attempted to win tactical battles by the manipulation of concepts. Both white Americans and Indians alike attempted to use all of their intellectual skills, as well as the oratorical and persuasive devices of their cultures, to sway the council in their own interest. The verbatim records of the proceedings are therefore primary sources for analyzing cultural concepts self-consciously utilized to gain diplomatic advantage. They are primary documents for the ethnohistorian, whose research combines historical methodology with the comparative and theoretical insights of anthropology.

One objection to the use of this material for historical or anthropological study is that it was inadequately or falsely interpreted from the original Indian languages. However, this is a futile objection. The interpreters were almost always named in the documents; most were mixed-bloods or non-Indian men married into an Indian tribe. They were the only interpreters the Indians had and their translations are as accurate as any ever obtained at that time. Significantly, after reading through a good number of the transcripts it is possible to pick out Indian idioms that are difficult to translate and that were therefore expressed in various ways in English, as well as standard words and phrases that were consistently translated in the same way but whose English glosses obviously did not accurately express the original idea in the Indian language. In many of these cases it is possible to postulate with a fair degree of certainty what the actual words were in the Indian original. Such difficulties in translation do not make the task of reconstructing ideological systems impossible; in fact, they make it easier, for it is in these areas where translation was difficult that differences in ideological systems are most clearly pointed up.

Solemn councils between representatives of both sides were the only acceptable means recognized by both Indians and whites for establishing formal relations between two peoples. For the Indians the council was the traditional way of making peace or negotiating with another people. For the white Americans it had been the custom, since the days of Jamestown, to counsel with the Indians. Under United States law, written treaties, signed by representatives of both sides, were the only legal means for dealing with Indian tribes, and councils evolved as the forum where treaties were presented to Indians and they were persuaded to sign them.[2]

But if the council as a diplomatic forum was commonly understood by both whites and Indians, the concept of the treaty was not. For plains Indians, the council was an end in itself. What was important was the coming together in peace, smoking the pipe in common to pledge the truthfulness of all statements made, and the exchange of opinions. Plains Indian political systems did not use voting as the mechanism for settling issues; consensus politics was the rule. Issues had to be discussed from all points of view until a clear consensus was reached. Until that occurred, no decision was made, and once it was reached, no vote was necessary. Thus, from the Indians' point of view, the council *was* the agreement.

For white Americans, the council with its associated feasts and gift giving was only a preliminary to the real agreement, which was embodied in written form. The success of the council depended not on what was said, but on whether or not the necessary leaders, or later, the requisite percentage of the male population, could be induced to sign the document.

"Touching the pen," the action of the Indian in touching the end of the pen while the scribe marked an *X* after his name, was frequently objected to by Indian leaders. They did not understand the process, were suspicious of it, and felt it unnecessary. Whites, on the other hand, considered it to be essential. For individual Indian leaders, touching the pen apparently signified that they were validating all they had said at a council; in many cases the record of the treaty proceedings makes it clear that the Indian leaders did not realize their signatures committed them to *only* those statements written in the treaty. Sometimes, it is equally clear, treaty commissioners played on this to trick Indians into signing documents containing provisions to which they had not agreed.

The predominant historical view of treaty making is that Indians were taken advantage of by whites, who usually presented them with documents prepared in advance which they were persuaded, bribed, or threatened into signing. There is a great deal of truth to this view, but it ignores an important aspect. American Indian leaders were not mere pawns of the U.S. government. They did use political strategies to combat whites on their own ground and sometimes they were able to gain important concessions. They were at other times unsuccessful, and frequently their techniques were too subtle even to be understood by the commissioners. But analysis of some of these means provides important insights into plains Indian diplomacy and opens new dimensions for understanding the fundamental conflicts between Indians and whites on the western frontier.

This paper draws upon examples of treaty making among the Sioux, Kiowas, Comanches, Cheyennes, and Arapahoes from 1851 to 1892. First the 1851 Fort Laramie treaty council is examined as representative of plains treaty councils and as illustrating the symbolic perspective in ethnohistory. Then various examples of Indian diplomacy are presented to illustrate the range of strategies that can be abstracted from the verbatim proceedings and to demonstrate the value of this approach.

The 1851 Treaty Council

The 1851 treaty council held near Fort Laramie may be taken as a model of plains treaty councils.[3] It was on a larger scale than most since an estimated ten thousand Indians were present representing ten bands of Sioux as well as Cheyennes, Assiniboins, Shoshones, Arikaras, Gros Ventres (Hidatsas), Mandans, Arapahoes, and Crows. The encampment lasted nearly three weeks, from September 1 to September 21. During this period the commissioners met the Indians in council only about eight days. The rest of the time was occupied with the Indians counseling among themselves while the commissioners drew up a map of tribal territories, in Sunday recesses, and in waiting for the wagon train that was bringing the presents to be distributed after the treaty was signed.

Three general features of the council suggest a minimal model for plains treaty councils. The first is the ritual aspects, as practiced by both Indians and whites; the second is the recitation of both sides' demands and requests; and the third is the distribution of presents.

Ritual aspects. The ritual aspects of this council are fairly well recorded and are extremely significant for reconstructing the event in its fullest context. The Sioux and Cheyennes made the first gesture by erecting a large council lodge composed of several tipis to form a kind of amphitheater. This was the usual form for the council lodge when various bands came together and so was the culturally prescribed stage for serious deliberations. The U.S. commissioners took the next step by erecting a large tripod on which to hoist the American flag.

Preparations for the council were completed on a Saturday, but the commissioners announced that since the next day was "the white man's Medicine Day," no business could be transacted. The council began on Monday. Only headmen were allowed to enter the council lodge, and the order of their seating, by tribe, was arbitrarily decided by the commissioners. The council was called to order each day by the firing of the cannon and raising of the flag. The council began and ended with the smoking of the pipe by all the Indians and the commissioners. Colonel D. D. Mitchell, the chief commissioner, made an opening speech to set the moral tone of the meetings:

> I am sent here to transact business with you. Before commencing that I propose to smoke all around with you. The ceremony of smoking I regard as an important and solemn one, and I believe you all so regard it. When

white men meet to transact important business, and they desire to test their truth and sincerity, they lay their hands on the Bible, the Book of the Great Spirit—their Great Medicine—and take an oath. When the red man intends to tell the truth, and faithfully fulfill his promises, he takes an oath by smoking to the Great Spirit. The Great Spirit sees it all and knows it. Now I do not wish any Indian to smoke with me that has any deceit or lies in his heart—or has two hearts—or whose ears are not bored to hear what his Great Father at Washington has to propose, and perform whatever is agreed upon. All such will let the pipe pass. I don't want them to touch it.[4]

At least three important points about this speech should be noted. First, the commissioner attempted to speak to the Indians in terms they would understand. The reporter who covered the council remarked on this aspect as follows: "His [Mitchell's] expressions were short, in simple language, such as they could readily understand, in many cases adopting various forms, and employing their own hyperbolical mode of thought. Between sentences he paused to see that the interpreters understood him correctly, and to allow time for them to communicate it to their respective tribes."[5] Second, the commissioner made it clear that he considered the Indian form of oath by smoking the pipe to be a legitimate one, comparable to the white man's swearing on the Bible. Third, the use of the term *Great Father at Washington* must be considered to have been at least ambivalent. To some Indians it may have seemed a white man's claim that the Great Spirit lived in Washington, a boast that the whites enjoyed a closer relationship to God than did the Indians.

The smoking of the pipe by the commissioners was a self-conscious bow to Indian custom. In return the commissioners demanded at the end of the council that the Indians defer to the white man's custom of touching the pen to the treaty paper. Since they had already sworn themselves to truth, signing the treaty was redundant for the Indians, but they clearly understood it as an important ritual for the white men.

The other impressive bit of ceremony on the part of the whites was the celebration on the second Sunday of a Roman Catholic mass. In a large tipi in the half-breed camp, Father P. J. De Smet said mass and preached to the assemblage in French. The pomp and ceremony of the event was as impressive to the St. Louis newspaper reporter who accompanied the treaty commission as it was to the Indians. Of De Smet the newspaper man wrote: "The Indians regard him as a Great Medicine man, and always regard him with marked respect and kindness."[6]

Throughout the council the Indians reciprocated rituals by holding dog feasts, warrior society dances, and displays of horsemanship.

Demands and requests. The second aspect of the council, the exchange of demands and requests, was done in the usual formal manner. On the first day Colonel Mitchell delivered a speech outlining the commission's intentions in visiting the Indians and enumerating the points of the proposed treaty. On ensuing days the Indian chiefs were allowed to give their responses. These were not spontaneous speeches, but were developed out of council meetings in the various tribal camps, and were essentially tribal or band position statements. Toward the end of the meeting the commissioners read the treaty, article by article, and the Indians were asked to sign. The only contribution that the Indians had been allowed to make to the actual content of the document was in terms of tribal boundaries. At this treaty council there was no real negotiation, in part because the Indians were not being asked to give up any land.

The Arapaho and Sioux responses to the 1851 treaty council are representative of two distinct strategies used by plains tribes to attempt to win favor and gain concessions from the United States. The Arapaho attitude may be characterized as conciliatory and the Sioux attitude as defiant. It must be clearly understood that these are descriptive of diplomatic strategies, not of individual emotions.

The Arapaho chiefs decided to go along with the whites in their various demands. They expressed particular gratitude that there would be an end to all warfare. Addressing Mitchell, Cut Nose, an Arapaho chief, stated: "You, Grandfather, are doing well for your children in coming so far and taking so much trouble about them. I think you will do us all much good; I will go home satisfied. I will sleep sound, and not have to watch my horses in the night, or be afraid for my squaws and children."[7]

The oldest of the Arapaho chiefs, Authon-ish-ah, in a speech addressed to the Arapahoes themselves, seemed to take the tack that the chiefs alone could no longer take full care of the people, and that they would have to rely on the whites. He said: "Fathers and children, we give you all up to our white brethren, and now we shall have peace, the pleasantest thing in the world. The whites are friends to us, and they will be good to us if we don't lie to them. . . . The whites want to be good to us; let us not be fools, and refuse what they ask."[8]

The Arapahoes agreed to appoint Little Owl as head chief of the tribe, and through him to transact all business with the whites. Cut Nose addressed Mitchell as follows: "We have chosen our chief as you requested us to do, Father. Whatever he does, we will support him in it, and we expect, Father, that the whites will support him." The Arapahoes clearly pointed out the reciprocal nature of the agreement as they understood it. Cut Nose requested that the whites pick out a country for themselves to live in, and not trespass into Arapaho hunting grounds. He also suggested that the whites "should give us game for what they drive off."[9]

The Arapaho position, then, established rigid reciprocity between whites and Indians, the Arapahoes symbolically acknowledging the white men's power and binding them through the treaty to support the Indians. From the Arapaho viewpoint, the treaty worked to their advantage.

The Sioux attitude was very different. From the beginning they refused to cooperate in the matter of choosing a head chief. Blue Earth, the old Brulé chief, told Mitchell: "We have decided differently from you, Father, about this chief for the Nation. We want a chief for each band, and if you will make one or two chiefs for each band, it will be much better for you and the whites. Then we will make soldiers of our young men, and we will make them good men to the whites and other Indians. But Father, we can't make one chief."[10]

However, Mitchell was unyielding. He demanded that the Sioux bands all come together and unite as a single nation. Regarding bands he said: "Your Great Father will not recognize any such divisions." In the end Mitchell had to select representatives from each of the ten bands to be chiefs, and then select one of them to be head chief. His candidate, Frightening Bear, was then duly elected to the office by all of the band chiefs. The new head chief was not eager for the position. He said: "Father, I am a young man and have no experience. I do not desire to be chief of the Dahcotahs. . . . If you, Father, and our Great Father, require that I shall be chief, I will take this office."[11] It is very clear that the whites had imposed a new political office on Sioux society, one unlike any they had ever had before. Since it potentially entailed great power, Frightening Bear publicly spoke of his worry that he would be assassinated out of jealousy. Certainly the Sioux did not accept the idea of having a head chief.

The Sioux also objected strenuously to drawing boundaries around tribal territories. Blue Earth said, "We claim half of all the country; but, we don't care for that, for we can hunt anywhere."[12] Black Hawk, an Oglala, told the council:

> You have split the country and I don't like it. What we live upon we hunt for, and we hunt from the Platte to the Arkansas, and from here up to the Red But[t]e and the Sweet Water. . . . These lands once belonged to the Kiowas and Crows, but we [the Oglalas, Cheyennes, and Arapahoes] whipped these nations out of them, and in this we do what the white men do when they want the lands of the Indians.[13]

Mitchell explained that the boundaries were not intended to limit the tribes in any way, so long as they remained at peace. Nonetheless, the Sioux never accepted the boundaries.

The Sioux presented the council with a number of demands of their own. Big Yancton asked for horses, cattle, and fowl to make reparation for damages done to the Indians. A chief of the Blackfoot Sioux asked for a hundred wagonloads of goods each year, and asked that they be sent more buffalo as well. The latter request may have represented a challenge to the white men's claim to have been sent to the Sioux by the "Great Father."

Painted Bear, a Yankton Sioux, may well have summarized the dominant Sioux attitude of the time in the following words: "Father, this is the third time I have met the whites. We don't understand their manners, nor their words. We know it is all very good, and for our own good, but we don't understand it all. We suppose the half breeds understand it, and we leave them to speak for us."[14]

Many of the Sioux did not want to have any dealings with the United States. Their chiefs continually expressed their inability to understand the whites as well as their reliance on the mixed-bloods for advice. Unlike the Arapahoes, they refused to put trust in the whites and continued to pressure them for specific demands and concessions.

Distribution of presents. The third aspect of the council was the distribution of presents. Token presents were given in advance to the headmen of each tribe to redistribute to their followers. This served to validate their status in the tribe by giving tangible proof of the esteem in which they were held by the whites. At the end of the council, after the treaty was signed, the wagon train came up and the bulk of the presents were distributed. This was the most significant part of the council for most of the Indians present. The event is memorialized in Sioux winter counts as "The winter of the big distribution."[15] The whites at the council clearly understood the importance of the gift-giving aspects of the event. The reporter wrote: "It is a standing rule with all Indians, that whenever they meet, especially upon occasions of this character, they must have presents of some kind or other. . . . . Without these no man living—not even the President of the United States—would have any influence with them, nor could he get them into council, or keep them together a day."[16]

Plains Indian Diplomacy

This general model of treaty making—ritual, counseling, and gift giving—holds from the earliest plains treaty councils with the Lewis and Clark expedition down through the various commissions that negotiated with the tribes beginning in the 1880s for the breakup of reservations by agreeing to the allotment of lands in severality and the sale of "surplus" land for white settlement. The elaborateness of gift giving and ritual decreased, on the whole, through time, and the extent of negotiation somewhat increased, but the treaty council remained a relatively stable institution throughout the period.

Perhaps the single most frustrating aspect of the entire history of treaty making was the inability of the two sides to communicate with one another meaningfully. Both whites and Indians used the councils to deliver speeches composed in advance. Specific objections or questions by Indians were rarely answered when they were raised, but were answered a day or more later in the course of lengthy speeches. Many questions went unanswered, and many objections were simply ignored. Treaty commissioners frequently excused this practice by saying that the Indians' speeches were being recorded to be taken back to Washington. The commissioners told the Sioux in 1865, "We will take back all your words, and the Great Father will read all you have said."[17] But in reality neither the Great Father nor anyone else ever read them. Most remain unpublished or generally unavailable.

Examination of these documents solely from the perspective of reconstructing chronological history is quite disappointing. Usable historical data often seem to be altogether lacking in the speeches, replaced instead by rhetorical devices. Rarely do the speeches, white or Indian, rely on logic. These are not intellectual debates about matters that can easily be discussed. They are the records of more dramatic conflict between mutually exclusive ways of life.

Study of Indian diplomatic techniques provides a wealth of data on tribal cultures. Some trends may be seen over time that are suggestive of deeper changes in Indian cultures. One such trend involves the expressed attitude toward land. At the 1851 treaty council there seems to have been, from the white man's point of view, a rather practical attitude put forward by the Indians. They were capable and eager to discuss boundary issues. In the quote from Black Hawk given earlier, the idea of landownership by right of conquest is clearly articulated. Later, when the whites returned to ask the Sioux for more land for roads, they refused. At an 1865 council Lame Deer, a Miniconjou chief, stripped off his clothes and said to the commissioners: "I stand here naked and this is my condition. Why will you trouble me for my land, my brothers? You told me you would not ask me for anything."[18] Other leaders tried other strategies. Some claimed the land because they were born on it, because the bones of their forefathers lay in it, or because it had been given to them by God. One That Killed the White Buffalo Cow, a Lower Brulé chief, told the commissioners in 1865: "Who does all this country here belong to? It is ours. It belonged to our fathers and our fathers' fathers." Yet at the same time, Iron Nation, another Lower Brulé chief, said of his people, "The older ones came from Minnesota. There we were born."[19]

The council proceedings suggest that Indians thought about land according to its utility; it was not measured or conceived of in the white man's way. When the 1865 commission asked Lone Horn, the Miniconjou chief, if he would like to live on the Missouri River, he answered simply, "When the buffalo comes close to the river, we come close to it. When the buffaloes go off, we go off after them." The same commission asked the Indians where Frog, the Lower Brulé chief, lived. Iron Nation answered, "Everywhere; where he is."[20] The attitude expressed seems to suggest that land was not seen as the constant—people and animals were the constant features. Hence the justification for Indian ownership of land tended to be expressed in terms of people and buffalo.

Later, when the Indians' land base was already severely eroded and tribes became more specifically tied to land in the form of reservations, purely religious reasons tended to be adduced to argue for retaining that land which was left. A typical example is the statement of Iseo, a Kiowa leader, in 1892: "Mother earth is something that we Indians love. . . . We do not know what to do about selling our mother to the government." Another example is this statement by Spotted Horse, a Cheyenne, in 1890: "We look upon this land as a home and as our mother and we don't expect to sell it." Old Crow, another Cheyenne, told the same commission: "The Great Spirit gave the Indians all this country and never tell them that they should sell it. . . . If you have had any such word from the Great Spirit that gave them this land I would like to hear it."[21]

The point here is to suggest that detailed study of the treaty council proceedings may provide more data than might at first glance be expected on such complex and abstract issues as changing attitudes toward land.

Tactics

A survey of Indian diplomatic tactics that repeatedly occur in treaty council records reveals an interesting variety as well as significant differences among tribes. A few examples will be discussed here to illustrate the variety and nature of these tactics, as well as the value of such data to an understanding of Indian cultures.

Sometimes religious and moral justifications were presented by Indian orators to treaty commissioners in order to explain the Indians' perspective on the white man. An excellent example of this type of diplomacy is provided by a council in November 1866, held in Kansas at the Big Bend of the Arkansas River. Commissioners were investigating the Indian situation on the southern plains and preparing for a great council that would be held the following year at Medicine Lodge Creek. The commissioners counseled with Lone Wolf, head chief of the Kiowas, and a delegation of headmen in order to discover information about past hostilities and to impress on the Indians the necessity of peace.

> Colonel J. H. Leavenworth told the Kiowas: The Great Chief at Washington has heard some bad news about you and he has sent out two of his chiefs to see if they are true. . . . The names of those that have acted badly we have put on a piece of paper, and we shall tell the Great Chief what we know about them and he will decide whether they live or die. If any of your people go to Texas or Old or New Mexico and commit depredations the Great Chief will not forget it, but he will send an army of his men and exterminate you.[22]

These threats were not well received by the Kiowas. They had long heard whites boast of the power of the Great Chief or the Great Father in Washington, but they had never experienced it themselves. They were skeptical and they were angered to be ordered not to raid the whites to the south since it was economically important to them and also provided them with the regular means by which young men gained status to raise themselves in the social hierarchy.

Rather than take a stance blatantly antagonistic to that of the commissioners, Lone Wolf allowed White Bird, an old medicine man, to make the first speech in reply to the whites. The record of the proceedings reads as follows:

> The Indians then laid two circular pieces of paper on the floor; one blue and one white. Otank or White-bird, an old Indian then went through a form of prayer and spoke as follows to Lone Wolf in Kiowa, who repeated it to the Interpreter in Comanche.
>
> Lone Wolf—That piece of paper (pointing to the white) represents the earth. There is a big water all around the earth. The circular blue paper is the sky. The sun goes around the earth. The sun is our father. All the red men in this country, all the Buffalo are all his (old man's). Our Great Father the sun told us that the white man would kill all of them, there is no place for us to hide because the water is all around the earth. When my time comes to die I intend to die and not wait to be killed by the white men. I want you to write to the Great Chief and tell him that I understand my Great Father the sun, that my Great Father the sun sent me a message, that I went around the prairie poor and crying and the Great Father the sun sent me a message that I can read. A long time ago when I was little I began to study medicine and when we make a treaty with the white man I see it and know whether it is good or not. I am the man that makes it rain, I talk to the Great Father. If I have any difficulty with anyone and wish them to perish with thirst I stop the rain and if I wish them well I cause it to rain so that the corn can grow. My Great Father the sun told me that fire and water were alike, that we cannot live without either of them. This is all the old man's talk, he wishes to go to Washington.
>
> He (Lone Wolf) then said that he wished to talk for himself. I do not know what the Great Chief at Washington will think of the old man's talk.
>
> Capt. Bogy—We have similar men among us who converse with the Great Spirit.[23]

White Bird's speech is significant in several ways. It lays out an entire cosmology and belief system which is in direct contradiction to that of the whites. It puts the Great Chief in Washington into perspective under the power of the true Great Father, the sun. White Bird claims an especially close relationship to the sun, manifested in his power to control rain. Implied in his speech is his own belief that he is closer to the Great Spirit than is the white man's Great Chief. His desire to go to Washington was very likely motivated by a feeling that if he could but meet this Great Chief face to face he could best him with his power, matching him trick for trick.

Diplomatically, this speech was a good choice because it led into the refusal by the Kiowas, at least for the moment, to commit themselves to follow the will of the president, and provided moral and ethical grounds on which to do so. Unfortunately, it was probably ineffective. Bogy's comment relegates the speech to mere mysticism. Doubtless the commissioners simply missed the point. But the speech provides a good model of the Kiowa world as they presented it to oppose the view of the world propounded by the whites.

The use of kinship terms was another diplomatic tactic manipulated by Indians and whites alike. The 1865 treaty commissioners told the Miniconjou Sioux: "Your Great Father, the President, has selected us to come out to this country to visit his red children, the Dahcotahs. . . . The President, your Great Father, has not sent us to make peace because he is weak. . . . On the contrary, he pities his red children."[24]

Lone Horn, the Miniconjou head chief, seems to have felt the need to maneuver around the father-child relationship established by the commissioners, clearly limiting the father role to the president and excluding the commissioners from it. He therefore addressed the commissioners as follows: "My friends, I will begin my speech with claiming relationship to all of you. I will call you my brothers." This is significant since the relationship between brothers in Lakota society was the closest of all family relationships; one could not refuse anything to a brother without giving mortal offense. The Sioux in particular, reflecting the great emphasis placed in their culture on kinship, were adept at manipulating kinship metaphors in order to attempt to jockey whites into positions where they would be forced to make concessions. Later in his speech Lone Horn chided the commissioners: "It is good that you, my friends, my brothers, make peace with me, but it seems to me you are holding back, and do not like to make peace freely."[25] Unfortunately, the whites probably never understood the kinship strategy. Even in the example discussed here the commissioners failed to pick up on the significance of Lone Horn's statement and did not reciprocate by calling him brother. If they had, they would have placed themselves in the reciprocal brother relationship and would have improved their own bargaining position as well.

Government commissioners frequently used the expression "our red children" to put Indians into a subordinate position. Just as frequently, Indian orators exploited the father-children metaphor to ask for favors. In plains Indian cultures this relationship was a very important one in which the father gave freely to his children. At a Sioux treaty council in 1856, Bear Rib addressed General W. S.

Harney as father: "My Father! What is there better to wish for than a father." Much later, in 1892, Lone Wolf, the Kiowa chief, used the metaphor ironically to make his point that Indians should be protected from land allotment. He said to the commissioners: "You will believe me when I say we were like babies not knowing how to get up and take care of ourselves."[26]

Kinship terms used at treaty councils are significant symbols. They functioned as diplomatic devices that must be explored in order to understand the dynamics of the event. They are not merely paternalistic, racist, or subservient designations to be ignored in favor of what was really being said. Especially from the Indians' point of view, the use of kin terms was not a mere token, but embodied the real message of what was being communicated.

Another diplomatic tactic frequently used was to set up an equivalence between Indians and whites to provide a moral basis from which to ask that Indians be treated the same as whites. Eagle Drinking, a Comanche, told a commission in 1865: "I bear in my mind and heart the same feelings as the Great Father at Washington. I speak to my people as the Great Father at Washington does to his." In 1867 the Comanche chief Ten Bears told the commissioners: "My Great Father at Washington has the same heart that I have although I live on the prairies." In the same year the Comanche chief Rising Sun told the commissioners: "The Great Father is warm hearted, so am I."[27]

It would be easy to proliferate examples, but the tactic was the same. By establishing the common humanity of whites and Indians, a moral base was established from which to negotiate for concessions. Many other tactical devices were also frequently manipulated for diplomatic advantage, among them the use of writing, factionalism, dependence on the government, shaming the government for broken promises, and emphasizing tribal differences.

Treaty council proceedings are valuable documents for reconstructing the symbolic expressions of Indian cultures as Indian orators attempted to use their skill to best the white man at diplomacy. These documents are major resources for the study of plains Indians, reflecting cultural changes through time. The publication of treaty council proceedings and thorough studies of them will vastly enrich our understanding of native American cultures on the plains and allow some reconstruction of the Indians' points of view as they were threatened with cultural extinction in the face of white American expansion.

Notes

1. This paper is a preliminary report on work currently being done to edit for publication the records of the 1860s peace commissions that visited and made treaties with most of the plains tribes. See also Raymond J. DeMallie, "American Indian Treaty Making: Motives and Meanings," *American Indian Journal* (Washington, D.C.: Institute for the Development of Indian Law) 3, no. 1 (January 1977): 2–10. I am indebted to the Institute for the Development of Indian Law (IDIL), which supported this work. My thanks go especially to Kirke Kickingbird, director of IDIL, to Lynn Kickingbird, and to the staff of IDIL for their continued encouragement.

2. The best concise discussion of treaty making is in Wilcomb E. Washburn, *The Indian in America* (New York: Harper and Row, 1975), pp. 96–103, 234–40.

3. For published accounts of the 1851 council, see D. D. Mitchell's reports in the *Annual Report of the Commissioner of Indian Affairs, 1851*, House Executive Document 2, 33d Cong., 1st sess., pp. 288–90, 322–26, and LeRoy R. Hafen, *Broken Hand: The Life of Thomas Fitzpatrick* (Denver: Old West Publishing Co., 1973), pp. 284–301. The record of the council proceedings was published in the *Missouri Republican* (St. Louis), October–November 1851.

4. *Missouri Republican*, October 26, 1851.

5. Ibid.

6. Ibid., November 9, 1851.

7. Ibid., November 2, 1851.

8. Ibid.

9. Ibid.

10. Ibid.

11. Ibid., October 26, 1851; November 23, 1851.

12. Ibid., November 2, 1851.

13. Ibid., November 9, 1851.

14. Ibid., November 2, 1851.

15. For example, see the Big Missouri winter count in the Buechel Memorial Museum of St. Francis Mission, St. Francis, South Dakota.

16. *Missouri Republican*, October 6, 1851.

17. *Proceedings of a Board of Commissioners to Negotiate a Treaty or Treaties with Hostile Indians of the Upper Missouri* (printed document, n.d.), p. 42 (hereafter cited as *1865 Proceedings*).

18. Ibid., p. 22.

19. Ibid., pp. 41, 44.

20. Ibid., pp. 34, 37.

21. "Transcripts of Councils of Cherokee Commission . . . Kiowa, Comanche, Apache," pp. 5, 14, 45, Irregularly Shaped Papers 78, Office of Indian Affairs, Record Group 75, National Archives.

22. "Proceedings of a Council . . . with the Kiowa Indians . . . Nov. 26,

1866," Treaty no. 364, Documents relating to ratified treaties, Office of Indian Affairs, Record Group 75, National Archives, Microcopy T494, roll 7.

23. Ibid.

24. *1865 Proceedings*, p. 18.

25. Ibid., pp. 18, 19.

26. *Council with the Sioux Indians at Fort Pierre,* House Executive Document 130, 34th Cong., 1st sess., p. 23; "Transcripts of Councils of Cherokee Commission . . . Kiowa, Comanche, Apache," p. 32.

27. *Annual Report of the Commissioner of Indian Affairs, 1865*, House Executive Document 1, 39th Cong., 1st sess., p. 533; "Proceedings of a Council held with the Comanche Indians . . . November 12th, 1866," Treaty no. 364, Documents relating to ratified treaties, Office of Indian Affairs, Record Group 75, National Archives, Microcopy T494, roll 7.

Plainsmen of Three Continents: Volga German Adaptation to Steppe, Prairie, and Pampa

Timothy J. Kloberdanz

"Wie schön ist das ländliche Leben, / ein Häuschen auf grüner der Flur" ("How pleasant is life in the country, / with a small house on the green plain"), sing Volga Germans in the opening lyrics of an old and favorite folk song.[1] Like so many things typically *Wolgadeutsch,* the song persists even though it sometimes must be appreciated in an entirely new context. The Volga German grain farmer in western Kansas who looks out over a sweeping landscape of knee-high winter wheat and shimmering church spires will attest to the old-country sentiment of the above song, as will the ruddy-faced Canadian farm woman of Volga German extraction who powers a modern harvester in Saskatchewan, and the Volga German *labrador* who leisurely sips maté while surveying his fields of flax on the fertile pampas of central Argentina. For Volga Germans, much has changed in their two-hundred-year history as a distinct ethnic group, but for many the ever familiar scene of an unobscured horizon remains the same.

This paper focuses on the adaptation of Volga German settlers to three of the world's major grassland areas: the Russian steppes, the North American Great Plains, and the South American pampas. As used throughout this paper, the term *adaptation* denotes a process whereby a population alters itself or its relationship to its habitat in order to make that milieu "a more fit place in which to live." The various ways human beings adapt to their physical, sociopolitical, and intellectual environment have long been the concern of anthropologists but only recently has this ecological "way of seeing" gained "currency in modern cultural anthropology."[2]

Obviously, it is impossible to identify and discuss in this paper all of the important variables that underlie Volga German adaptation in three different areas of the world. What follows is a descriptive overview of various aspects of Volga German adaptation that were largely influenced by the colonists' long sojourn in Russia.

From their earliest pioneering days on the steppe, the Volga

Germans modified traditional institutions and created or borrowed new ones in response to existing needs. Yet, while the colonists displayed varying degrees of technoeconomic flexibility, their religious and social institutions reflected considerable stability and conservatism. Thus, by the time of their emigration to the pampas and prairies of the New World, the Volga Germans had already experienced a century or more of maintaining themselves economically, politically, and socially in a foreign land.

The Volga Germans comprise the largest of several German-speaking groups who once lived in predominantly agrarian colonies in Russia.[3] The *Wolgadeutschen* are sometimes confused with—or erroneously thought to encompass—various other but no less interesting German enclaves in pre-Revolutionary Russia such as the Black Sea Germans near Odessa, the Chortitza-Molotschna Mennonites, the Crimean Germans, the Bessarabian Germans, or the Volhynian Germans. While all of these groups often are lumped together as Russian Germans, German Russians, or simply Germans from Russia, there are distinct historical, linguistic, and social differences that need to be taken into careful consideration before any generalizations can be made. Today, possibly as many as one million or more Volga Germans and their descendants can be found throughout North and South America, western Europe, and the Soviet Union.[4]

The Steppes

In the years 1764–67, approximately seven thousand families, principally from Hesse, the Rhineland, Baden, Alsace, Bavaria, and the Palatinate, emigrated to Russia. Most of these emigrants were lured eastward into Russia by a manifesto of Catherine the Great which promised free land, freedom of religion, exemption from military service, and numerous other privileges. After two thousand miles of difficult travel by ship and wagon, the first Volga colonists reached what was to be their future home and experienced immediate disillusionment. "We looked at each other with fear," an early participant of the great migration to the Volga remembered, "to find ourselves in a wilderness, which, as far as the eye could see, showed . . . nothing but withered grass."[5] Shortly after their arrival, a few homesick colonists attempted to return to the verdant valleys and wooded hills of their homeland, but were turned back by Russian officials. One group of distraught men, women, and children who headed westward were murdered by their native guides on an island in the Volga River.[6]

By the fall of 1767, the Volga Germans had established 104 mother colonies on both sides of the lower Volga near the modern-day Russian cities of Saratov and Kuibyshev (formerly Samara). Forty-four of these colonies were located on the west side of the Volga (called the hill side, or *Bergseite*) and sixty were situated on the east side (known as the plains side, or *Wiesenseite*). Approximately two-thirds of all the colonies were composed of Protestant villagers, while the remainder were solidly Roman Catholic.[7]

In 1769, the original colonist population of an estimated 27,000 had dropped to 23,109. Six years later, only 5,502 pioneer families survived of the 7,000 who originally journeyed to the Volga. According to existing accounts of the colonization, the emigrants endured numerous hardships: bitterly cold winters and searing summer temperatures, epidemics, raids by nomadic bands of Kirghiz and organized groups of outlaws, crop failures, spring floods, and other calamities. "The dark winter days and the long nights," wrote one early colonist, "seemed never to end. We were separated from all mankind, and we lived miserably and in greatest need."[8]

The demands of an arid, continental climate necessitated many changes in the agricultural practices, housing, clothing, diet, and social organization of the Volga Germans. Once they realized that there was no hope of returning to their homeland, they began the tedious process of trial-and-error adjustment. In their first months on the steppe, few Volga Germans had the necessary building materials (promised by the agents of Catherine the Great) to construct adequate shelter. Thus, from the Russians and other neighboring peoples, the Volga Germans learned how to construct subterranean homes called *zemlyanky* in the black earth of the steppe. Some of these dwellings were built in the same manner as those of certain native inhabitants, complete with smoke vents and small windows fashioned from animal bladders. Later, when the promised building materials and Russian carpenters finally arrived, the new homes of logs or clay bricks often had a distinctive eastern European flavor. Eventually, few German homes on the Volga were without an enclosed entryway, called a *Krilitz* (after the Russian term *kriltso*).[9] Other Russian influences included large stoves of sun-dried brick in the central portion of the home and the practice of building a separate summer kitchen to keep the main dwelling cool during the suffocating months of summer.

Volga Germans quickly adopted many items of Russian clothing, ranging from long sheepskin coats to thick felt boots. Inside the Volga German homes, Russian foods like borsch, *blini*, and *pirozhki* (called *Bierock* by the colonists) were served, along with *kvas* (a fermented drink made from black bread or barley meal).[10] Russian loan words were incorporated into the various German dialects on the Volga and included representative terms such as *ambar* (granary), *arbus* (watermelon), *kardus* (cap), and *nushnik* (outhouse).

In the realm of agriculture, the Volga Germans combined traditional practices "with a number of entirely new traits resulting directly from the new ecological adaptation."[11] Thus, the wooden hook plow of the Russian peasant gradually gave way to an altered form of the German moldboard plow; Russian pole wagons were replaced by German rack wagons; the scythe and cradle (*Reff*) was used in place of the sickle; and the wooden harrow of the Russian was improved upon until the Volga Germans had developed one with strong iron teeth. Russian varieties of wheat, barley, and oats that were suited to the climate of the steppe were borrowed by the Volga Germans, while the colonists, in turn, introduced the cultivation of tobacco and potatoes.[12]

One of the most important Volga German innovations was the discovery of a heating fuel known as *Mistholz*. This "manure wood" was a conglomerate of barnyard straw and animal manure that was moistened, mixed, and allowed to dry in the sun. After curing, the accumulation was cut into small blocks and stacked in the same manner as firewood.[13] *Mistholz* had a high heat value and made further utilization of the treeless steppe possible for both German and Russian settlers.

During their first years on the Volga, the colonists had to be relatively self-sufficient. Various skills were important not only in supplementing their agricultural income, but in creating an economic pattern of diversified subsistence. Unlike other German agrarian groups in Russia (such as the Black Sea colonists who settled near Odessa in the early 1800s), the Volga Germans came from a variety of occupational backgrounds. The first Volga colonists were not required to submit proof of agricultural expertise, as were the later German emigrants who went to Russia. Thus, the lack of agricultural knowledge among many Volga Germans meant that the first years of colonization were exceedingly difficult, but it also allowed numerous individuals to put their specialized skills to use in fashioning tools that were unavailable on the Volga.

One of the many important home industries that developed in the German colonies was the manufacture of a popular gingham material called *sarpinka*. The weaving of this cloth was introduced to the Volga Germans by a group of Moravian Brethren whose village on the Volga was considered a "show colony" by Russian officials. *Sarpinka* looms were constructed in numerous Volga German homes and helped provide cash income during the long winter months.[14]

By the early nineteenth century, the Volga Germans had undergone innumerable changes in their life-style. The mere appearance of their homes, granaries, gardens, clothing, agricultural implements, and modes of travel reflected the extent of their adjustment to life on the Volga frontier. J. G. Kohl, an adventuresome traveler who visited German settlements throughout Russia during the early 1840s, was favorably impressed with the progressive character of many of the villages. He remarked that the difficult task of pioneering had left its mark on the German farmers, for they "smacked of the steppe."[15]

Despite laudatory observations by Kohl and other European travelers, occasional references to the static nature of Volga German culture were made by certain early writers and sometimes are still echoed today. One American scholar cited the German colonists on the Volga as a "good example of arrested development." Another writer, an early-twentieth-century journalist, described the Volga Germans of czarist Russia as a living fossil and actually compared them to a frozen mammoth on display at the museum in St. Petersburg. Such notions (often the impressions of non-Volga Germans) were just as erroneous as those espoused by later descendants of the Volga Germans who defended the culture of their forefathers as pure and devoid of Slavic influence. One modern-day Volga German American, for example, wrote of his ancestors: "Despite their sojourn of over 100 years in Russia, there was nothing Russian about them."[16]

The adaptive strategy of the Volga Germans was one that encouraged technological flexibility. Practically anything that promised to make the Volga colonists more efficient farmers was tried and tested, regardless of whether it came from within or outside the colony. The first years on the steppe had taught struggling Volga Germans to adapt or perish and this experience colored many aspects of their daily life.[17] In order to survive, Volga Germans had to work, and in this regard they adapted with vengeful determination. The German colonists glorified hard work in their songs, proverbs, and other folklore to the extent that one of their favorite expressions was *"Die Arbeit schmeckt süsser als Essen"* ("Work tastes sweeter than food"). Their dialectal word for *work* was not the standard German verb *arbeiten*, but rather *schaffen*, which means "to produce, to create."[18]

While Volga Germans adjusted to the rigorous demands of their physical environment, they displayed less flexibility in responding to external forces in their sociopolitical milieu. However, one way in which they were able to maintain their ethnic identity was through a Russian system of land tenure known as the mir (or village commune) that periodically reapportioned its arable lands on the basis of the number of "male souls." This system of land tenure, which was adopted by the colonists in the late eighteenth century, fostered large patriarchal extended families in many Volga German colonies. One disadvantage of the mir was that while the population steadily increased, the available landholdings became correspondingly smaller. However, this land shortage was sometimes relieved by out-migration and the subsequent establishment of daughter colonies, which was a vital adaptive process.[19]

The Russian mir made it possible for Volga Germans to insulate themselves from the surrounding Russian peasantry. No outsiders (other than occasional German brides from neighboring villages) could gain entrance into the colony without special approval of the village commune. Thus, the mir gave rise to the development of closed corporate communities among the Germans on the Volga. Eric R. Wolf has described such communities as "corporate organizations, maintaining a perpetuity of rights and membership; and . . . closed corporations, because they limit these privileges to insiders, and discourage close participation of members in the social relations of the larger society."[20]

Within the colonies on the Volga, the German language, religion, social customs, and ancestral folklore were important aspects of the intellectual environment. Among Roman Catholics and Lutherans, church ritual and magico-religious practices occupied prominent places in their daily lives. Individual rites of passage and group rites of intensification also accentuated social solidarity.[21] Those Volga German pietists who shunned elaborate church rituals as worldly, periodically participated in emotion-charged religious movements that swept the Volga countryside.

Village schools in the Volga colonies also cultivated a deep respect for the religion, language, and historical traditions of the colonists. Within the home, small Volga German children learned the oral traditions from grandparents who talked and sang as they labored at the spinning wheel or *sarpinka* loom. The family members, schoolmaster, pastor, and peers all reinforced the individual's self-concept and ethnic consciousness. Thus, the village protected the Volga German from the outside world and the colonist reciprocated by remaining loyal to its values and traditions.

For more than a century, Volga Germans in Russia tilled the

black soil of the steppe and altered their farming methods to suit ever changing needs. Drought, famine, and other hardships sometimes stalked the Volga region, but the colonists usually had adequate grain reserves and the important home industries to fall back on during the lean years.

In the early 1870s, the Volga Germans faced new challenges in adjusting to their sociopolitical environment. Czar Alexander II abrogated numerous privileges of the German colonists, including exemption from compulsory military service. Other Russification measures that angered many Volga Germans were enacted. At about the same time, crop failures and worsening land shortages also gave cause for alarm. The out-migration of colonist families that had always relieved population pressure in the Volga region now reached staggering proportions. This time, however, the migrants were moving, not into new daughter colonies on the Volga steppe, but to distant lands in Siberia and the New World.

The Prairies

Few Volga Germans were eager to leave behind the security of their colony in exchange for something about which they knew so little. Thus, massive meetings were called in Russia that attracted thousands of Volga German representatives. At these gatherings, scouts (*Kundschafter*) were selected and sent to survey farm lands in the United States. In 1874, for example, five scouts from colonies on the eastern side of the Volga toured parts of the American Great Plains. When they returned to Russia, they brought with them a pound of Nebraska earth, a handful of prairie grass, and other items that inspired numerous families to emigrate. In the summer of 1876, a large body of nearly fifteen hundred Volga German colonists left Russia and settled on the plains of Kansas. Their arrival marked the beginning of a wide-scale migration that was to attract thousands of Germans from the Volga for the next thirty-eight years.

In 1877, the first large Volga German contingent set out for Brazil but were instead taken to Argentina, where, the emigrants were told, "you will find clear pampas where the land is as good as that which you had in Russia."[22] Volga Germans also emigrated to the western prairies of Canada as early as 1893, but the largest number did not move there until the early 1900s. There is little doubt that most of the early Volga German emigrants preferred to settle in areas that closely paralleled the level topography of their own homeland. One Volga German historian wrote of these emigrants:

"When they came to the New World they sought out regions that offered them the livelihood in which they and their forefathers had been engaged on Russia's steppes. They were drawn to the prairies of North America and the pampas of Argentina, and there was a saying that every hillock was a thorn in their eyes."[23]

This deliberate attempt on the part of Volga German emigrants to settle in a physical setting similar to the one they had left behind was characteristic of many other emigrant groups. The term *latitude pull* has been used to describe a similar phenomenon in which emigrants are drawn to new areas that possess the same climatic features as those of their old homeland.[24] This intriguing but perhaps simplistic view fails to explain adequately the initial direction of most Volga German immigration. The German colonies on the Volga were located between 50° and 52° north latitude. This same latitude area in the New World includes portions of Saskatchewan and Alberta that, in fact, attracted Canada's largest number of Volga Germans. However, most Volga Germans in North America settled in the central plains states of Kansas, Nebraska, and Colorado, which lay between 38° and 42° north latitude. The majority of South America's Volga German population established homes in the pampas region between 31° and 38° south latitude. While these regions differ climatically in many ways, it is nonetheless remarkable how similar the Volga steppes, Canadian prairies, American plains, and Argentine pampas are in regard to soil composition, natural vegetation, and topography.[25] Moreover, all four regions are considered among the most productive grain-producing areas in the world.

At about the same time as large numbers of Volga Germans began contemplating immigration to the New World, railroad companies in the United States sent agents into Russia to recruit settlers and publicize the existence of vast tracts of cheap land. To the Germans from the Volga, such opportunities were far more enticing than the dispersed settlement created by individual homesteads in the American West. A century on the steppe had convinced these colonists that nucleated settlements were vitally important in an alien land.

Volga Germans began establishing settlements in the United States as early as 1874, particularly in the states of Kansas and Nebraska. Large groups of Volga German Protestants chose Nebraska as a suitable area for settlement, with Lincoln acting as an early distribution center. The jumping-off place for Volga German Catholics in Kansas was Topeka while the area of greatest settlement was in the central portion of the state. The agrarian hamlets established by Volga Germans in Ellis and Rush counties near present-day Hays, Kansas, perhaps best illustrate the type of settlement the colonists wished to establish on the American Great Plains. From 1876 to 1900, some 1,320 Volga Germans made their homes in the Hays area. The majority of these settlers were from the *Wiesenseite* (plains side) of the Volga and they marveled at how similar the Kansas prairie was to their former homeland in Russia. Like their fore-fathers a century before, the Volga Germans in Kansas faced numer-ous hardships. But this time there was a difference: they were pre-pared. Their heavy Russian clothing proved effective during the first harsh winters in Kansas, as did their experience with the building of earthen *zemlyanky* and houses of sun-dried clay brick. Many families who settled on the more fertile soils in the county did not do so accidentally. Before purchasing farm land, one Volga German chewed a bit of the soil to see if it "tasted after grain."[26] While these settlers brought with them much knowledge and many skills for living in a plains environment, they also possessed the agricultural flexibility that characterized their life-style in Russia. For example, the emigrants brought with them quantities of seed from the Volga, but their spring wheat, tobacco, and watermelons did not do well in central Kansas. As soon as the settlers were able to accumulate sufficient funds, they purchased winter wheat and other varieties of seed that were better suited to the climate of the central plains.

While some Volga German families homesteaded 160-acre tracts in Ellis County, many others bought land from the Kansas Pacific Railroad that was unbroken by individual farms. This made possible the establishment of settlements very similar to the closed colonies on the Volga. As in Russia, the Kansas settlers built their homes around the church square and walked or rode to their outlying fields. In the early years of settlement, the Volga Germans in Ellis County implemented the mir system, but this communal ownership soon gave way to the formation of "Town and Grazing" companies (based on shares of the total capital investment) that were legally chartered by the county government. The notion of private ownership did not become important among many Volga Germans in Ellis County until as late as the 1920s.[27]

Within each of the nucleated Volga German settlements in Ellis County, the strong in-group attitudes that characterized German colony life on the Volga predominated for decades. These village allegiances were so strong that Volga German Catholics of neighbor-ing hamlets did not begin to intermarry until after World War II. Albert J. Peterson, Jr., a cultural geographer who made an in-depth study of settlement patterns in Ellis County during the late 1960s, concluded: "The German-Russian adjustment to the landscape—his establishment of a rural ghetto—is a manipulation of a deeply ingrained German-Catholic culture that has prolonged the acculturation of these people into the mainstream of American society."[28]

Not all Volga Germans in the United States were able to transplant as much of their old way of life as did the Ellis County pioneers. Though many Volga German emigrant groups searched for a level topography that was conducive to group settlement, few who came after 1880 actually found such ideal conditions. Most Volga German emigrants were faced with two choices: either to obtain homesteads or move into the prairie towns as railroad workers and sugar beet laborers. A majority chose the latter, perhaps because the social cohesion of the old country proved more crucial than something as tempting to a German Russian as free land. Unlike the Black Sea German emigrants, who swarmed into Dakota Territory and anxiously filed homestead claims, the Volga Germans exhibited widespread reluctance to do so. This can be understood when one considers the different economic backgrounds of the two groups. In Russia, the Black Sea Germans followed the Ukrainian inheritance rule of ultimogeniture and thus were accustomed to finding new farm lands for older sons. This practice contrasted sharply with the communal nature of Volga German land tenure and its ramifications. Historians of the German-Russian immigration to the United States have noted that approximately 95 percent of the Black Sea Germans became farmers, while only 50 percent of the Volga German immigrants chose agriculture as their primary occupation.[29]

The story of the many thousands of Volga Germans who emigrated to America's midwestern cities and towns is still little known. Most studies of the Volga Germans have characteristically portrayed them as being either wheat growers or sugar beet farmers. However, many early Volga Germans quickly adapted to an urban setting, perhaps owing to the influence of the important home industries on the Volga that made it easier to adjust to long factory hours in the city. Many Volga Germans who labored at the *sarpinka* loom in Russia welcomed similar types of employment in cities like Chicago, Lincoln, and Denver. Their experience in Russia had taught them that factory jobs—like the old-country home industries—perhaps assured them of greater economic security than crops, which were susceptible to drought, heat, and insects. An additional factor related to Volga German success in the urban areas is that many emigrants from Russia were able to maintain local ties better in the city than on isolated homesteads. Thus, even in densely populated cities like Chicago, small communities of Volga Germans were established according to ancestral affiliation. One writer even reported a "closed colony" of Volga German factory workers in the heart of Chicago as late as 1930.[30]

Still another illustration of the economic flexibility of Volga Germans in the central plains is their important role in the sugar beet industry. In the early 1900s, Volga Germans were especially important in the beet fields of Nebraska and Colorado, and eventually in Wyoming, Montana, and other states. By this time, railroad lands and even individual homesteads were no longer available. Thus, thousands of Volga Germans became involved in the cultivation and production of sugar beets. In the beginning, most Volga Germans were hired by American farmers as manual laborers to thin, hoe, and harvest in the beet fields. The old-country mir had encouraged large patriarchal extended families, and these social units proved adaptive in the beet fields, where a large work force was required. The transition from beet laborer to farm operator was a gradual one, made easier for Volga German families who temporarily left their homes in the so-called "Rooshun" areas of town to seek employment in the beet fields each spring. This system paralleled the old-country practice of working in the outlying fields most of the summer and returning to the village on weekends for religious services and socializing. By 1930, more than one-half of "all the sugar beet farms in Colorado, Nebraska, Montana, and Wyoming were in the hands of Volga German farmers."[31]

Mobility was another characteristic of Volga German adaptation in the New World. Although the German emigrants from the Volga valued permanence, they often had to wander from one place to another in search of a suitable home for their families. "Our people," wrote one New World descendant of the colonists, "sit like birds on a branch, always ready to fly off and establish a new settlement." [32] As a result, one finds Volga German communities in various parts of all the plains states as well as in Iowa, Illinois, Idaho, Ohio, Oregon, Michigan, Wisconsin, California's Fresno Valley, the wheat-producing section of eastern Washington, the onion fields of New York state, and numerous other areas. The innovative minds and adaptive skills of steppe-bred Volga Germans were put to many uses in the United States and proved important in as many places.

Canada attracted a relatively small number of Volga Germans, and most of these emigrants settled in the prairie provinces of Alberta and Saskatchewan during the early 1900s. Many Volga

Germans were wary of settling in Canada, owing to the existence of Dominion Acts, which, like the homestead laws in the United States, required residence on dispersed farm lands. Nevertheless, the offer of free land in a region so similar to the old homeland eventually drew numerous Volga Germans to the Canadian prairies. Volga German Protestants settled in eastern Saskatchewan and near Calgary, Alberta. Volga German Catholics settled in greater numbers on the Saskatchewan-Alberta border west of Saskatoon in an area known as St. Joseph's Colony.[33] Besides the level landscape and excellent soil, another special attraction of this region was the advantage of settling in close proximity to one another. The early settlers built houses of sod, clay, and green poplar—sometimes with thatched roofs of straw or reeds—and farmed much as they did in Russia. However, the virgin Canadian soil often was rocky, which made the first plowing difficult. Some Volga German homesteaders found it expedient to hitch three oxen to their plows in order to prepare their land for planting.[34] Initially, Volga Germans in Saskatchewan took advantage of the long winter months by building looms and weaving in their homes. This industry was especially important in a harsh land where snow sometimes fell in May and similar agricultural setbacks occurred.[35]

The Pampas

The German-Russian emigrants who settled in the Southern Hemisphere provide unusually rich insights into Volga German adaptation. In the fall of 1876, a small delegation of Volga Germans visited Brazil to investigate settlement conditions there. Of all the available lands for colonization, the group was most impressed with the grasslands in the Brazilian state of Parana. Here several members of the delegation expected to raise wheat and other crops just as they had done on the steppes of their homeland. Brazilian officials encouraged the Volga Germans to settle in more fertile areas that were forested, but the colonists adamantly refused to settle in such unfamiliar terrain. The Volga German delegation not only persuaded Brazilian officials to allow them to settle in Parana but were also given permission to establish closed colonies based on communal ownership of land. Less than a year later, a large number of Volga German families had established villages in southern Brazil, but the grasslands there did not prove as fertile as they had anticipated. Like their forefathers in Russia, the emigrants had to make major adjustments in traditional agricultural practices. Volga German settlers in Brazil eventually cultivated new crops that were more suitable to the soil conditions and climate, such as corn and manioc. Many of those who had settled in Brazil soon joined a much larger emigration to the pampas of Argentina.

In September of 1877, Volga German delegates met with officials of the Argentine government and were granted numerous privileges that made possible the establishment of closed colonies in Argentina. By 1878, the first Volga German colony was founded in the province of Buenos Aires. The rich grasslands of Argentina provided a refreshing—and comforting—scene to weary Volga Germans in search of a new home thousands of miles from the undulating Volga steppes. Said one German colonist as he happily surveyed the level terrain bordering the wide waters of the Parana River: "As I look out over this expanse of country, I feel as if I were back in Russia, in our old homeland."[36]

Although the Argentine pampas reminded many Volga Germans of their *Wolgaheimat*, the subtropical climate in South America posed special problems. Poor transportation and other hardships also made the early years of settlement exceedingly difficult. During their first months on the pampas, the colonists lived in tents or lean-tos and cooked their meals in the open just as they had done during planting and harvest time on the Volga. Volga German women, eager to have their own freshly baked bread in Argentina, constructed crude, makeshift ovens in the overhanging portions of river banks until more permanent ones could be built. Yeast for the bread dough was obtained by soaking Argentine *galletas* (dried biscuits) in water until the solution soured. No farming equipment was available to the emigrants and thus they had to construct their own agricultural implements and means of transportation. Although two-wheeled carts were popular in Argentina, the Volga Germans preferred to build four-wheeled farm wagons like those used in Russia. The emigrants sawed cross-cuts from tree trunks and used these disks of wood as crude wagon wheels. Many settlers fashioned lined pieces of horse harness from the heavy sheepskin coats they had brought with them from the Volga. Harrows and soil-turning plows were also made by Volga German craftsmen and were rapidly put to use by settlers eager to test the fertility of the pampas. Horses obtained from local officials and the native inhabitants were often wild or freshly broken and had to be tamed by the Volga German colonists. Those settlers who used oxen as draft animals soon discovered that the "neck yokes employed on the Volga frustrated and balked the South American beasts; these had to be hitched to the horns."[37]

The Volga Germans in Argentina built their houses in much the same manner as they had in Russia. A few of the earliest emigrants built subterranean homes like the old *zemlyanky* of their ancestors. These dwellings quickly won one group of Volga Germans the name *vizcacheros,* given them by Argentine natives who thought the settlers resembled the ubiquitous burrowing rodents of the pampas. Later homes were built of adobe or sun-baked clay bricks. The winterproof Russian *Krilitz* (entryway) seldom was built in Argentina, but—owing to the hot climate—the practice of building a small summer kitchen outside the home survived.[38]

Although Volga Germans were unable to maintain a completely closed colony existence in South America, their geographical isolation and small nucleated settlements did enable them to preserve many distinct values and ancestral traditions. The Argentine government had reluctantly agreed to allow many Germans from Russia to settle in groups, but Spanish-language instruction was required in the village schools as early as 1878. Government inheritance laws (which stipulated that land must be divided equally among surviving children) also hindered Volga German efforts to maintain the type of social life they had known in Russia.[39]

Within a few decades after their arrival in South America, the Volga Germans assumed an important role in Argentina's agricultural production. Wheat, flax, barley, alfalfa, and corn were grown successfully by thousands of Volga Germans. Many of the colonists in South America preferred diversified farming and were able to remain largely self-sufficient. Even when the price of grain was low, the economic security of families remained relatively stable, thanks to a supplemental cash income from sales of poultry and milk products.[40]

Perhaps the greatest difficulties that Volga Germans faced in adapting to the pampas were posed by incongruities in their new intellectual environment. One Russian-born Volga German who had sojourned in Argentina before settling on the prairies of western Canada complained that in South America "everything seemed upside down."[41] Indeed, early Volga Germans on the pampas often felt disoriented while celebrating weddings in the chilly month of July and observing their important Christmas traditions in the hot summer month of December. Explained one writer: "The constellations of the north had vanished . . . while those of the Southern Cross and nebulous Milky Way emerged. At noontime the sun stood in the north, the moon waxed and waned on different sides, and the cold wind, the *pampero*, came out of the south!"[42]

Much of the traditional folk cosmology and seasonal folklore of the Volga Germans underwent significant change in the subtropical areas of central Argentina, just as their old-country clothing and agricultural practices did. But the settlers fiercely retained their ethnic identity as Germans, although—like their countrymen in the United States and Canada, who were invariably called "Rooshuns"—the Argentine colonists sometimes were derided by surrounding natives as *rusos*.[43] Volga German emigrants in the New World did not disavow their Russian birthplace, but they would repeatedly exclaim: *"Sei ich im Schweinstall gebore, sei ich immer noch Deitsch!"* ("Had I been born in a pigsty, I would still be German!")[44]

While the climate and stars and moon in South America seemed very different from what Volga Germans remembered in Russia, the emigrants found comfort in the realization that at least they had their own compact villages and churches in Argentina.[45] Furthermore, the pampas and the wheat fields that surrounded them provided an additional sense of familiarity. One Volga German poet in Argentina, perhaps echoing his people's proud sense of accomplishment, wrote in the new language of his adopted country:

> Y en esta tierra inmensa
> Escribí con la reja del arado
> El magnífico poema del trabajo.[46]
>
> . . . On this immense land
> I inscribed with the blade of my plow
> The magnificent poem of work.

Today a growing number of Volga Germans in many parts of Canada, the United States, and South America are actively cultivating an interest in their history and ethnic heritage. For the most part, they are indistinguishable from other New World descendants of European extraction, unlike the original German emigrants from the Volga who arrived in Topeka, Lincoln, Saskatoon, and Buenos Aires wearing their conspicuous sheepskin coats, felt boots, and homespun clothing. Perhaps modern-day Volga German descendants in the New World no longer "smack of the steppe," but their greatest numbers are still concentrated in the grassland regions of North and South America.

One cultural ecologist who studied ethnic adaptation in South America succinctly described the unusual history of the German Russians as a "natural experiment that gauges the response of a particular group of people to alterations in their environment." [47] Although many Volga German emigrants desired to settle in areas of the New World that were physically similar to their former surroundings, all needed to make at least some adjustment to new economic, sociopolitical, and intellectual realities.

Notes

1. For the complete German lyrics and English translation of this folk song, see Norbert R. Dreiling, *Unsere Leute: Exodus to Freedom* (Hays, Kans.: Volga German Centennial Association, 1976), p. 12.

2. Yehudi A. Cohen, Introduction to *Man in Adaptation: The Cultural Present*, ed. Yehudi A. Cohen, 2d ed. (Chicago: Aldine Publishing Co., 1974), p. 3; Robert McC. Netting, *Cultural Ecology* (Menlo Park, Calif.: Cummings Publishing Co., 1977), p. 7.

3. Some comprehensive sources on the historical background of the Volga Germans include the following: Gerhard Bonwetsch, *Geschichte der deutschen Kolonien an der Wolga* (Stuttgart: J. Engelhorns Nachf., 1919); Gottlieb Beratz, *Die deutschen Kolonien an der unteren Wolga in ihrer Entstehung und ersten Entwicklung*, 2d ed. (Berlin: Verlag des Verbandes der wolgadeutschen Bauern, 1923); Hattie Plum Williams, *The Czar's Germans*, ed. Emma S. Haynes, Phillip B. Legler, and Gerda S. Walker (Lincoln, Nebr.: American Historical Society of Germans from Russia, 1975); Adam Giesinger, *From Catherine to Khrushchev: The Story of Russia's Germans* (Battleford, Sask., Canada: Marian Press, 1974); Fred C. Koch, *The Volga Germans: In Russia and the Americas, from 1763 to the Present* (University Park: Pennsylvania State University Press, 1977); and Victor P. Popp and Nicolás Dening, *Los Alemanes del Volga* (Buenos Aires, Argentina: Gráfica Santo Domingo, 1977).

4. This estimate is mine and is based on population figures given in a number of key sources, especially Richard Sallet, *Russian-German Settlements in the United States* (1931), trans. La Vern J. Rippley and Armand Bauer (Fargo: North Dakota Institute for Regional Studies, 1974), p. 112; Giesinger, *From Catherine to Khrushchev*, p. 37; Koch, *The Volga Germans*, pp. 294-95; Popp and Dening, *Los Alemanes del Volga*, p. 185.

5. Emma Schwabenland Haynes, "Pioneer Stories from the Volga," *American Historical Society of Germans from Russia Work Paper*, no. 9 (Oct. 1972), p. 22. For additional information regarding initial German colonization on the Volga, see Adam Giesinger, trans., "Early Chroniclers among the Volga Germans," *Journal of the American Historical Society of Germans from Russia* 1 (Spring 1978): pp. 25-30.

6. Koch, *The Volga Germans*, p. 47.

7. All of the German colonies on the Volga were noninterdenominational except two, the Protestant villages of Katharinenstadt and Beauregard in the province of Samara. Both had a minority of Roman Catholic settlers.

8. Koch, *The Volga Germans*, p. 35; George J. Eisenach, *Pietism and the Russian Germans in the United States* (Berne, Ind.: Berne Publishers, 1948), pp. 27, 28 n. 7.

9. Koch, *The Volga Germans,* pp. 25, 26.

10. Ibid., p. 50.

11. This phrase is borrowed from Stephen I. Thompson, *Pioneer Coloniza-tion: A Cross-Cultural View,* Addison-Wesley Modules in Anthropology, no. 33 (Reading, Mass.: Addison-Wesley Publishing Co., 1973), p. 15.

12. Williams, *The Czar's Germans,* pp. 140, 141.

13. Koch, *The Volga Germans,* p. 77.

14. Ibid., p. 65.

15. J. G. Kohl, *Russia: St. Petersburg, Moscow, Kharkoff, Riga, Odessa, the German Provinces of the Baltic, the Steppes, the Crimea, and the Interior of the Empire* (London: Chapman and Hall, 1842), pp. 438–39 n.

16. Williams, *The Czar's Germans,* p. 97. Francis H. E. Palmer, *Russian Life in Town and Country* (New York: G. P. Putnam's Sons, 1901), p. 176. Victor C. Leiker, Foreword to *Conquering the Wind* by Amy Brungardt Toepfer and Agnes Dreiling (Garwood, N.J.: Victor C. Leiker, 1967), p. v.

17. A similar strategy of "adapt or get out" has been described for the American plains by Carl Frederick Kraenzel, *The Great Plains in Transition* (Norman: University of Oklahoma Press, 1955), pp. 283–88.

18. Koch, *The Volga Germans,* p. 4.

19. Out-migration as an adaptive process is briefly mentioned by John W. Bennet in "Social Adaptation in a Northern Plains Region: A Saskatchewan Study," in *Symposium on the Great Plains of North America,* ed. Carle C. Zimmerman and Seth Russell (Fargo: North Dakota Institute for Regional Studies, 1967), p. 188.

20. Eric R. Wolf, "Closed Corporate Peasant Communities in Mesoamerica and Central Java," in *Peasant Society: A Reader,* ed. Jack M. Potter, May N. Diaz, and George M. Foster (Boston: Little, Brown and Co., 1967), p. 231.

21. Volga German rites of passage are described in Timothy J. Kloberdanz, "The Volga German Catholic Life Cycle: An Ethnographic Reconstruction" (Master's thesis, Colorado State University, 1974).

22. Koch, *The Volga Germans,* p. 225.

23. Ibid., p. 2.

24. The interesting theory of "latitude pull" was first brought to my atten-tion by Dr. Michael Kenny, a cultural anthropologist at the Catholic University of America, Washington, D.C.

25. For example, see C. Langdon White, George T. Renner, and Henry J. Warman, *Geography: Factors and Concepts* (New York: Appleton-Century-Crofts, 1968), pp. 239–94.

26. Albert J. Petersen, Jr., "The German-Russian Settlement Pattern in Ellis County, Kansas," *The Rocky Mountain Social Science Journal* 5 (April 1968), pp. 52, 55.

27. Ibid., p. 55.

28. Ibid., p. 53. Also see Albert J. Petersen, Jr., "German-Russian Catholic Colonization in Western Kansas: A Settlement Geography" (Ph.D. diss., Louisi-ana State University, 1970).

29. La Vern J. Rippley, Introduction to Sallet, *Russian-German Settlements in the United States,* p. 7; also Karl Stumpp, "Das Russlanddeutschtum in Uebersee," *Heimatbuch 1963* (Stuttgart: Landsmannschaft der Deutschen aus Russland), p. 8.

30. Sallet, *Russian-German Settlements in the United States,* p. 62.

31. Frederick C. Luebke, "Ethnic Group Settlement on the Great Plains," *Western Historical Quarterly* 8 (October 1977): 414; Sallet, *Russian-German Settlements in the United States,* p. 49.

32. Jakob Riffel, *Die Russlanddeutschen insbesondere die Wolgadeutschen am La Plata (Argentinien, Uruguay und Paraguay),* 2d ed. (Lucas González, Argentina: published by the author, 1928), p. 21, cited in Koch, *The Volga Germans,* p. 234.

33. This area also attracted a large number of Black Sea German Catholics from Russia and the Dakotas. See W. Schulte, *St. Joseph's Colony, 1905-1930,* trans. Lambert and Tillie Schneider (Battleford, Sask.: Marian Press, 1976). For a shorter but more comprehensive discussion, see Adam Giesinger, "Germans from Russia in Western Canada," *American Historical Society of Germans from Russia Work Paper,* no. 7 (December 1971), pp. 37-42.

34. Much descriptive information about the pioneering experiences of early Volga German homesteaders in western Saskatchewan is contained in a 186-page handwritten German manuscript by Michael Stang (n.d.). It is currently being translated into English for publication by Dr. Joseph S. Height, Franklin College, Indiana.

35. Schulte, *St. Joseph's Colony, 1905-1930,* pp. 109-10.

36. Giesinger, *From Catherine to Khrushchev,* p. 350; the direct quotation is an English translation of Riffel, *Die Russlanddeutschen,* p. 47, cited in Iris Barbara Graefe, *Zur Volkskunde der Russlanddeutschen in Argentinien* (Vienna: A. Schendl, 1971), p. 20.

37. Graefe, *Zur Volkskunde der Russlanddeutschen,* p. 22; Iris Barbara Graefe, "Germans from Russia in South America," *American Historical Society of Germans from Russia Work Paper,* no. 24 (Fall 1977), p. 26; Koch, *The Volga Germans,* pp. 226, 227.

38. Iris Barbara Graefe, "Zur oekologischen Einpassung der Wolgadeutschen in Argentinien und Brasilien," in *Rendezvous mit Tier und Mensch,* comp. Otto Koenig (Vienna: Molden, 1974), p. 45; Graefe, "Germans from Russia in South America," p. 28.

39. Graefe, *Zur Volkskunde der Russlanddeutschen,* p. 133.

40. Ibid., pp. 96-97; also Graefe, "Germans from Russia in South America," p. 29.

41. From an interview with a Volga German Canadian informant near Macklin, Saskatchewan, August 24, 1977.

42. English translation of Graefe, "Zur oekologischen Einpassung der Wolgadeutschen," p. 43.

43. Graefe, *Zur Volkskunde der Russlanddeutschen,* p. 131.

44. I have heard this dialectal expression many times in Volga German

areas of settlement stretching from western Saskatchewan to the prairies of southeastern Colorado.

45. For an interesting description of the ongoing process of Volga German assimilation and its most recent ramifications in South America, see Iris B. Graefe, "Cultural Changes among Germans from Russia in Argentina, 1967-1977," in *Germans from Russia in Colorado,* ed. Sidney Heitman (Fort Collins, Colo.: Western Social Science Association, 1978), pp. 58-69.

46. M. E. Rau, quoted in Jose Brendel, *Hombres Rubios en el Surco* (Buenos Aires: Editorial Guadalupe, 1961), p. 123. A similar English translation of this verse appears in Al Bitz and Richard Gross, "The German Russians of South America," *Heritage Review* (North Dakota Historical Society of Germans from Russia), no. 19 (December 1977), p. 6.

47. Graefe, *Zur Volkskunde der Russlanddeutschen,* p. 129.

Prairie Bound: Migration Patterns to a Swedish Settlement on the Dakota Frontier

Robert C. Ostergren

A topic that is frequently addressed in settlement studies is the process of frontier migration. The fact that new settlers on the frontier had to come from somewhere else naturally raises questions about the origins of these people, the timing of their migrations, the routes they followed, and the communication process that motivated them. Moreover, the widespread occurrence of culturally homogeneous immigrant communities, especially on the homestead frontiers of the American Middle West, gives rise to a curiosity about the significance of migratory experiences and associations in explaining immigrant settlement behavior. To a certain extent, the selection of a place to live and the choice of one's neighbors must have been a product of experiences with places and people along the way.[1]

The study of historic patterns of movement to the American frontier, however, is not easily accomplished. Detailed information about the travels and stopping places of large numbers of immigrant settlers does not generally exist. When people are on the move they tend to make a far fainter imprint on the historical record than when they put down roots. Consequently, it is often possible to make only generalized comments about the migration patterns of frontier populations. Available data, for the most part, are place oriented. We know when people arrived in a certain place and when they left that place, but lack the connecting evidence necessary to determine where they came from or where they were going to. Faced with such data problems, most studies of frontier migration have dealt with the frequency of migration rather than the pattern. These "turnover" studies have yielded a great deal of information about population mobility rates in a variety of places and time periods.[2] They tell us little, however, about the cumulative migration experience of individuals and groups.

On occasion material does surface that lends itself to the detailed study of migration patterns for a particular population. This type of material usually appears in the form of collected pioneer autobiographies or life histories. A recent and seminal example of the use of material of this nature is an article by John Hudson that delimits frontier migration patterns to the state of North Dakota on the basis of pioneer autobiographies collected in the late 1930s.[3] Hudson uses a sample of one thousand autobiographies to test and flesh out various notions about migration and mobility in American life. His article deals with these questions on a very broad scale in that the sample population is widely scattered in both time and space. It reflects the entire North Dakota frontier experience from the 1870s to the 1910–20 period. The patterns revealed are interesting in a comparative sense and hint at what might be achieved in working on a smaller scale.

This paper focuses on the migration experience of the early population of a single frontier settlement. The population is a group of 206 immigrant Swedish settlers who made their way in the late 1860s and early 1870s to the same place in southeastern South Dakota—the Dalesburg settlement of Clay County. The tracing of their presettlement activities is made possible by the existence of an uncommonly rich data source. In the 1930s a local resident wrote, as a hobby, detailed histories of all the homesteaders in the settlement.[4] What makes his collection of histories so rich is the remarkably consistent attention paid to the moves and domiciles of its subjects. The information allows a nearly complete view of the migration experience of each homesteader from the time he left the home parish in Sweden until his death, whether it was on the homestead in South Dakota or elsewhere. The aim of this paper is to describe the migration experience of the Dalesburg settlers and to relate that experience to the early settlement patterns and associations that occurred in the community.

The Dalesburg Settlement

The destination of the 206 Swedish settlers and their families who are the subject of this study was an area of rolling prairie situated on the east side of the valley of the Vermillion River, a sluggish tributary of the Missouri River located in Clay County, Dakota Territory (fig. 1). Clay County was opened for settlement around 1860, roughly about the time that the rapidly moving pre–Civil War frontier began to push up the major river valleys into Nebraska and Dakota territories. A combination of Indian troubles, the Civil War, drought, and grasshopper plague caused the advance of

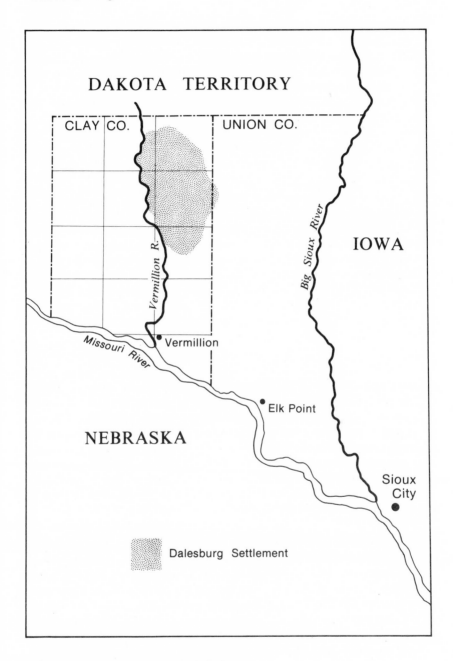

Figure 1. Clay County, South Dakota

settlement to halt just short of the area, which meant that until the late 1860s the only sizable population in the county was located at the town site of Vermillion.

With the return of better times, the lure of free homestead land, and the construction of the Dakota Southern Railroad up from Sioux City, the area underwent a boom period. From 1868 to 1873 settlers flooded into the county, advanced up the Vermillion Valley, and spread out onto the prairies. The influx was dominated by settlers of Scandinavian origins who, like most immigrants, segregated themselves in the process of settling the region. The Norwegians settled largely to the west of the Vermillion River, the Swedes to the east of the river, and the Danes formed a number of communities in various locations across the county.

The Swedish settlement area became known as the Dalesburg settlement—the name given to the first post office in that part of the county. The name, which was originally spelled *Dahlsborg*, came from the fact that many of the original settlers hailed from the Swedish province of Dalarna.[5] At its greatest extent, the settlement stretched for about fifteen miles from north to south along the east side of the Vermillion River and extended eastward from the river for a distance of six to eight miles.

The map in figure 2 shows the location of most of the early Swedish homesteads in the settlement. The arrows, which were drawn on the basis of the dates when homesteads were claimed, show the general manner in which settlement progressed across the community. The creeks that emptied into the Vermillion clearly played an important role in determining the settlement pattern. The advance of settlement tended to move up the creeks and the homesteads tended to cluster near the creeks, which represented the only convenient source of water and wood on the prairie. Two areas along the Vermillion, labeled "Cabbage Flats" and "Vermillion Bottom" on the map, were poorly drained and generally avoided in the settlement process.[6]

The settlement was organized socially around the religious institutions that were founded within its boundaries. The first and largest of these was the Dalesburg Lutheran Church, which was founded during the winter of 1871. The Lutheran church could by no means command the allegiance of the entire community, since a great deal of religious dissension apparently existed from the beginning. The dissension resulted in the establishment later that year of a rival organization, the Bloomingdale Baptist Church, just two miles away.[7] Later on, a Mission Covenant church was organized in the

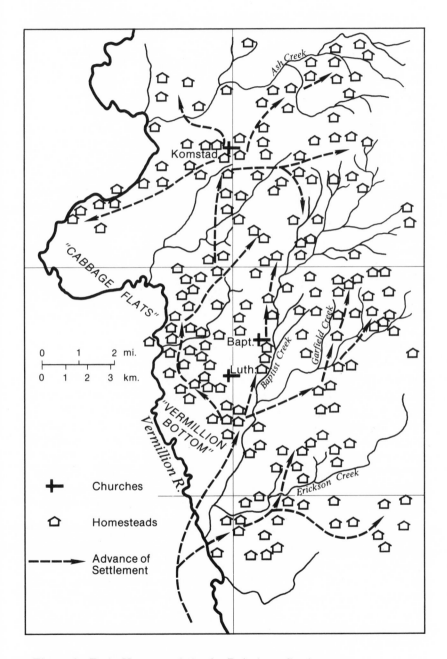

Figure 2. Early Homesteads in the Dalesburg Settlement

northern part of the settlement near the Komstad post office. All three churches functioned vigorously throughout the early history of the settlement, serving as focal points for the social associations of the settlers.

Origins in Sweden

With few exceptions, the people who would eventually settle in Clay County began leaving Sweden in the mid-1860s. Their departure was a part of the ground swell of emigration that took place in Sweden as that decade drew to a close. A series of bad harvests in Sweden, coupled with good times in America, provided the impetus necessary for the mass migration. Most of the Dalesburg migrants (75.6 percent) left during the period 1868–70, the three peak years in the Swedish emigration curve for that period.

Of perhaps greater interest, in terms of differentiating the experience of the migrants, is the exact location of their points of departure. The map in figure 3 shows the distribution of parishes from which the Dalesburg people emigrated.[8] The "emigration field" covers nearly all of Sweden, but concentrations of activity occur in certain areas. For purposes of analysis, it is useful to regionalize the pattern. Three distinct regions delimited on the map serve to group those emigrants that seem to have had a common cultural background.

The first of these culture groups is made up of those who emigrated from the forested regions of Upper Dalarna and similar districts in northern Värmland. This group, comprising sixty-eight primary emigrants and their dependents, will hereafter be referred to as the Upper Dalarna culture group. A second group, consisting of sixty-one primary emigrants and their dependents, emigrated from the coastal and lower river valley parishes of the Bothnian Coast. The third group hailed from the old province of Östergötland and adjacent districts in northern Småland (forty-three emigrations). The remaining thirty-three emigrations were from scattered locations, although it should be noted that there is a rather weak fourth group (ten emigrations) from the province of Skåne.

There is every indication that the emigrants left Sweden quickly. There are but one or two cases of children being born in Swedish coastal towns or cities, and in nearly all cases the records show that the emigrants arrived in America the same year that they left Sweden. Most proceeded to the larger Swedish ports and sailed first to England and then to America. The majority entered the United

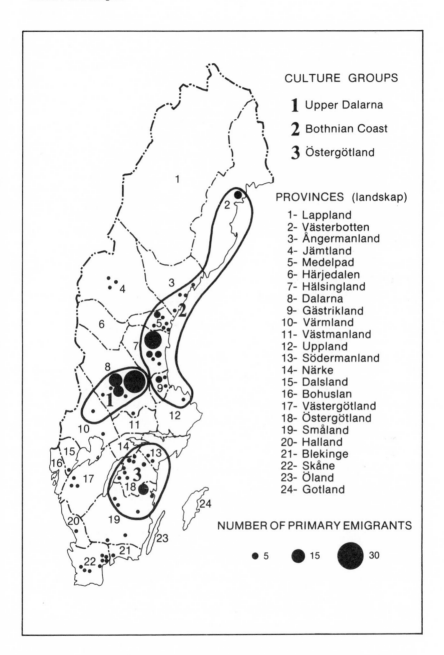

CULTURE GROUPS

1 Upper Dalarna

2 Bothnian Coast

3 Östergötland

PROVINCES (landskap)

1- Lappland
2- Västerbotten
3- Ångermanland
4- Jämtland
5- Medelpad
6- Härjedalen
7- Hälsingland
8- Dalarna
9- Gästrikland
10- Värmland
11- Västmanland
12- Uppland
13- Södermanland
14- Närke
15- Dalsland
16- Bohuslan
17- Västergötland
18- Östergötland
19- Småland
20- Halland
21- Blekinge
22- Skåne
23- Öland
24- Gotland

NUMBER OF PRIMARY EMIGRANTS

● 5   ● 15   ⬤ 30

Figure 3. Parish Origins in Sweden of Clay County Settlers

States through the port of New York. The major difference in their experience, up to that point, is that their cultural backgrounds differed, depending upon the part of Sweden they were from.

The Movement to Clay County

Most scholars agree that the business of moving to the frontier was a serious undertaking that required planning and the acquisition of reliable information about one's destination.[9] To be sure, the very first inhabitants of a newly opened area may have come there by happenstance, but the waves of settlers that filled the area in were the product of a complex communication system. Potential migrants were prompted to act by the receipt of information through both public and private channels. Many areas were widely advertised in newspapers and pamphlets or promoted by agents representing land and railroad companies. Even more reliable was the information that came through relatives and acquaintances.

For a substantial number of the Dalesburg migrants, the receipt of information about the Dakota frontier must have taken place in Sweden and prompted the decision to emigrate. The speed and directness with which many made the move is indicative of this. Eighty-one of the emigrants (39.3 percent) proceeded directly from a U.S. port of entry to Clay County. They made no intervening stops, which suggests that they knew exactly where they were going. The remainder (125 migrants) moved indirectly to Clay County, stopping at least once along the way for a period of a month or more. It is uncertain whether or not those who moved indirectly had information about their ultimate destination, but we can assume that many did because information about the Dakota frontier was widespread in Sweden at the time.[10]

The fact that some moved directly to Clay County while others did not is an intriguing one. What could explain this difference in behavior? The time of arrival of direct and indirect migrants in Clay County follows no particular pattern. Therefore, the explanation is not that the early migrations were indirect and that the later migrants, who possessed better information, were able to move more directly. Nor do variables such as age or marital status have any bearing on the way in which people moved to Clay County. The proportion of direct migrants to indirect migrants remains fairly constant over time. Furthermore, single migrants were just as apt to move directly as were married men burdened by dependents. There was some difference in age. The average age of the direct migrants tended to be somewhat greater than that of the indirect migrants (34.5 years vs. 29.8 years), but the difference is not large enough to explain the divergence in behavior.

The explanation lies in the channels of personal information flow that individuals may have been following. It is reasonable to assume that if an immigrant was in contact with a relative or friend that had preceded him to America, his first action would be to go to that person. He could then proceed westward, with the encouragement and advice of trusted friends who knew what lay ahead. Moreover, the rigors of the journey could be lessened by following in the path of others who had left the settlement for points west in earlier years.[11]

If one considers the emigration history of the culture regions from which the Dalesburg people emigrated, it becomes clear that the probability of having such contacts was greater for some than it was for others. Emigration, for instance, began relatively late in the forested upland parishes of Dalarna and northern Värmland. The Dalesburg people who left the Upper Dalarna area in the late 1860s were among the first to leave the region. The opportunity for them to go to established settlements where they might have contacts was not great. Most immigrant Dalacarlian communities were located in places that were settled about the same time as Dalesburg or later. The Bothnian Coast, on the other hand, is a region that experienced earlier migration. One might expect emigrants from there to have had a greater opportunity to make intervening stops. The Östergötland region experienced the earliest emigration. Its later emigrants probably faced the greatest prospect of proceeding to the American frontier by way of a place where they knew someone.

In fact, the migrations followed exactly that pattern. The proportion of indirect migration was very low for those that emigrated from Upper Dalarna (38.2 percent) and considerably higher for those who emigrated from the Bothnian Coast (70.5 percent) and Östergötland (76.7 percent). Table 1 and the map in figure 4 show the distribution of initial stops for the 125 migrants that proceeded indirectly to Clay County. Certain places figured prominently in the migration process for certain groups. Of special importance to the Bothnian Coast group is Allamakee County, Iowa, an important 1850s settlement of Hälsingland people. Keokuk, Iowa, was an important Östergötland settlement, and the Galesburg-Andover-Moline district of western Illinois embraced settlements from Östergötland and the Bothnian Coast area. The cities of Chicago, Council Bluffs, Sioux City, and Omaha had Swedish populations of mixed origins

TABLE 1
Indirect Migrations to Clay County, South Dakota
(Heads of Households)

Initial Stops	Total Pop.		Upper Dalarna		Bothnian Gulf		Öster- götland		Others	
	No.	%	No.	%	No.	%	No.	%	No.	%
Allamakee Co., Iowa	22	17.6	— —		18	41.9	3	9.1	1	4.3
Andover, Ill.	16	12.8	5	19.3	— —		10	30.4	1	4.3
Chicago, Ill.	15	12.0	2	7.7	— —		5	15.2	8	34.7
Sioux City, Iowa	13	10.4	5	19.3	4	9.3	1	3.0	3	13.4
Moline, Ill.	10	8.0	— —		5	11.7	5	15.2	— —	
Council Bluffs, Iowa	10	8.0	— —		9	20.9	— —		— —	
Galesburg, Ill.	6	4.8	4	15.4	1	2.3	1	3.0	— —	
Keokuk, Iowa	4	3.2	— —		— —		4	12.1	— —	
Omaha, Nebr.	4	3.2	— —		1	2.3	1	3.0	2	8.7
Stockholm, Wis.	3	2.4	— —		— —		1	3.0	2	8.7
Dakota City, Nebr.	3	2.4	2	7.7	— —		— —		1	4.3
Rio, Wis.	3	2.4	3	11.5	— —		— —		— —	
Isanti Co., Minn.	2	1.6	2	7.7	— —		— —		— —	
Madrid, Iowa	2	1.6	— —		2	4.7	— —		— —	
Le Seuer, Minn.	2	1.6	— —		— —		— —		2	8.7
Boonesboro, Iowa	2	1.6	— —		1	2.3	1	3.0	— —	
La Porte, Ind.	2	1.6	1	3.8	— —		— —		— —	
Kandiyohi Co., Minn.	1	0.8	— —		1	2.3	— —		— —	
Wapello Co., Iowa	1	0.8	— —		— —		— —		1	4.3
Oakland, Nebr.	1	0.8	— —		1	2.3	— —		— —	
San Franciso, Calif.	1	0.8	— —		— —		— —		1	4.3
Detroit, Mich.	1	0.8	1	3.8	— —		— —		— —	
Unknown	1	0.8	1	3.8	— —		— —		— —	
Totals	125	100.0	26	100.0	43	100.0	33	100.0	23	100.0

and served as staging areas for frontier-bound immigrants. The Missouri River towns of Omaha–Council Bluffs and Sioux City were especially important to Dakota-bound immigrants. About 10 percent of the indirect migrants made second and third stops. In most cases these stops took place in these gateway towns of the Missouri Valley.

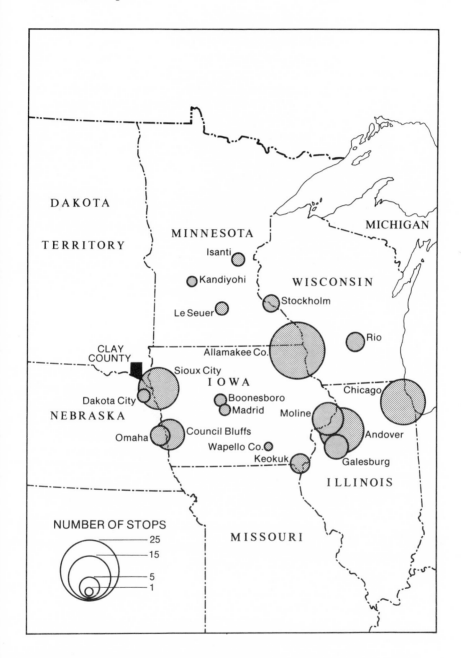

Figure 4. Initial Stops of Indirect Migrants to Clay County

The difference between culture groups in their potential for stops on the way westward would have the effect, in addition to varying their experience, of varying their time of arrival on the frontier. It was pointed out earlier that most of the Dalesburg migrants left Sweden at roughly the same time and proceeded directly to America. The graph in figure 5 shows how similar their emigration curves were. In contrast to that is the graph in figure 6, which shows the arrival curves for each of the three culture groups. The effect of intervening stops was to delay the arrival of the people from the Bothnian Coast and Östergötland. It should be pointed out, however, that there were also direct migrants in both the Bothnian Coast and Östergötland groups that arrived right alongside the earliest settlers from Dalarna. On the other hand, the Upper Dalarna lead was enhanced by the fact that the indirect migrations of the people from Dalarna were delayed for a shorter time on the average than those from the other groups. The average time from emigration to settlement for the indirect Dalarna migrant was 1.48 years. Migrants from the Bothnian Coast took an average of 1.9 years and those from Östergötland took 3.5 years.

Settling the Dalesburg Community

The collection point for settlers arriving in Clay County was the town of Vermillion, where the land office was located. It was customary for land seekers to leave dependents and possessions there while they went out to have a look at the land. Often this was done in small parties, since there were men who were in the business of guiding people out to survey the countryside.[12] In some cases, parties came up from Sioux City to find land and file claims. They would then return to Sioux City for their dependents and baggage.[13] These land-seeking parties were a key element in determining the spatial pattern of homesteading, for it was the timing of an immigrant's arrival in Vermillion, along with the associations he had made with other migrants back in Sweden or along the way, that often determined the make-up of land-seeking parties and collective trips to the land office.

The map in figure 7 indicates that to a remarkable extent culture group associations played an important role. There was a clear tendency for those with common backgrounds to congregate along certain creek beds. People from Upper Dalarna colonized the areas along Erickson Creek, Garfield Creek, and the lower and central reaches of Baptist Creek. Immigrants from the Bothnian Coast area

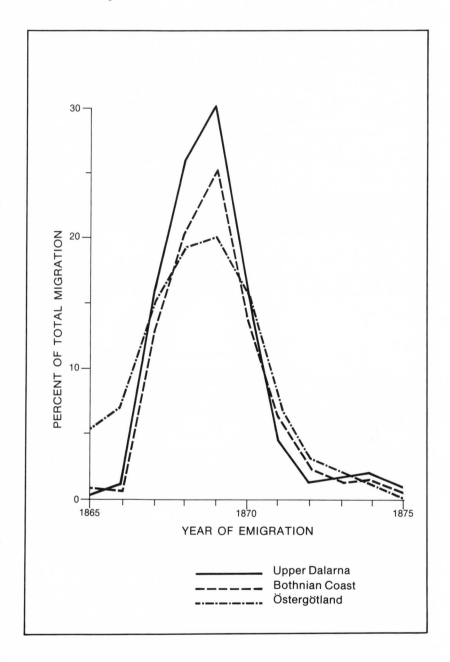

Figure 5. Emigration Curves by Culture Group

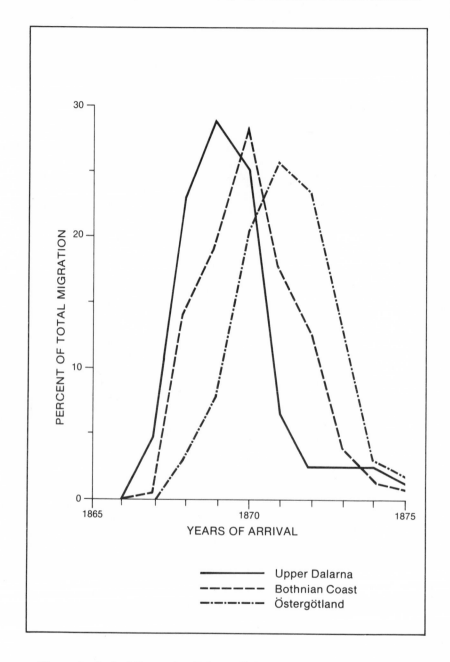

Figure 6. Arrival Curves by Culture Group

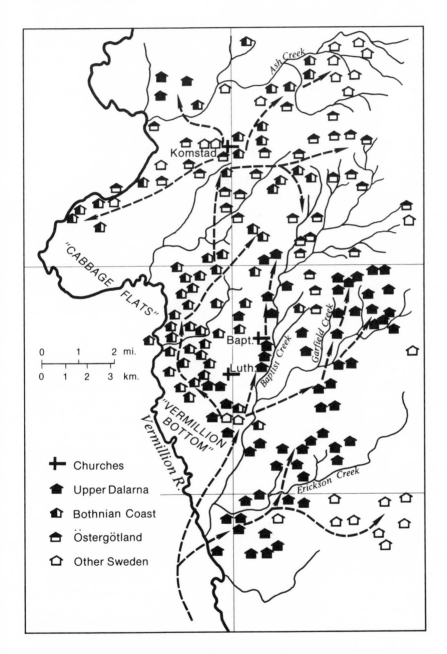

Figure 7. Homesteads by Culture Group

concentrated very heavily along the small unnamed creek that flows into the Vermillion River between Cabbage Flats and Vermillion Bottom. Others scattered northward along the Vermillion and some of its upriver tributaries. The Östergötland group occupied the area at the headwaters of Baptist Creek and along the unnamed creek directly to the west (near Komstad post office).

The importance of personal associations within the culture groups is evident if one inspects more closely the patterns outlined above. For instance, the Upper Dalarna people that settled along the lower reaches of Garfield Creek were all from the same place—the parish of Gagnef. Those that settled along Erickson Creek were largely from the parish of Svärdsjö, while residents of the neighborhood that emerged along Baptist Creek hailed largely from the parish of Rättvik. Each of these groupings reflects associations that were made back in Sweden.

At another level, the Östergötland people who occupied the headwaters of Baptist Creek and the area around Komstad post office had, for the most part, the common experience of spending time near Andover in Henry County, Illinois. The large concentration of Bothnian Coast people located to the west of the Lutheran church came from widely scattered locations in Sweden, but had, in most cases, proceeded to Clay County by way of Allamakee County, Iowa. Most of the Bothnian Coast people settling to the northeast of Cabbage Flats had moved as a group to Clay County, stopping at Madrid and Council Bluffs, Iowa.[14] All of these are examples of associations made or strengthened by common experience in moving west toward the homestead frontier.

A remarkable thing about this clustering process is that not all the homesteads in each of the neighborhoods were taken simultaneously. There was usually a three- or four-year lag between the time that the first settler and the last settler of a neighborhood cluster filed his claim. During that period, the fringe of settlement would have advanced a considerable distance beyond. The formation of such distinct units was the product of conscious effort rather than the simple availability of land. A settler that was interested only in acquiring good land might well have made his choice elsewhere.

Conclusion

The degree to which these associations were perceived within the Dalesburg settlement and influenced the later life of the community is an important question. To investigate it is beyond the scope of this

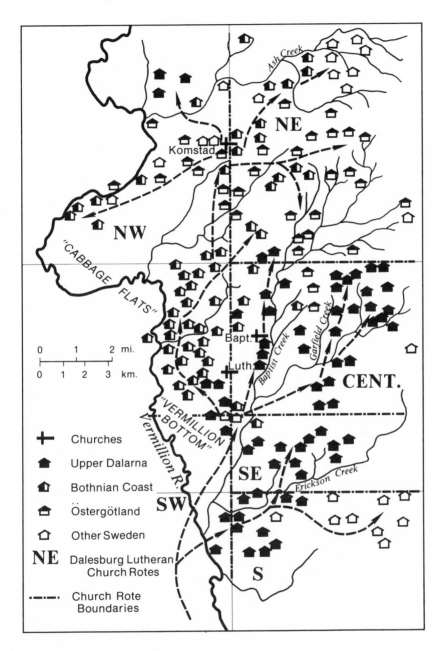

Figure 8. Dalesburg Lutheran Church *Rotes*

paper, but a possible line of inquiry would be a study of the religious structure of the community. A quick survey of the membership rolls of the Dalesburg churches suggests that church membership cut across neighborhood lines. A look at the internal organization of one of the churches, however, is more revealing. The Dalesburg Lutheran Church divided its membership into administrative districts called *rotes*. Although the boundaries of the rotes shifted somewhat during the history of the church, the map in figure 8 gives a fairly good approximation.[15] The districts correspond reasonably well with many of the neighborhood clusters identified above. One may conclude that there was an official acknowledgment here of a community social organization that was older than the community itself.

The social organization of the Dalesburg community was the product of associations made or strengthened by common experience in making the journey from Europe to the homestead frontier. People who had known one another before the emigration began or who came to know one another at stopping points along the way grouped themselves into clusters or neighborhoods when they took their land. It was the communication and migration axes that connected home districts with intermediate settlements in the Middle West and eventually Dalesburg itself that guided the entire process and promoted the spatial concentration of homogeneous groups that is associated with ethnicity on the agricultural frontiers of the Great Plains.

Notes

1. The literature on the segregation of culture groups in the American Middle West is large. Some examples are John G. Rice, *Patterns of Ethnicity in a Minnesota County, 1880-1905* (Umeå, Sweden: Department of Geography, University of Umeå, 1973); Robert C. Ostergren, "Cultural Homogeneity and Population Stability among Swedish Immigrants in Chisago County," *Minnesota History* 43 (Fall 1973): 255-69; and Peter A. Munch, "Segregation and Assimilation of Norwegian Settlements in Wisconsin," *Norwegian-American Studies and Records* (1954): 102-40. Questions about the migration process have become especially prominent in recent years as scholars have begun to view movement as possibly a more significant factor in explaining the American experience than the frontier institutions of Turner's celebrated thesis. See George W. Pierson, *The Moving American* (New York: Alfred A. Knopf, 1972).

2. Knowledge about the comings and goings of people is normally extracted from place-oriented sources such as manuscript censuses, church registers, city directories, etc. An early example of a study that dealt with population turnover in a frontier community is Merle Curti et al., *The Making of an American Community* (Stanford, Calif.: Stanford University Press, 1959).

3. John C. Hudson, "Migration to an American Frontier," *Annals of the Association of American Geographers* 66 (June 1976): 242-65.

4. August Peterson, *History of the Swedes Who Settled in Clay County, South Dakota and their Biographies* (Vermillion, S.Dak.: Swedish Pioneer and Historical Society of Clay County, South Dakota, 1947). The book actually contains 242 life histories, but the number used in this study was pared down to 206 by the elimination of multiple homesteads within the same family and a number of entries for which information was scant. The 206 individuals studied here are the heads of the families that homesteaded in the area.

5. Lloyd R. Moses, ed., *Clay County Place Names* (Vermillion, S.Dak.: Clay County Historical Society, 1976), p. 45.

6. Ibid., pp. 34, 134-35.

7. Herbert S. Schell, *History of Clay County* (Vermillion: S.Dak.: Clay County Historical Society, 1976), p. 149.

8. The emigrations shown are those of primary emigrants. It was often common for other members of a family to emigrate later. These later emigrations are not shown, since they are viewed in this paper as a continuation of the first person's emigration.

9. This is well demonstrated in Hudson, "Migration to an American Frontier," pp. 244-56.

10. Approximately one month is considered for the purpose of this paper to be a significant stop. Staying in one place for that length of time or longer implies that fairly permanent lodgings and perhaps employment had to be found. The type of employment sought during extended stops would be an interesting piece of information, but it is not uniformly available for this population.

Agents representing the railroads and immigration commissions of the plains states and territories were present in Sweden during the late 1860s and early 1870s. In addition, there were letters home from Swedes living in the Midwest, where information about the Dakota frontier was widespread. Examples of letters may be found in Bjorn Hallerdt, ed., *Emigration från Dalarna* (Falun: Falu Nya Boktryckeri AB, 1968).

11. An important feature of settlement in the Middle West was the strings of communities that were linked by bonds of kinship. When the population of a community grew beyond the capacity of the land to support it, surplus population commonly left the community in search of land, establishing daughter communities farther west.

12. Schell, *History of Clay County*, p. 111.

13. Homesteaders who had filed in Clay County often returned to Sioux City in order to find work, especially if they filed too late in the season to break ground and plant a crop.

14. A relatively large group of emigrants from the parish of Gnarp in Hälsingland traveled together as far as Council Bluffs and then dispersed. These people were part of that group.

15. The map is based on information obtained from Pastor Robert G. Lundgren, Dalesburg Lutheran Church, Vermillion, South Dakota.

The Old Order Amish on the Great Plains: A Study in Cultural Vulnerability

John A. Hostetler

The Amish have been in America for approximately two and one-half centuries. During this time they have formed unique communities, communities which were different from those in their European homeland in Switzerland and Alsace. In Europe there was no toleration for nonconformists like the Amish, hence they had no privileges of landownership. But in America they thrived. Although a significant number of marginal communities have failed, they have formed substantial, long-lasting communities in geographic areas where they can meet the basic requirements for continuous social life.

The Amish came to the New World in two immigration movements. The first was in the eighteenth century (ca. 1727–70), when they settled in Pennsylvania. From the Pennsylvania settlements new communities have spread to most of the twenty states where the Amish live today. The second period of emigration was in the nineteenth century (1816–45), with Amish coming from Alsace, Lorraine, Bavaria, Hesse, and the Palatinate to Ohio, Indiana, Illinois, Iowa, and Nebraska. Upon their arrival they found the Amish of Pennsylvania stock more traditional than themselves, and consequently soon began to associate with the Mennonites. Most Old Order Amish today derive from the eighteenth-century groups. The term *Old Order* emerged in America as the forces of assimilation began to affect nineteenth-century life.

The Old Order Amish are those who live by the traditional pattern of horse-and-buggy scale. Against their wishes they have been featured in Sunday supplements and newspapers depicting men wearing black broad-brimmed hats and women wearing long dresses and bonnets. Amish groups who have accommodated to modernity generally consider themselves Amish Mennonite, identifying themselves as Mennonite of Amish background. Most Mennonite communities living on the Great Plains today derive from a Dutch-Prussian-Ukrainian background, with small groups of Swiss here and there.

No one knows how many Amish immigrants there were. From a population of about 8,000 in 1900, the Old Order Amish have increased to about 85,000 in 1978. With a natural increase of 3.019 percent per year they have doubled their population every 23 years.[1] Despite the break-aways of individuals and families from Old Order factions to Protestantism that occur about every generation, the Old Order continue to increase by having large families.

The Amish communities, it may be hypothesized, are located today in those geographic areas where community self-realization can be maximized. The many extinct Amish settlements attest to a great deal of trial and error in the formation of new communities.[2] In keeping with the theory of limited possibilities, we may observe that 75 percent of the Amish population is concentrated in three states—Pennsylvania, Ohio, and Indiana. Many of the settlements started in a different climate and at great distance from the mother communities have not endured. They have either returned to the mother settlement or have assimilated.

Any discussion of viability among the Old Order Amish must consider the maximizing values of Amish life. What are their ultimate values, their *wert rational*, and their understanding of the redemptive process? The relationship between subsistence, culture patterns, and ritual process gives rise to a distinctive charter in the case of the Old Order Amish.[3] The charter is expressed concretely in the formation of a community. Communities bound by this charter prosper better in some areas than in others. Basic to the charter is the maintenance of a small human scale rather than a large and rational bureaucratic scale of human association.

The Old Order Amish work constantly to keep scale. Their *Ordnung* (community rules) functions to keep the physical environment limited, modeled after the Garden of Eden and the valleys of Switzerland. All their social structures proclaim that "small is godly."[4] Their limitations on transportation (automobile, truck, airplane), their limitations on the telephone, their limitations on farm equipment and electricity, make large-scale operations dysfunctional. Their economic structure (labor-intensive family farms) and their social structure (married couples, children, and intergenerational family) maladapts them for large-scale agriculture. Their work socialization trains them for small-scale, family-sized, diversified, intensive farming on varied soils and terrain. Supportive of the small scale are a common faith, dialect, simplicity, neighborliness, and consumptive austerity.

The function of scale is dramatically illustrated by contrasting the Old Order Amish with the Hutterian Brethren. Although the two groups have a common Anabaptist origin, the functioning of their communities is very different. Hutterites emigrated to America from the open landscape of the Ukraine. Their social structure is modeled after a colony and not a family scale of subsistence activity. Large acreages and great distances between communities are common to their social structure. Although Hutterite *Ordnung* greatly restricts personal possessions and conveniences, it does not restrict ownership of large acreages, rational work organization, large-scale machinery, or interchanges between great distances.[5] The Hutterites are located altogether on the Great Plains in the United States and Canada, whereas the Old Order Amish are clustered largely east of the Mississippi on family-operated farms. The average acreage of a colony (with perhaps fifteen families) in South Dakota is 5,387 acres, in Alberta, 8,892, and in Lancaster County, Pennsylvania, the average holdings of an Amish farm is about 48 acres.

Throughout Old Order Amish history there have been many attempts to establish communities outside of their present large settlements. There are extinct communities in virtually all of the states where the Amish live today, and in such faraway states as Mississippi, New Mexico, California, and Oregon. We shall review several, but by no means all, of the attempts of the Amish to settle in the Great Plains. The central concern is to identify those aspects of small-scale Old Order culture that are vulnerable when transplanted to the Great Plains. We shall begin with early extinct settlements and then examine a Kansas Old Order community that has survived for over a century.

Early Settlements

Nebraska. The first Old Order Amish to enter the Great Plains were Pennsylvania Amish (from Juniata and Mifflin counties) who settled in Gosper and Phelps counties, Nebraska, in 1880.[6] A few single Amish men had traveled to Nebraska in the previous year, found a location, and erected frame buildings. Their post office was Bertrand, located twenty-five miles southwest of Kearney. The economic incentive was homesteading. The settlement grew to thirteen families, mostly named Yoder. Three brothers homesteaded 320 acres, which they parceled into three farms. In retrospect one member of the Nebraska settlement wrote: "Had they known more about this land and its climate, they should each have acquired . . . 320 acres." Besides tilling the soil for grain farming, they also raised sheep. The bishop, Yost H. Yoder, was called back to Mifflin County, Pennsylvania, to help resolve a church dispute.[7] By 1904 the settlement had dissolved. During the twenty-four-year life of the settlement there were three Amish weddings. As the young grew up, many left for other Amish settlements in search of companions. The families joined other settlements in Pennsylvania, North Dakota, Oklahoma, and Kansas.

No other Old Order Amish settled in Nebraska until 1977, when two Old Order Amish families, those of Atlee Miller and Levi Troyer of Ohio, moved to Pawnee County in the hope of founding a community. Ten of their seventeen children are of school age and are currently being tutored at home by Mrs. Troyer, who was an Amish teacher in Ohio. As of this date the parents have been arrested and fined for not having the children taught by a certified teacher.

North Dakota. The fever to move to North Dakota hit Indiana Amish families in 1893 and Mifflin County, Pennsylvania, families in 1896.[8] A substantial movement of plain people occurred in 1895, when members of the Church of the Brethren and Amish from Indiana, Ohio, moved to North Dakota. The Mifflin County families, consisting of Amish Mennonites as well as Old Order Amish, boarded a special train for North Dakota in 1903. They settled in Rolette and Pierce counties, filing claims on government lands. At its peak, this Old Order community consisted of two church districts and about fifty families. After 1909 many families dispersed to other Old Order settlements that had been established in Colorado, Kansas, and Montana, and some returned to their previous communities. Several reasons were given for the failure: severe winters, limited medical services, and inability to adjust to the environment. Most of the families who stayed joined Amish Mennonite congregations nearby, but three Old Order members, including the bishop, remained there until 1956. There is no record of any serious "church trouble." Bishop Eli J. Bontreger served from 1901 to 1910, and after he moved away, he returned twice each year until 1938 to serve as their bishop. In his autobiography Bontreger says, "We always got along well in the church, as we had a united ministry at all times."[9] He also says, "The novelty of farming those prairie lands, where four to six horse teams were needed, wore off after a number of years and a desire for farming on a smaller scale grew more or less on some of us." It was the cold, severe snowstorms and the low crop yields that loom large as the causes for the decline of the Amish community.

Montana. North Dakota Amish families began to settle in Montana in 1903, locating in Dawson County, thirty miles north of Glendive. Homesteading land was available, and land could be bought for $2.50 per acre from the railroads.[10] Although most of the Amish came by train, two families took their livestock and grain overland, a distance of three hundred miles. At least thirty-six families lived here during the thirty-two years of the life of the settlement. In 1935 the last of its members died. Several members had affiliated with the nearby Bloomfield Mennonite Church and others moved away. The community always had ministers. Environmental problems differed from those in North Dakota. Large ranchers resented the Amish and other settlers who moved into the area, for they could no longer use the land as free range but had to build fences. The area lacked trees; hence there was no natural source of lumber, fence posts, and wood fuel. Coal, however, was abundant. When there was rainfall the lush prairie grass was good pasture and excellent for raising livestock and sheep. The major crops were alfalfa, wheat, oats, barley, and flax. Hail, drought, and fire were unpredictable disasters. Although there were excellent yields in some years, the large acreages meant that threshing required labor over several months. Since the closest grain elevators were thirty miles away, transporting the grain was very time-consuming. The Amish community, like the one in North Dakota, ceased to attract settlers, gradually declined, and died a slow death. Homesteading had run out.

Colorado. Three separate Old Order Amish settlements were established in this state early in the twentieth century. The first of these was in Elbert County, near Limon, when Atlee Weaver and his family moved there in 1908 from Ohio.[11] The appeal was good cheap land, a land of sunshine and good health. The Amish lived in full view of Pike's Peak, as Jacob M. Yoder wrote to the folks back home:

> Now if a home you wish to seek,
>   Come where you can view old Pike's peak.
> To the land where plain and mountain meet.
>   And our farmers grow maccoroni wheat.

Transportation to Colorado was no problem, for twenty-four passenger trains passed through Limon each day. The many visitors to the Amish community had easy access, for it was twelve miles from the railway station. Individual families were attracted from a variety of older settlements, from Indiana, Kansas, Michigan,

Oklahoma, and Iowa. Some moved out before others moved in. Altogether seventeen families moved to Elbert County, but there were never more than twelve families living there at any one time. Farm sizes ranged from 160 to 320 acres, and the Amish purchased wide-open land with the intention of transforming it into large grain fields. The soil was a brown loam mixed with sand, and once the sod was broken, it was worked with horse-drawn machinery. As in Montana, the Amish hired steam-powered plows to break the tough prairie sod. They took comfort that there were no trees to cut down and no stumps to pull. Although wheat was a major crop, they also grew alfalfa, millet, rye, oats, barley, flax, potatoes, and corn.

The dwellings built here were "next to shacks," according to former residents—small, simple, and unfinished in the interior. The settlers were families who had tried to make a go of it in other communities but had failed. They came to Colorado with determination and little money. They worked hard and lived simply. Since there were no apples with which to make apple butter, they made pumpkin butter. With no maple trees for making maple syrup, they made syrup from corn cobs.

There were hardships and natural disasters—drought, hail, flies, Russian thistles, and cyclones. In the eight-year life of the settlement, there were no ordinations or resident ministers. Although several ministers visited the country "to take a look," none moved into the settlement. Worship services were held whenever there was a visiting minister or about every four weeks when one came from Cheyenne County. During the final years, ministers from other areas avoided going to Elbert County when it was learned that no communion service could be held because of "some difficulty." As long as there was disunity there could be no ordination. After most of the Old Order Amish had moved away, a few of the members joined the Mennonite church at La Junta. The Mennonites founded a congregation near Limon in 1922.[12]

Sixty miles south of Limon, in Crowley County, near Ordway, another Amish group began to settle in 1910.[13] The development here was a realtor's dream. Families were urged to buy five-acre plots in the Arkansas River valley and by irrigation produce cash crops that would make the owner "independent for life." Testimonial advertisements signed by Amish persons were promoted by the realty company. The purchase price of a plot was $600 and the company was asking $125 down and monthly payments of $10. Within two years ten Amish families, including a minister, had moved in. Most had come from Kansas. Instead of buying five-acre plots and settling in a village, as planned by the realty company, they bought twenty to forty acres of land per family. Crowley County stood in contrast to the two other Amish settlements in Colorado, which were located on treeless prairie. With irrigation in the Arkansas Valley there were orchards—cherry, plum, apricot, and apple trees. Instead of grain, sugar beets, alfalfa, and cantaloupes were raised. Alfalfa and sugar processing plants were constructed. Irrigation ditches carried water from the river to the fertile soil.

The production of alfalfa provided intensive work for the Amish settlers. In summer they raised and harvested the crop, and in winter they transported hay to town. Acres of cantaloupes also kept the families occupied with planting, thinning, cultivating, harvesting, packaging, and transporting them to the railway station. Mexican migrant workers were hired to assist.

The Crowley settlement existed for seven years. Although ceremonial and church life was harmonious, some bad features emerged in the "garden spot." Several of the Amish members contracted typhoid fever from the contaminated irrigation water, and two died. The Amish complained that the water was turned into the irrigation ditches late Saturday or on Sunday. They did not want to work late Saturday night and would not work at all on Sunday. The realty company denied that there was any such problem, but former residents still insist that the situation existed. The settlement broke up when families trickled back to Kansas and Oklahoma. By 1917 all fourteen of the Amish families had disappeared.

The third settlement in Colorado, which took shape simultaneously with the two described above, was situated in Cheyenne County near Wild Horse and Kit Carson. Homesteading was the major attraction, and families came from as far away as Indiana and Oklahoma. A person could file for 320 acres, build a small house, fence 40 acres, and break sod on 20 acres. Although some Amish had traded their farms in Indiana or Kansas for Colorado land and had some financial resources, there were others whose means were slight. The Amish assisted non-Amish homesteaders who had no horses or cows by giving them employment or by sharing food with them. Of the three settlements in Colorado, the one in Cheyenne County was the most hard-pressed. The winters were severe, the cattle ranchers cut the fences of the Amish and let their cattle graze the homesteaders' crops to the ground, Russian thistles had to be used for feed, and hundreds of cattle and sheep froze to death. One Amishman made an ox yoke and cultivated the soil with a team of oxen. Fish in the nearest lakes supplemented the food supply.

Although the settlement existed only from 1909 until 1914, one of the residents later wrote, "For a while we had a real nice church at Colorado with close to twenty families."[14]

Kansas. Western Kansas was the site of three Amish settlements, one located in Ness and two in Ford County. They existed at approximately the same time. Two families from Indiana settled in Ness County in 1893, but they left and returned with more Amish families in 1902.[15] They were joined by Amish families from other parts of Kansas and North Dakota. The farms, located near the villages of Ransom and Arnold, were in a region of true prairie. Although there are gently rolling slopes with cottonwoods along the creeks in this part of Kansas, there are miles of open space. The Amish built two-story houses and small barns, and planted plum, cherry, mulberry, and evergreen trees, as well as currant bushes and grapevines. The women raised a variety of vegetables by irrigating their gardens with well water. Although rainfall was very limited, the Amish found aspects of the weather in Ness County to their liking. The nights were cool, and with a low humidity, they seldom suffered the extremes of heat in the summer or cold in the winter. The long, sunny days in autumn were delightful.

Nevertheless, there were a variety of adversities. Dust storms and tornadoes appeared with little or no warning and brought sudden disaster. Periodic drought the Amish undersood, but in Kansas dry, hot winds appeared very quickly, withering all green plants. In winter blizzards were fierce and unpredictable. Famished jack rabbits raided feedlots and invaded granaries. Prairie fires were a threat to the homes and farm buildings in summer.

By 1922 the harsh, unpredictable weather had forced the Amish of this area to move away. Little is known about the church life or the size of the community. Ness County had exceptional rainfall (23 inches annually) during the first five years the Amish were settling in the area. If they took that to be typical, they were misled. The difference in rainfall between eastern and western Kansas may not have been appreciated by the Indiana Amish who were afflicted with "Kansas fever." The long growing season and beautiful autumns did not prevail over the harsh and unfavorable climate.

The settlement in Ford County began in 1904 and was extinct by 1921.[16] This settlement, located southeast of Dodge City near Bucklin, Kansas, was initiated by two families from Davies County, Indiana, who were joined by families from several states, primarily North Dakota and other Kansas Amish communities. At least forty-five families made Bucklin their home during a seventeen-year span. The wheat harvest was bountiful during the first several years. Most of the Amish had rented their land, although three of the ministers owned their farms. The Amish also tried to raise row crops, especially corn. Many Amish boys from other states, some of whom were not in good standing in their church, came here to get employment during the harvest, and "the ministers had their share of trouble with these wild boys." During the life of this settlement there were thirteen marriages and six ordinations.

The informants who lived in the community describe the many problems, of which dust storms were the worst, lasting sometimes for three days. "The beds were so dusty you couldn't sleep till you shook it all off." In church, the dust "came so thick and dark the preacher could hardly see to read the Bible." When there was a shortage of meat, the boys shot jack rabbits. Tumbleweeds lodged in the fences, making drifts as high as the fence. The crops were damaged by hot winds, and clouds of grasshoppers destroyed everything green in their path. The dry ground cracked open, and after ten years of crop failure many of the residents began moving out. With the outbreak of World War I, there were threats of violence against the Amish because they spoke German and were pacifists. These threats hastened decisions to move elsewhere—to other areas in Kansas, to Indiana, Ohio, Oklahoma, Michigan, and Delaware. The families left behind a cemetery of sixteen graves, none of which had been for adults. In 1939 a group of Amish from Reno County, Kansas, took up the bodies and reburied them in the Amish cemetery near Partridge.

Surviving Settlements

We turn now to the surviving Old Order communities on the plains. The largest consists of three church districts located in Reno County, near Hutchinson, Kansas. A second, located in Anderson County in eastern Kansas, near Garnett, was founded in 1903 as an offshoot from Reno County. A third settlement is located in Mayes County, Oklahoma, and has been in existence since 1910.

The Amish in Reno County, Kansas, have survived for slightly more than a century. Reno County has had two Old Order settlements, the one centering on Partridge and the other on Yoder.[17] Yoder, Kansas, is named after Eli Yoder, the son of an Old Order Amish bishop in Maryland who homesteaded here in 1870. A railway ran through the northeast corner of his farm, separating about five acres from the rest of his farm. On this plot he built a store, and he established a post office in his own house. The first Old Order Amish homesteaders came from Indiana and other states in 1883. In 1918 there were four Amish church districts and about ninety families. Today three Old Order districts remain, two at Yoder and one at Partridge. Wheat farming is the major income-producing activity, but livestock and dairy farming are other sources of income.

Aside from the motive of cheap land, there were push factors resulting in westward migration to Kansas. Drinking, bundling, and the use of tobacco were problems many Amish families wished to leave behind. A deep concern for the spiritual life of their children spurred them to find a tolerable community. These considerations are reflected in the Kansas *Ordnung* and in the leadership of the group, particularly at Partridge.

Amish leaders began to hold Sunday school in 1888 in their homes during the summer months. Newcomers, of the traditional type, sought to abolish it. Although the Sunday school was discontinued several times, it has survived to the present time. Daniel E. Mast, from his ordination as deacon in 1891 and minister in 1914, exerted a strong influence until his death in 1930. Through extensive Bible study and reading and writing for Amish publications he implanted deep spiritual concerns and strong opposition to alcohol and tobacco. His influence was keenly felt by the Amish not only in the West but in all of the regions east of the Mississippi as well.[18]

As soon as the early settlers arrived, they adopted carpets, window curtains, buggy tops, gasoline engines, binders, and headers—all prohibited in the eastern churches.[19] Changes in technology to permit a larger scale of farming are also reflected in the Kansas *Ordnung*. Enterprising lay members frequently bought new farm machinery before it became an issue in the church. When tractors and combines came up for discussion in 1924, the eastern bishops were called in to settle the dispute. Their decision was negative. Several members declared it a hardship to feed horses, especially during the dry years, and non-Amish landlords told their Amish renters that they would have to use a tractor or discontinue farming. Finally two Amishmen bought tractors, but felt that combines were "one of the most worldly things you can get." Both had owned threshing machines. The bishops argued that tractors would lead to bigger farms, and bigger farms would lead to the use of trucks. They were probably right, for after combines were permitted in 1935, then the question of pneumatic tires loomed up. The first solution was to allow rubber casings to be bolted to the wheels, but by 1945 pneumatic tires were permitted on the front wheels of a tractor and three years later they were allowed on the rear wheels. They were accepted for reasons of economy, adaptability, and more efficient use of energy.

In recent years, with the growing scarcity of land, the Amish have entered nonfarming occupations. Retail and repair shops, farm and lawn equipment, and a Dutch Kitchen restaurant are some of the businesses operated by the Amish at Partridge. Farming families have turned to specialization. This trend has compounded the problem of transportation and of energy for dairy and grain production. Gradually the tractor with a two-wheeled trailer replaced the horse and buggy as the common means of weekday transportation. This change began when one Amishman built a trailer with an air vent and a door but stopped short of making windows. By 1954 tractors were used by the young people to attend their weekly meetings. The horse and buggy was used for travel on Sunday. The Amish at Partridge in 1954 agreed to the use of electricity as an aid to farming operations. House appliances, except washing machines and irons, were forbidden, and air conditioners were allowed only for reasons of health. Prohibitions against multiple-bulb fixtures, yard lights, and globes were adopted as safeguards against vanity.

Social concerns and participation in the wider world accompanied changes in transportation. Symbolic of the growing awareness of the outside world was a three-month tour of Europe and Bible lands taken by two Old Order members, Raymond and Willie Wagler, in 1937. Young men who had served as conscientious objectors during World War II returned home with new experiences. They had formed associations with Christians of other denominations, experienced new surroundings, and many returned with visions of what could be done to improve their home, church, and community. A weekly young peoples' meeting was held despite the objections of the older members. A committee was elected to support a national Amish Missions Conference. Young men began to volunteer for foreign relief and missionary projects in Mennonite organizations. A few served in Puerto Rico, France, and Germany. Although there was opposition, it was never sufficiently strong enough to stop members from publishing tracts and articles. The first Amish person to attend nearby Hesston College, a Mennonite institution, was a girl who enrolled in a Bible course in 1948. Since that time several young men and women have attended both Hesston College and Eastern Mennonite College.

The Reno settlement represents a group of Amish families who shared fellowship in a common *Ordnung*. Some families stayed, some moved to other western settlements, some returned to their home settlement, and others adapted to scale, building a meetinghouse. The Yoder Mennonite Church was organized in 1918, the Plainview Mennonite Church in 1948, and the Center Amish Mennonite Church in 1958. The latter is affiliated with the Beachey Amish denomination. The charter members of these churches were Old Order Amish.

Exclusiveness may be more difficult to practice successfully in a rural sparsely populated plains area characterized by friendliness and interdependence than in places like Switzerland and Pennsylvania. Relationships between the Old Order Amish and the Mennonite-related groups are cordial. The Old Order Amish do not practice the same strict type of avoidance as do their spiritual brothers in eastern states. Former members who choose to affiliate with more progressive groups are not shunned. Ordained persons from the Center Church (Beachey) and from Mennonite congregations who attend meetings or funerals among the Old Order churches are frequently asked to speak. The degree of openness and mutuality between Kansas affiliations contrasts sharply with the exclusiveness of similar groups in the eastern states.

Conclusions

Western fever captured more than a few Amish during the late nineteenth and early twentieth centuries. Adventurous people were willing to leave their friends and well-established communities for the sake of adventure and colonization. In some cases "church trouble" at home forced them to leave for the Great Plains. A keen interest in cheaper lands, a love for peaceful and unmolested habitation, and willingness to take up hard labor attracted many of these Amish to western country. A few families were clearly of the roving type, for unlike the Lancaster County, Pennsylvania, Amish, they moved across the United States from six to eight times.[20] The widely known bishop Eli J. Bontreger, described himself as having "a kind of roving disposition." When his own boys had become teenagers in their small Wisconsin settlement and "their associates, both boys and girls, were not of our people and . . . had no church affiliation at all, we sensed danger ahead for our family."[21] About that time the older ministers in Shipshewanna, Indiana, asked him to return to his native community.

Many of those returning to their former communities did so reluctantly, for they seemingly enjoyed pioneering. After leaving

behind his life in North Dakota and Wisconsin, Bishop Eli J. Bontreger wrote with deep feeling: "The neighbors helped load the car. . . .
As the train pulled out we waved goodbye to each other as long as
we could see each other, then I watched the town disappear, and
when the familiar places had all disappeared, I fell down on my face
and cried like a child. The church, the brethren and sisters, and
kind neighbors, the good country, the natural advantages of climate
and land all drew like cords at my heart, and I felt that I was leaving
the best and happiest part of my existence when leaving Exeland,
Wisconsin."[22]

While living in the West many of the Amish became accustomed
to church rules that were more relaxed than those of their brethren
east of the Mississippi. When they returned, their progressive stance
became the object of tension, and, in the Nappannee, Indiana, settlement, a cause for division. Samuel Christner in 1930 "frowned on
the liberalizing tendencies of the Amish families returning to Nappannee from the drought- and poverty-ridden settlements of the
Great Plains during the depression."[23] Against the sympathetic views
of most ministers, Christner instituted an exclusive group that later
moved to Mercer County, Pennsylvania.

The Amish were not pioneers in the sense of being the first to
possess new lands or territory. As pacifists, they are ill-equipped to
cope with frontier situations requiring the use of force or coercion.
They are builders and conservators. Consequently, they have followed others, improving and gardening the soil after others have
moved on, and in recent decades they have successfully farmed in
areas where the soil had been depleted by their non-Amish predeces-
sors.

In conclusion we shall examine the basic hypothesis of small
scale as a basic requirement for Amish life. Vulnerability and the
problems of scale on the great plains can be summed up as follows:

1. Amish life thrives in a moderate climate on soils reasonably
fertile for general farming and livestock raising. The extinct settlements we have described were burdened with extreme temperatures,
blizzards, and wind storms. Great Plains soil and climate are suited
to specialized farming. The Amish, however, prefer general farming
with a diversity of crops and livestock.

2. Amish life requires that farm acreages be adapted to intensive
farming and fitted to scale for horse-drawn equipment and family
labor. Small acreages are insufficient to produce enough income for
survival and large acreages cannot be cultivated and harvested by
horse power.

3. Amish life requires a population of sufficient size and age distribution to provide for a potential mating population. The settlements we have described were too small and often the population was too inbred to permit the number of marriages necessary for continuity. Pioneering was challenging and it was enjoyed by some families, especially during the child-rearing stage of life. But for others it was a financial disaster, and in some cases the children did not remain Amish.

4. Amish life requires that the members of the community, especially household heads, who are sufficiently compatible with each other, to maintain a common discipline (*Ordnung*) as the basis for harmonious living. Several settlements failed for want of such consensus.

5. The Amish who have remained on the Great Plains have accommodated to their environment by allowing greater freedom in the use of technology for grain production, and by social assimilation. The present three small communities in Kansas and Oklahoma have survived not without considerable adaptation from a small- to a large-scale technology. All the surviving communities permit tractor machinery suitable for grain production beyond that possible with horse power. Even so, the population here has been declining during the past sixty years. The Old Order Amish during this time have been the seed bed of several Amish Mennonite churches.[24]

In spite of the vulnerability of the Old Order communities on the Great Plains, the overall growth of the population is stable. Throughout their history the Old Order Amish have resisted large-scale or bureaucratic organization, whether in schooling or in agriculture. For more than forty years the Old Order have resisted almost singlehandedly the forces of rural school bureaucracy and consolidation. They will not tolerate the removal of their children to a distance from their homes, where they are placed in large groups with narrow age limits, taught skills that are useless to their way of life, and exposed to values and attitudes antithetical to their own. These conditions develop when schools become large and bureaucratic. In a landmark decision (*Wisconsin* v. *Yoder*, May 15, 1972) the United States Supreme Court upheld the Amish school system and restrained the states from requiring compulsory high school attendance.[25]

When oil was discovered on Amish farms in Reno County, Kansas, the Amish sold their farms and abandoned their community. The road to wealth, leisure, and greed was antithetical to Amish life. According to a newspaper account, the Amish abandoned their farms to "greedy oil drillers."[26] If Old Order Amish religion is too inflexible to adapt to plains agriculture, it is precisely because the members are committed to the proposition that "small is godly."

Notes

1. The Old Order population is estimated on the basis of 511 church districts, using 168 as the average number of people per district. The rate of natural increase (for Ohio) was reported by Harold Cross and Victor McKusick, "Amish Demography," *Social Biology* 17 (June 1970): 83-101.

2. In Pennsylvania alone, Maurice A. Mook researched ten former communities; see his "Extinct Amish Mennonite Communities in Pennsylvania," *Mennonite Quarterly Review* 30 (October 1956): 267-76. David Luthy and Joseph Stoll have published on still other extinct settlements and we hope their effort will continue. I am indebted to them for much of the original research on Great Plains Amish settlements.

3. For a discussion of the charter, see J. A. Hostetler, *Amish Society* (Baltimore, Md.: Johns Hopkins University Press, 1968), chap. 3.

4. The phrase was suggested to me by Gertrude Enders Huntington.

5. For the agricultural management practices of the Hutterites, see the works of John W. Bennett, *The Hutterian Brethren: The Agricultural Economy and Social Organization of a Communal People* (Stanford, Calif.: Stanford University Press, 1967) and *Northern Plainsmen* (Chicago: Aldine Publishing Co., 1969).

6. See J. A. Hostetler, "The Amish in Gosper County, Nebraska," *Mennonite Historical Bulletin* 10 (October 1949): 1. Reminiscences and facts about this community appear in a privately published account by Abraham S. Yoder, *My Life Story* (Belleville, Pa., n.d.), abridged in *Family Life*, January 1968, p. 11.

7. Yoder, *My Life Story*, p. 2. The Pennsylvania group that Yost H. Yoder joined was nicknamed Nebraska Amish and is to this day the most conservative Old Order Amish group to be found anywhere. For a discussion of the group, see Maurice A. Mook, "The Nebraska Amish of Pennsylvania," *Mennonite Life* 17 (January 1962): 27-30.

8. *Mennonite Encyclopedia* (Scottsdale, Pa.: Mennonite Publishing House, 1954), s.v. "North Dakota Amish." More background material appears in the following sources: Eli J. Bontreger, "County Status Aided by Amish Mennonites," *Turtle Mountain Star* (Rolla, N.Dak.), June 22, 1938, p. 58; Floyd E. Kauffman, *History of Fairview and Spring Valley Congregations in North Dakota* (Minot, N.Dak., 1949); Floyd E. Kauffman, "Amish in North Dakota," *Mennonite Historical Bulletin* 14 (January 1953); David Luthy, "The Amish in Foster County, North Dakota," *Family Life*, February 1977, p. 19; David Luthy, "The Amish in Ward County, North Dakota," *Family Life*, March 1977, p. 15; idem, "The Amish in Rolette County, North Dakota," *Family Life*, April and May 1977, p. 17; and "Letters from North Dakota Pioneers," *Family Life*, June 1977, p. 19.

9. Eli J. Bontreger, "My Life Story," mimeographed (Shipshewanna, Indiana, June 1953), p. 15.

10. David Luthy, "Amish in the Treasure State," *Family Life*, July 1974, pp. 17-20.

11. David Luthy, "Colorado, beside the Rocky Mountains. Part One: The Amish in Elbert County," *Family Life*, October 1973, pp. 14-17.

12. *Mennonite Encyclopedia*, s.v. "Limon."

13. David Luthy, "Colorado, beside the Rocky Mountains. Part Two: The Amish in Crowley County," *Family Life*, November 1973, pp. 15-18.

14. Mrs. Will P. Miller, "Life in Colorado," *Family Life*, March 1968, pp. 37-39.

15. David Luthy, "Amish in Ness County, Kansas, 1902-1917," *Family Life*, January 1972, pp. 21-24.

16. Joe Stoll, "Life on the Kansas Prairies. Part I," *Family Life*, January 1971, pp. 20-23; ibid., "Part II," February 1971, pp. 24-26.

17. These communities are discussed by Gideon G. Yoder in "The Oldest Living American Mennonite Congregations of Central Kansas" (M.A. thesis, Phillips University, 1948); D. Paul Miller in "Amish Acculturation" (M.A. thesis, University of Nebraska, 1950); and David Wagler in "History and Change of the Amish of Reno County, Kansas" (term paper, Bethel College, 1968). The Partridge settlement was the subject of a thesis by James A. Knight, "Pluralism, Boundary Maintenance, and Cultural Persistence among the Amish" (Wichita State University, 1977). David Luthy, "Forced to Sell Their Farms," *Family Life*, January 1978, p. 19, treats the Reno County air base and the Amish. For other extinct accounts, see idem, "The Amish in Mead County, Kansas," *Family Life*, November 1977, p. 21; and idem, "The Amish in Sumner County, Kansas," *Family Life*, April 1978, p. 17.

18. A selection of Daniel E. Mast's articles were published in *Ausweisung Zur Seligkeit*, also appearing in translation as *Salvation Full and Free* (Inman, Kans.: 1955). Mast, along with Eli J. Bontreger, was a promoter of the periodical *Herald of Truth* launched in 1912. For a biography of Mast, see David L. Miller, "Daniel E. Mast (1848-1930): A Biographical Sketch," *Mennonite Historical Bulletin* 39 (January 1978): 2.

19. Wagler, "History and Change," p. 14.

20. The Amish of Lancaster County scarcely showed interest in the westward homesteading movement discussed here. Only two families moved to Kansas and both returned. See David Luthy and Gideon Fisher, "The Amish in Harvey County, Kansas," *Family Life*, May 1979, p. 17. One, who earned the nickname "Kansas Amos" for his persistent advocacy of Kansas, needed financial assistance to return. Their failure had a profound effect on the Pennsylvania Amish. The Lancaster Amish, who are located on fertile soil and who maintain a respected status among Amish communities, are less inclined to move than Amish farther west.

21. Bontreger, "My Life Story," pp. 14, 17.

22. Ibid., p. 17.

23. James E. Landing, "The Amish, the Automobile, and Social Interaction," *Journal of Geography* 71 (January 1972): 53.

24. Though not explicitly stated, many of the Mennonite congregations whose history is recorded by Paul Erb (*South Central Frontiers: A History of the South Central Mennonite Conference* [Scottdale, Pa.: Herald Press, 1974]) are of Old Order origin.

25. For the background to this decision, see Donald A. Erickson, *Public Control for Non-Public Schools* (Chicago: University of Chicago Press, 1969); and Albert N. Keim, *Compulsory Education and the Amish* (Boston: Beacon Press, 1975).

26. *Wichita Sunday Beacon*, March 8, 1936.

A Religious Geography of
the Hill Country Germans
of Texas

Terry G. Jordan

One of the more unusual European ethnic enclaves on the margins of the dry lands in North America lies in the subhumid Hill Country of south-central Texas. Between 1844 and the Civil War, a sizable migration of peasant farmers, artisans, and university-educated political refugees from western and central Germany was directed to this hilly frontier.[1] Today, a sizable German-populated district stretches northwestward from New Braunfels and the outskirts of San Antonio for one hundred miles, a district described by several students of German-American culture as "the most thoroughly Germanized portion of the United States" (fig. 1).[2]

The immigrant Germans had to cope with recurrent drought, excessive heat, rocky soils, isolation, and a largely alien flora and fauna. But the frugal, hard-working Germans perservered in this strange land and soon prospered. So distinctive was the result of interaction between German culture and a difficult environment that geographer Donald W. Meinig felt justified in designating the "German Hill County" as a culture region within Texas. In part, Meinig maintained, "it remains a distinctive region because of the success of those early colonists and their descendants in making a living out of a marginally productive country."[3] In part, too, the distinctiveness is a result of culture contacts among Germans, Mexicans, and hill southern Anglo-Americans, contacts that began immediately upon the Germans' arrival and persist to the present day.

This paper is a study of the progress of religious acculturation among the Germans of that environmental stress zone. Five aspects of religious culture are considered: church affiliation, residential segregation by sect, religious spatial organization, ecclesiastical architecture, and burial practices.

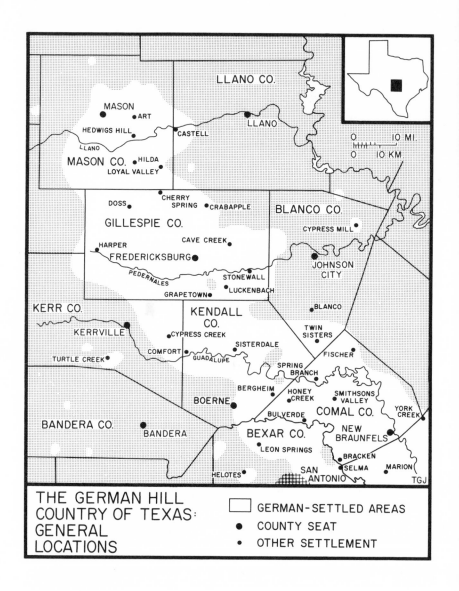

THE GERMAN HILL
COUNTRY OF TEXAS:
GENERAL
LOCATIONS

☐ GERMAN-SETTLED AREAS
● COUNTY SEAT
• OTHER SETTLEMENT

Figure 1.

Religious Affiliation

About two-thirds of the Germans who settled the Texas Hill Country were Protestants, mainly Lutherans but with smaller numbers of Calvinists, Zwinglians, Pietists, and members of the State Church of Prussia (a union of all Protestant groups). Perhaps as many as three in ten were Roman Catholic, even though the major Catholic strongholds in the Rhineland and south Germany were not major contributors to the migration. A small but vociferous and influential minority, perhaps 5–10 percent, were freethinkers, consisting mainly of university-educated political refugees.

TABLE 1

Religious Affiliations of the Hill Country Germans, 1890

Group	Number of Churches	Number of Members	Percentage of Churchgoing Population
Lutheran, General Council	3	490 ⎫	
Lutheran, Joint Synod of Ohio and Other States	1	800 ⎬ 2,090	34.5
Lutheran, Independent	1	800 ⎭	
German Evangelical Protestant	2	1,050	17.0
Methodist, North (Southern German Conference)	5	405 ⎫	
Methodist, South (German Mission Conference)	6	315 ⎭ 720	12.0
Protestant Total	18	3,860	63.5
Roman Catholic[1]	4	2,178	36.5
Freethinkers[2]	––	500	––

Source: *Report on Statistics of Churches in the United States at the Eleventh Census, 1890* (Washington, D.C.: GPO, 1894), figures for Blanco, Comal, Gillespie, Kendall, Llano, and Mason counties, Texas.

[1] The Roman Catholic figures probably include some non-Germans, and the Catholic membership criteria are more inclusive than those of the Protestant groups.

[2] This figure is an estimate, not derived from the census.

These various religious groups and philosophies imported from Central Europe all thrived in the Texas hills. The frontier experience nurtured a native German religious factionalism that had been mildly suppressed in Europe. While the splintered Protestantism of neighboring Anglo-American communities might suggest that the proliferation of church groups among the Germans represents acculturation, it is clear that the seeds of Teutonic factionalism had been sown long before, in Germany.

The situation at Fredericksburg, the principal German settlement within the hills, was typical. There an early attempt, in 1847, to unify all Protestants quickly came to grief. In 1852, six families withdrew from this *Vereins Kirche* to found a Lutheran church, expressing their distaste for the Zwinglian and Reformed elements in the union church by placing Lutheran journals and related publications in the cornerstone of their new building. The remnant Protestant union in Fredericksburg split again in 1887, one faction adopting the original Augsburg Confession and Luther's small catechism, the other displaying its preference by sealing a picture of Ulrich Zwingli in the cornerstone. By 1890, imported German Protestantism was represented in the Texas hills by four different denominations. One of these, the German Evangelical Protestant Church, "a body of Germans, liberal in belief, independent or congregational in polity, and without synodical organization," claimed over one thousand Hill Country members.[4] Today the various factions find expression in two Lutheran bodies and the United Church of Christ (Evangelical and Reformed, a successor to the State Church of Prussia). Individual congregations often changed their affiliation. For example, St. Martin's Church on the outskirts of New Braunfels, founded in 1851 as the first Lutheran parish in Texas, later joined the German Evangelical Synod of North America (State Church of Prussia) and still later affiliated with the American Lutheran Church. Some Lutheran congregations never affiliated with a synod, remaining fully independent in the manner of some rural Anglo churches.

Protestant diversity in the Texas hills was further intensified when German-speaking Methodist missionaries began preaching in 1849.[5] In fact, Methodist converts were the first to secede from the Fredericksburg Protestant union. Though clearly representing acculturation, the German Methodist movement in America had roots deep in Teutonic Pietism, a seventeenth-century rebellion against the formalism and worldliness of established Protestantism. Relatively few of the Texas immigrants were drawn from the main Pietist stronghold in southwest Germany, and the Methodists apparently won many or most of their converts from the established churches, rather than appealing only to the scattering of Pietists. Published genealogies of Hill Country German Methodist families suggest that, before conversion, most had been Lutherans, Catholics, or members of the State Church of Prussia.[6] Typical of the converts was a Catholic farmer in Comal County, who, curious about a Methodist camp meeting held in his neighborhood, sneaked up to observe the affair from the concealment of some bushes. He became so caught up in the emotional goings on that he emerged from his hiding place and converted.[7] The success of the Methodist missionaries was all the more remarkable because they required converts to refrain from drinking, dancing, and membership in the typically German clubs and societies.

By 1890, the Methodists claimed 12 percent of the churchgoing Hill Country German population, but factionalism divided them, too. After the Civil War, over half of the Hill Country Methodists affiliated with the northern church, while the remainder stayed loyal to southern Methodism. Each had its own separate German-speaking conference. Some small German communities in the Hill Country acquired two Methodist congregations in this manner. Not until the national reunification of the Methodists in 1939 was this local factionalism ended. A few years earlier, accelerated acculturation of the German Methodists in the Hill Country was assured when their conferences within the church were merged with others in the 1920s, placing Germans in the same conferences as Anglo-Americans.[8] The German-language Methodist newsletters ceased publication in the 1930s. Today there is little to distinguish Methodist German congregations from those of the Anglos. In one respect, however, the German Methodists are distinct from their Anglo counterparts. They have remained staunchly loyal to Methodism through every generation since their conversion, while Anglo-Texan Methodists have defected in droves to Baptist and other faiths in the twentieth century.

Freethinkers, too, thrived in the Texas hills. It is not uncommon to find German-American livestock ranchers who boast that Bibles have never been allowed in their homes. One resident of a German freethinker community, describing the sentiment of a half-century ago, recalled that "the attitude toward organized religion ran the gamut from mild anticlericalism to articulate, bitter denunciation." Missionaries made little headway with these freethinkers. One Lutheran preacher recalled his early visit to a rural community near New Braunfels, where the German settlers informed him "they did not want a missionary." The Methodists fared even worse in an agnostic bastion in Kendall County, where a persistent Wesleyan missionary was pelted with rotten eggs. An Episcopal observer in nearby Boerne, the seat of Kendall County, reported in 1867 that "no religious services are held" and lamented that even the school-house was "controlled by an infidel" who allowed no worship services to be held in the building. Even worse, he reported, "the holy day is violated, and cards, beer, and dancing occupy the place of preaching, praise, and prayer." The Kendall County German element, he concluded, "is the great fallow-ground to be broken up . . . —a hard soil, it is true, but one . . . the power of the Divine Spirit can soften and sublime."[9]

Segregation by Sect

Many, perhaps half or more, of the Hill Country settlers came from religiously diverse communities in Germany. The Hessian grand duchy of Nassau, one of the major contributing areas, was a veritable religious shatter zone. Others, particularly settlers from the Braun-schweig-Hannover area of Lower Saxony, were derived from an almost purely Lutheran setting.

In the Hill Country, German Protestants and Catholics coexisted peacefully from the very first, making no effort to segregate them-selves by quarters within the towns or by districts in the countryside (fig. 2). The tolerance born of the Thirty Years' War rests easily on the Texas hills. New Braunfels and Fredericksburg, together with the surrounding rural parts of Comal and Gillespie counties, still today display a chaotic mixture of Protestants and Catholics. The two groups share membership in the numerous shooting, bowling, and singing clubs in the region and often associate in the dance halls and beer parlors. Intermarriage is not uncommon.

A rather different spatial distribution characterizes the German Methodists. They are concentrated in the central Llano River valley, on the northern perimeter of the German-settled area (fig. 2). This compact district, roughly fifteen miles on a side, is the most purely Methodist region in Texas and perhaps in North America. All of the six rural churches existing within the district at the turn of the cen-tury, three of which survive today, were Methodist. Apparently the Methodist segregation occurred by design rather than accident. The original mission church in Fredericksburg lost a substantial part of its membership as converts left to settle the Llano Valley. The Methodist exodus from Fredericksburg occurred mainly in the

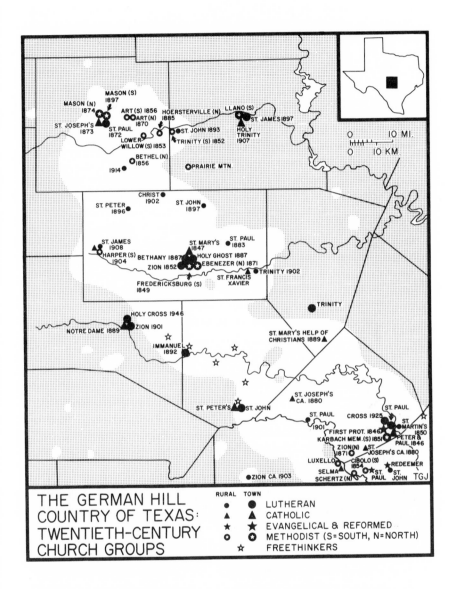

Figure 2. Note the relatively late founding dates of rural Lutheran and Catholic churches and the rural regionalization of Methodists and freethinkers.

mid-1850s, coinciding closely with the opening of the first brewery in the town. Seemingly, many Methodists withdrew, Mormon-like, to their Llano Valley Zion in order to escape the dance halls, saloons, and social clubs of their fellow Germans. The Methodist German communities in Mason and Llano counties are still today notable for the absence of such establishments. Cherry Spring, a largely Lutheran hamlet just across the line in Gillespie County, boasts the dance hall nearest to the Methodist stronghold, earning for it among the Mason Wesleyans the reputation of a den of iniquity.

The freethinkers, to a considerable degree, also segregated themselves. For example, a nineteenth-century Lutheran missionary working in the York Creek settlement near New Braunfels noted with disgust that "most of the seventy families of German descent pride themselves in being heathen." Perhaps most unusual were the "Latin settlements"—communities of highly cultured freethinkers educated in the universities of Germany. The Hill County boasted three such communities: Sisterdale and Tusculum in Kendall County and Bettina in Llano County.[10] Of these, only Sisterdale survives, and though it long ago lost its academic flavor, agnosticism still prevails.

Sisterdale is only one part of a major rural concentration zone of freethinkers. The valley of the Guadalupe River and its tributaries in Kendall and eastern Kerr counties, centered on Sisterdale and Comfort, is the only rural district in Texas in which the majority of the inhabitants are known to be agnostics (fig. 2). Comfort, an unincorporated Kendall County town of 1,400 inhabitants, had no churches during the first four decades of its existence, and even today most of its German-American residents remain freethinkers.

There is, then, considerable regionalization of religious groups within the German Hill Country. Each succeeding river valley brings the visitor into a different religious realm: the Llano Valley, with its stern, ascetic Methodists; the Pedernales Valley, peopled by hardworking, fun-loving Lutherans and Catholics; and the Guadalupe Valley, the stronghold of rural Texan agnosticism.

Spatial Organization

In the European experience of the Hill Country Germans, religious life had been centered in village- and town-based churches, each of which had a clearly defined membership territory. The word *Pfarrbezirk* connotes a village-situated church, including all the lands worked by the villager-members. Certain elements of this European spatial organization survived in Texas, but others were abandoned or modified.

The German colonists in the Hill Country quickly discarded the clustered farm village settlement pattern. By 1850, five years or less after the initial settlements were founded, most of the farmers had already dispersed over the countryside to live in typically American isolated farmsteads. Parish borders blurred and no longer dictated membership. In the process, however, the large majority of German settlers clung to the European tradition of town-based churches. Even as late as 1883, the thousand square miles constituting Gillespie County contained no German Lutheran or Catholic churches outside of the county seat, Fredericksburg (fig. 2). At that time, Fredericksburg was home to only one-fifth of the Gillespie population, and German settlement was well dispersed through the county.[11]

A similar organizational pattern initially developed in Comal County, in spite of the fact that the administrative seat and church town of New Braunfels was not centrally located, but instead lay near the eastern county line (fig. 1). To reach church, some German farmers and ranchers in Comal and Gillespie counties were obliged to travel forty miles or more round trip over poor roads and through difficult terrain. Occasionally, priests and ministers journeyed out to "preaching stations" in the remote valleys, but their visits were infrequent and did not overcome the religious isolation of the rural districts.

Retaining the village-church tradition in a situation where each county had only one "village" and the majority of the population was dispersed had several results. Attendance became irregular, baptisms and confirmations were often delayed, and the role of formalized religion in daily life decreased for some people in the outlying districts. Others coped with the problem by instituting the "Sunday house," a custom perhaps unique to the German Hill Country. On town lots in Fredericksburg, ranchers and farmers built small second residences.[12] Early on Saturday, the typical rural family traveled in from the country, took care of business and shopping needs, attended a Saturday evening party or dance, and spent the night in their Sunday house. After attending church on Sunday morning, they would return to the country. The back streets of Fredericksburg were dotted with Sunday houses, distinguishable from the residences of town folk by their smaller size. Many survive to the present. The Sunday house custom not only permitted access to church services, but also provided weekly social contacts, something the isolated rural folk, so recently and suddenly removed from the community life of their ancestral German villages, surely needed.

Beginning in the 1880s, the Hill Country Catholics and Lutherans were sufficiently acculturated to begin abandoning the village-church tradition. By 1882 two rural German Catholic churches had been established in Comal County. The first rural Lutheran church in the hills was founded in 1883 at Cave Creek community in Gillespie County. Some of these outlying churches still served substantial areas, particularly as the German-settled area continued to expand. At Cave Creek, for example, some parishioners received permission to build Sunday houses on church property, and certain others purchased small plots oˊ adjacent land for that purpose.[13]

The proliferation of rural churches in the German Hill Country continued until about World War I, with a peak of activity in the 1900–1910 period (fig. 2). Even so, the Lutheran and Catholic Germans never equaled the neighboring Anglo-Americans in the density of rural churches. Many rural communities remained without a church. In Comal County, the rural German-American population in 1920, numbering about 5,000, was served by only four rural churches.

In the German Methodist Llano River valley, a quite different spatial organization of churches prevailed from the very first, an organization inherently Anglo-American. A Methodist circuit rider initially served the scattered ranchsteads, and rural chapels were soon built. The overall Methodist ministry to the Germans was decidedly rural in character, because the church followed its converts as they left the towns to settle the countryside. Partly as a result of this rural concentration, Methodist churches were and are generally smaller in membership than other German parishes. In 1890, there was one church structure for every 65 German Methodists, as opposed to only one building for every 418 Lutheran members and one for every 544 Catholics. Even after the rural expansion of Lutheranism in Gillespie County, this proportion did not change. In 1960, the 3,963 Lutherans in Gillespie were served by nine churches—one for each 440 members. If only rural churches are considered, the 1960 Gillespie County average is still almost 200 members per church, and it should be noted that rural depopulation was well underway by that time. St. Paul Lutheran Church at Cave Creek in Gillespie County is representative of the rural parishes. St. Paul's baptised membership was 309 in 1889, 219 in 1940, 150 in 1950, and 125 in 1967.[14]

Clearly, then, those Germans who converted to Methodism quickly discarded the village-church tradition and adopted an Anglo-American Protestant spatial system. Those who remained true to Lutheranism and Catholicism clung for decades to a quasi-European ecclesiastical pattern, despite its impracticality, and they never fully adopted the Anglo Protestant concept of the small rural chapel.

Traditional Ecclesiastical Architecture

German church structures in the Texas Hill Country, regardless of denomination, differ in important architectural respects from those of the neighboring Anglo-Americans. These differences can be seen in both style and building materials. The following description of German-American church structures is based on an inspection of twenty traditional buildings erected before 1910. Of these, seventeen are still standing and fourteen remain in use.

Almost two-thirds of the German churches studied are built of native hewn limestone or sandstone, as are most traditional dwellings in the Hill Country (fig. 3). Catholics, Lutherans, Methodists, and Evangelicals alike preferred such construction. Another one-tenth of the structures, including the original 1847 union church at Fredericksburg and the St. Martin's Lutheran Church, built on the outskirts of New Braunfels in 1851, are of half-timbered (*Fachwerk*) construction (fig. 4). Both stone and half-timbered churches occur in the European source regions of the Texas settlers, and it is apparent that these techniques were imported.[15] It is noteworthy, however, that the nogging in the half-timbered walls of St. Martin's Church is typical Mexican adobe brick. By comparison, the large majority of Anglo-American churches in the surrounding counties are of frame construction. Only one-fourth of the German structures are frame.

In style, three-quarters of the German structures are Gothic or Gothic-inspired. Features of this style observed in the Hill Country include stepped towers, jagged steeples and pointed windows, and the elaborate use of stained glass. One church, the original St. Mary's Catholic at Fredericksburg, has the rare Gothic feature known as a helmet tower (*Helmturm*), a convex-sided crown atop the vestibule tower. The Gothic style is preferred by all German denominations in the Hill Country and prevails both in rural and town settings. Neighboring Anglo-Americans, by contrast, normally erected simple white frame chapels, devoid of ornamentation and symbols and generally lacking even a steeple or bell tower.[16] Four German-built

Figure 4. The original octagonal, half-timbered *Vereins Kirche* in Fredericksburg, dating from 1847. This remarkable structure was destroyed in 1897, shortly after this photograph was taken.

Figure 3. St. Joseph's Catholic Church in western Comal County, dating from 1910, is typical of many in the Hill Country. Hewn native limestone is the building material. Photo 1975.

chapels were noted, but these typically have steeples or bell towers, and one is of stone construction. In Mason County, the substantial rural German Methodist structures are easily distinguished from the humble board chapels of Anglo Methodists. The plain Anglo church houses can easily be mistaken for schools, but the Germans who became Wesleyan demanded places of worship that looked ecclesiastical and sanctified. In that regard, the German Methodists remained Central Europeans. Only in minor architectural features did the German Methodists accommodate the British-southern chapel style, as, for example, in the inclusion of two separate front doors—one for each sex—or in the erection of an adjacent tabernacle for camp meetings (fig. 5).

Another likely example of German influence in ecclesiastical architecture was the 1847 union church at Fredericksburg. Octagonal with half-timbered sides eighteen feet long, this *Vereinskirche* was topped by a cupola also of eight-sided design (fig. 4). In plan, the church is almost identical to the original cathedral of Charlemagne at Aachen, a type known to architects as the Carolingian octagon, and the Fredericksburg church could well have been copied from that well-known prototype. The octagonal form could also have an Anglo-Texan antecedent, since the type does occur in the American South.[17] Unfortunately, the *Vereinskirche* was demolished in 1897, though a replica was completed in 1935.

Cemeteries and Graves

In nineteenth-century rural Germany, as in much of Europe, cemeteries were usually located in the yard surrounding the church building, a location implied in the word *Kirchhof*. Even if the burial ground was not adjacent to the village church, it still lay within the settlement and enjoyed religious sanction. Family plots and private ownership of grave sites were unknown, and in fact it was common practice to reuse the site after some decades had passed. Burial in places other than the sanctified cemetery was uncommon.

German burial practices in the Texas Hill Country represent, in many respects, radical departures from Central European custom. Acculturation advanced rapidly as the Hill Country Germans adopted many Anglo-American practices. Perhaps most notably, the ancient custom of burial in sanctified ground was very early abandoned by the majority, particularly Protestants. As early as November of 1846, for example, a German geologist traveling through the Hill Country noted that the burial of a young immigrant girl was on her family's

Figure 5. United Methodist Church at Art, Mason County, was built in 1890 as the third structure housing the local German congregation of the Methodist Episcopal Church, South. Note the sandstone construction, separate entrances for men and women, and Gothic style. Photo 1970.

farm, following Anglo-American custom. Anglo influence was also seen in the fact that all people in the funeral procession were mounted on horseback. In the years that followed, isolated German family cemeteries became very common all through the Hill Country, often enclosed by sturdy rock walls (fig. 6). The difficulty of moving corpses from remote farms and ranches to the towns no doubt helps explain the German adoption of the family cemetery custom. But even in Fredericksburg, burials on private town lots were noted as early as 1848.[18] Curiously, the freethinkers of Kendall County established very few family cemeteries.

Church cemeteries were present almost from the very first in the Hill Country. In no case, however, were burials made surrounding the church. Two sites have church and cemetery enclosed by a single fence, but the more typical arrangement, also copied from Anglo-Americans, is for the church-related burial ground to be spaced away from the church building by a hundred yards or more. At St. Paul

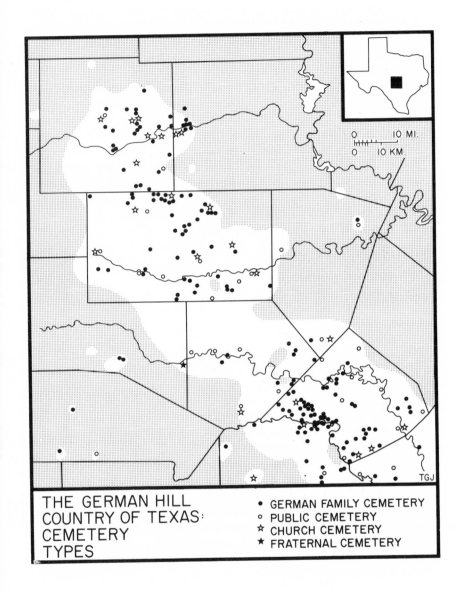

THE GERMAN HILL
COUNTRY OF TEXAS:
CEMETERY
TYPES

• GERMAN FAMILY CEMETERY
○ PUBLIC CEMETERY
☆ CHURCH CEMETERY
★ FRATERNAL CEMETERY

Figure 6.

Lutheran in Bulverde, for example, the cemetery is on the other side of a creek and upstream by several miles from the church, in a different county. For most Hill Country Germans, ecclesiastical cemeteries were unknown until the establishment of rural Lutheran and Catholic churches in the 1880–1910 period. For example, it was not until 1884, almost forty years after initial settlement, that rural Catholics in the community of Comal near New Braunfels petitioned the bishop in San Antonio to sanctify a burial site near their recently established church.[19]

Secular community cemeteries were laid out when towns were established in the Hill Country, and one was included in the original plat of Fredericksburg. Most town-dwelling Protestants use these community graveyards, as do many freethinkers. One fraternal cemetery, for members of the Order of the Sons of Hermann, is found in the Hill Country, just outside the freethinker stronghold of Comfort (fig. 6).

In all except sanctified Catholic cemeteries, typically Anglo-American family plots are the rule. Catholics permit only husband and wife to be buried side by side; in other respects the place of burial is determined by the annual sequence of deaths. Most Catholic graveyards, as well as some Lutheran and community cemeteries, have special children's sections, apparently a European practice.

Other typically Anglo-American features, such as scraped earth (grassless) plots, mounding of graves, decoration with shells, and burial of the husband on the right side of the wife, occur frequently in Hill Country German cemeteries (fig. 7).[20] As would be expected, the German Methodist graveyards display the greatest number of Anglo traits.

Distinctive German tombstone art persisted into the twentieth century in some Hill Country cemeteries. These are notable nineteenth-century examples displaying typical German folk art designs, such as the heart symbol (fig. 8). Here and there one finds exquisite wrought iron grave markers, including some dating from as late as the World War I period (fig. 9). Distinctive markers, either in stone or wrought iron, are not found in Methodist and freethinker cemeteries or on post-1920 burials. The community graveyard at Sisterdale, the freethinker stronghold, is almost totally devoid of Christian or folk symbolism of any kind.

Conclusion

Many facets of German religious culture survived in the Texas Hill Country. Resistance to acculturation is seen in church affiliation,

Figure 7. Shell-covered German grave mounds in the St. Martin's Lutheran Cemetery, located in the Hortontown neighborhood of New Braunfels. The use of shells as grave decoration was adopted from Anglo-Americans. Photo 1975.

since only about one in eight churchgoing German-Americans today belongs to a church different from that of his immigrant ancestors. Even the freethinker tradition survived in a rural Texas setting. Factionalism may have increased in Texas, but it likely represented freer expression of an inherently German religious divisiveness rather than Anglo influence. Indeed, even the conversion to Methodism may have been, for some, a natural outlet for suppressed German Pietism.

Resistance to acculturation is also seen in the remarkable survival, for several generations, of the church-town tradition among Lutherans and Catholics, groups which never fully accepted the Anglo-American rural chapel pattern. The Sunday house was one result. Ecclesiastical architecture provides an even clearer example of European cultural survival, in terms of both style and building materials.

Curiously, the Hill Country cemeteries, where we might expect Old World ways to prevail longest, reveal considerable acculturation.

Figure 8. The heart motif, so common in German folk art, appears on an 1877 tombstone in the Catholic cemetery at Fredericksburg. Photo 1977.

Figure 9. A distinctive wrought iron grave marker in the St. Paul Lutheran Cemetery at Cave Creek in rural Gillespie County. Photo 1977.

Normally, superstitious rural folk are reluctant to change time-tested methods of laying the dead to rest, but Hill Country grave-yards of every religious stripe display many Anglo-Texan practices. Perhaps most notable was the almost immediate adoption by the Germans of burial in unsanctified ground, especially in rural family cemeteries.

Overall, the religious acculturation of the Hill Country Germans progressed slowly and remains incomplete. Considering the level of environmental stress and the frequency of contacts with non-Germans, one can only describe the survival of religious ethnicity in the Hill Country as remarkable.

Notes

1. A good general source is Rudolph L. Biesele, *The History of the German Settlements in Texas, 1831-1861* (Austin, Tex.: Von Boeckmann-Jones, 1930), pp. 66-110.

2. John A. Hawgood, *The Tragedy of German-America* (New York and London: G. P. Putnam's Sons, 1940), p. 142; Gilbert G. Benjamin, *The Germans in Texas* (New York: D. Appleton, 1910), p. 55.

3. Donald W. Meinig, *Imperial Texas: An Interpretive Essay in Cultural Geography* (Austin: University of Texas Press, 1969), pp. 93, 102-3.

4. Robert Penniger, *Fredericksburg, Texas: The First Fifty Years*, trans. C. L. Wisseman (Fredericksburg, Tex.: Fredericksburg Publishing Co., 1971), pp. 63-65; *Report on Statistics of Churches in the United States at the Eleventh Census: 1890* (Washington, D.C.: GPO, 1894), p. 401.

5. See Bruno C. Schmidt, "A History of the Southern German Conference" (B.D. thesis, Southern Methodist University, 1935); Ervin M. Jordan, "The Work of the Methodist Episcopal Church, South, among the Germans in Texas" (M.A. thesis, Southern Methodist University, 1935).

6. See, for example, Dan Fischer, *The Willmanns in America—1853-1953* (n.p., 1953); Selma M. Raunick et al., *The Kothmanns of Texas, 1845-1931* (Austin, Tex.: Von Boeckmann-Jones, 1931); and Gilbert J. Jordan and Terry G. Jordan, *Ernst and Lisette Jordan: German Pioneers in Texas* (Austin, Tex.: Von Boeckmann-Jones, 1971).

7. Oral family tradition among Mason County descendants of Anton Willmann (1809-91).

8. *Der Missionsfreund* (Fredericksburg, Tex.) 36 (January 22, 1932): 3 (the semimonthly newspaper of the German Methodist Llano District).

9. Vera Flach, *A Yankee in German Texas* (San Antonio, Tex.: Naylor, 1973), pp. 30-31; H. C. Ziehe, *A Centennial Story of the Lutheran Church in Texas, 1851-1951*, 2 vols. (Seguin, Tex.: South Texas Printing), 2:132; *Der Missionsfreund* 32 (April 7, 1927): 1; Andrew F. Muir, "No Sabbath in West Texas: Missionary Appeals from Boerne, 1867-1868," *West Texas Historical Association Year Book* 31 (1955): 117, 118, 121.

10. Ziehe, *Centennial Story,* 2:132; Louis Reinhardt, "The Communistic Colony of Bettina," *Texas State Historical Association Quarterly* 3 (July 1899): 33-40; A. Siemering, "Die lateinische Ansiedlung in Texas," *Der deutsche Pionier* 10 (1878): 57-62.

11. Terry G. Jordan, *German Seed in Texas Soil* (Austin: University of Texas Press, 1966), p. 160; idem, "The German Element of Gillespie County, Texas" (M.A. thesis, University of Texas, Austin, 1961), pp. 70, 81.

12. *St. Paul Lutheran Church, Cave Creek, Texas, 1883-1968* (n.p., [ca. 1968]), p. 1; Samuel E. Gideon, "Sunday Houses in Texas," *Pencil Points,* April 1931, pp. 276-81; Jordan, *German Seed,* p. 161.

13. W. Bonenkamp et al., eds., *Schematismus der deutschen und der deutsch-sprechenden Priester sowie der deutschen Katholiken-Gemeinden in den Vereinigten Staaten . . .* (St. Louis: B. Herder, 1882); *St. Paul Lutheran,* pp. 1, 10; State of Texas historical marker at Cave Creek, Gillespie County.

14. *A Century of German Methodism in the Llano River Valley of Texas* (Fredericksburg, Tex.: Fredericksburg Publishing Co., 1952); Gilbert J. Jordan, "Texas German Methodism in a Rural Setting," *Perkins Journal* 31 (Spring 1978): 1-21; *Official Minutes of the Constituting Convention of the Southern District of the American Lutheran Church* (n.p., 1960); *Report on Statistics of Churches;* *St. Paul Lutheran,* pp. 6, 17, 18, 25.

15. Anneliese Siebert, *Der Baustoff als Gestaltender Faktor niedersächsischer Kulturlandschaften* (Bad Godesberg, W. Germany: Bundesforschungsanstalt für Landeskunde und Raumordnung, 1969), pp. 101-22.

16. Jordan, "German Element," pp. 182-83; Terry G. Jordan, "The Traditional Southern Rural Chapel in Texas," *Ecumene* 8 (1976); 6-17.

17. Elise Kowert, *Old Homes and Buildings of Fredericksburg* (Fredericksburg, Tex.: Fredericksburg Publishing Co., 1977), pp. 132-35; Clay Lancaster, "Some Octagonal Forms in Southern Architecture," *Art Bulletin* 27 (June 1946): 103-11.

18. Ferdinand von Roemer, *Texas,* trans. Oswald Mueller (San Antonio, Tex.: Standard Printing, 1935), p. 212; Kowert, *Old Homes,* p. 59.

19. Oscar Haas, *History of New Braunfels and Comal County, Texas, 1844-1946* (Austin, Tex.: Steck, 1968), p. 205.

20. Donald G. Jeane, "The Traditional Upland South Cemetery," *Landscape* 18 (Spring-Summer 1969): 39-41; Sara Clark, "The Decoration of Graves in Central Texas with Seashells," *Texas Folklore Society Publications* 36 (1972): 33-43.

Folk Religion as Ideology for Ethnic Survival: The Hungarians of Kipling, Saskatchewan

Linda Dégh

Studies of ethnic groups in the modern industrial world may benefit particularly from the approach of folklorists who seek special insights from subjective, intentional expressions of persons about themselves and their views of the world. In their effort to understand the existential bases of American ethnic communities and the ethnic behavior of their individual members, folklorists endeavor to bridge the gap between the scholar's *objective* and the informant's *subjective* definition of ethnicity. In the dynamics of social life, the symbols of ethnicity develop differently in each place as a result of the interaction of innumerable factors. Local groups naturally depend upon their unique rearrangement of inherited, borrowed, and newly created cultural expressions. They retain loyalty to traditional ways, and yet the ancestral heritage is changed as it is adapted to new cultural settings and social realities in different ways.[1]

Elements of local heritage seem to be stronger than those of the national stereotype. That is to say, peasant immigrants represent the culture of their native village, town, or region more than that of their nation. Under feudal conditions peasants could not develop either a fatherland concept or devotion to the larger political entity in which their home village was located. Thus people in the new-country settlements, immigrating from diverse regions in the same old country, continue to identify themselves by their disparate imported traditions. Tension growing out of regional differences naturally results and sometimes leads to open conflict. It intensifies and develops further through a set of symbols of self-identification. The ethnic identification marks, often exhibited consciously by group members with reference to old-country norms, belong more to the irrational than to the rational sphere of life. They are manifested in the formulation of a specific local folk religion, the ideology of which is explicated through myths about the foundation of the settlement, and which functions as a regulator of community life and work ethos.[2] Because religion functions as a cohesive as well as divisive force (not only in the spiritual but also in the social and cultural life of American ethnic enclaves), it also plays a leading role in the stimulation of discord between the adherents of diverse religious traditions. These points may be observed in the experiences of Hungarians who settled in Kipling, a small town on the plains of Saskatchewan, Canada.

Kipling is a small town, isolated from the rest of the world by large parcels of cultivated land. The farmsteads are linked to town by an intricate labyrinth of gravel roads that have been cut up by farm machinery and trucks. A similarly intricate and extensively used telephone network connects farmsteaders with the townsfolk on a closed-circuit information exchange. The pattern of this settlement complex is rather inconspicuous. It developed naturally from the original land parceling done by the Canadian Pacific Railway at the turn of the century in order to accommodate immigrant settlers, who cleared the woods and broke up the soil for cultivation.[3] The landscape still preserves relics of the efforts of the founding fathers. Remnants of old sod-covered log and adobe buildings interrupt the monotony of greening wheat fields pampered by sophisticated modern agricultural technology. Briar and saskatoon hedges hide old water dugouts. Similarly, they decorate piles of rocks that farmers lifted from the ground and hauled away to make the land arable. To the ethnographer the landscape itself appears as a gigantic open-air museum, paying tribute to the pioneer ancestors and documenting the gradual transformation of the postfeudal peasant into a commercial farmer.

Kipling, with a population of 1,000–1,200 persons, is a typical prairie service center for wheat farmers. Its aerial view, printed in color and sold as the only available postcard, could be that of almost any other community in the area. The most prominent establishments, all necessary for running the farm business, are the elevator, the freight train depot, service stations, farm equipment repair shops, and the hotel, which has the only restaurant licensed to sell alcoholic beverages. But the unpaved main street has more to offer to fill the immediate needs of the residents. People running errands often show up there more than once a day during the mild season. While looking after their business at the grocery or dry goods store, the bank, the post office, or the laundromat, they exchange news and gossip about local and world affairs, considerably weakening the attraction of the *Kipling Citizen*, the local weekly newspaper. It has never been able to compete with the speedy spread of whispered news anyway. The recreation center is the meeting place of senior citizens; young people are regular patrons of the movie theater and of the only hamburger place in town. Above all, however, the entire population is most visibly structured according to their participation in the religious and social activities of eleven churches. The latest one, a Baptist church, was erected in a conspicuously rotund shape so that "the Devil should not hide in the sanctuary."[4]

The religious beliefs and practices of most Kipling Hungarians differ from those of most church goers. Even though many had themselves baptized as adults in the Baptist, Pentecostal, or Adventist church, they retained their membership in the Hungarian Calvinist church into which they had been baptized as infants.[5] People commonly attend the services of more than one church and participate frequently in church-related activities such as Bible class meetings, choir rehearsals, and interdenominational get-togethers at private homes. The high point, of course, is the Sunday worship. These services start in the early morning in the Baptist church and continue in the Calvinist church, which is naturally the focus of attraction and the home base for all. It is where devotion, positive and negative emotions flare up. On rare Sundays or high holidays when two services are performed (a Hungarian in addition to the English) by a visiting pastor, the avid churchgoers attend both. In the afternoon the people reconvene at the Pentecostal or the People's church. They find justification for their ecumenical behavior, as for so many things, in the Bible.

Whoever enters into conversation with the older members of the community will have to cope with the presence of passionate, although not always standard, religiosity. The metaphysical super-saturation of Kiplingians is manifested in almost all of their statements or gestures, suggesting the extent to which religion dominates members of the older generation, whose daily lives are filled with convincing, edifying experiences that have top priority in the minds of the people.[6] "We all worship one God" is one of the often heard expressions intended to render acceptable certain behaviors, such as the easy reconciliation of dogmatic contradictions. "This is the work of Satan" is another slogan used to explain other kinds of behavior, such as the complete refusal to deal with spiritualism, diverse kinds of spiritualistic beliefs, atheism, and even politics. God and Satan thus vie with each other on the streets and in the homes of Kipling, day by day, hour by hour. Some persons express strong, almost aggressive, belief in something, while others argue against it with similar vehemence. One person might say, "There are no revenants," whereupon another might answer: "There are spirits, but to conjure them up is the working of the Devil." A third person would just smile forgivingly at this kind of controversy, thereby indicating his enlightened superiority, which often turns out to be a similar kind of belief disguised in modern wrapping. Religion proper, regardless of formal organization, is the focus of concern among the people of Kipling.

Only a minority of active farmers (those also engaged in other enterprises) reside in town. Most of the neat, comfortable, ordinary frame houses of Kipling are inhabited by retired farmers who are well into their eighties but who still share farm work with their children. Mutual aid acts as a cement strengthening ties between the generations within families. Farmsteaders repay parental help by providing produce and by assisting with the maintenance and repair of the "old folks'" house and yard in town. On the other hand, school-age children of the farmsteaders are boarded by their grandparents until their graduation from the Kipling high school.

Surface features of practical life in Kipling are much like those in other prairie towns similarly isolated from each other and remote from urban centers. Yet, like other communities, Kipling strives for the recognition of its distinctiveness. In the short and modest history of the town even a dull and forced place name legend—claiming that the town was named for Rudyard Kipling, who once traveled through the region and accidentally looked out the window when his train passed through—seems of some significance. The Hungarian community, nevertheless, has another, officially unrecognized, but, for the settlers, more meaningful and romantic name: Békevár (Bastion of Peace). This name was assigned by the pioneers to the original, all-Hungarian nucleus of the town with a school and a church in its center, which lies some four miles north of today's Kipling.[7] The name was indicative of the mood of the founders, who viewed the cluster of their staked-out properties of 160 acres, hewn from the wilderness by each of them, as the fulfillment of the dream of their poor peasant ancestors and as a haven in which peace and industry would lead to prosperity and happiness for the long line of progeny. Nevertheless, the two names do not characterize the spirit of the town. Most inhabitants do not know who Kipling was, and peace and harmony do not dominate their lives.

Kipling-Békevár is essentially a Hungarian village, the largest and oldest rural settlement of Magyars in North America. Although there are residents in the town of British and other ancestry, they do not blur the conspicuous visibility of the Magyar concentration.[8] Inevitably, the ethnicity-conscious community, as well as the outside researcher, describes the town as homogeneously Hungarian, composed of people who share a common national tradition. There are some objectively visible traits to support that view, such as loyalty to language, Old World peasant-style religiosity, eating habits, and kinship cohesion. The people often deliberately emphasize these traits for the outside observer.

The basic components of homogeneity consist of several interdependent characteristics. There were no class or essential educational differences between the settlers. All were peasants or peasant-craftsmen in the old country and are now farm entrepreneurs, possessing from several hundred to several thousand acres of land. As once in the old country, the farms are owned and operated by large families on the basis of organized division of labor. Farming is viewed by all as the essential and ideal way of life, and people display a subjective, passionate, almost worshipful identification with the soil they cultivate.[9] Their rapture and humility is almost metaphysical; they feel it is a duty and a privilege to raise many children because large families can produce more crops under the leadership of wise elders.

The settlers imported their Calvinist faith from the old country and developed a puritanic sectarianism in their worship system and personal relationship with God. According to their religious philosophy, farmers "are closer to the Lord" than others, and more subject to his reward and punishment. Rigid principles of industry, frugality, and religiosity regulate individual and group life, and this is particularly expressed in the plainness of home decoration, simplicity of clothing, and the suppression of some worldly types of folklore. The level of participation by Kipling Hungarians in provincial politics and community administration is strikingly lower than that of the other ethnics: they limit their community services and interest in running for office mainly to farm and church-oriented organizations.

Social conformity, in general, is not broken down by mere personal and in-group disagreement, quarrels, the formation of interest groups, rivalries, slanderous gossip, or lasting feuds. In the Kipling-Békevár case, however, small personal sensitivities develop along the line of essential ethnic differences. Under the surface of this idyllic agrarian paradise united by religious and work ethics are wide and deep divisions. The signs of discord are of diverse nature and magnitude. Sometimes they seem trivial and, transferred to other sociocultural contexts, would seem senseless.

By observing interpersonal relationships and the formation of friendship and neighborhood circles in Kipling-Békevár, one can detect a definite pattern in who visits whom, who calls whom by telephone, who attends whose Bible hour, who avoids whose company, who shares secrets with whom, who exchanges kitchen recipes with whom, and who trades gossip with whom and about whom. Animosities arise out of these patterns and delineate a division between the members of two rival groups: the Highlanders and the Lowlanders.

Persons take offense at trifling incidents that would not even be noticed if they had not occurred between members of opposing groups. Instead, the incidents are widely discussed and dramatized in order to increase tension. Mrs. N. carries a grudge against the usher who seated her at a "disgraceful" place at the Sunday service in order to humiliate her; Mr. K. tells a long story about how he was bypassed when the hymnals were distributed among the congregation; and old Mrs. F. will never forget the loss of her cat because "this woman" lured it to her granary full of mice by leaving the door ajar, just to annoy her.

These and similar indications of a basic and irreconcilable cleavage within the Kipling society reveal the persistence of regional identities within the two groups of the original settlers. The question arises naturally, Why is it that after seventy-five years of living together, the descendants of the original settlers, so similar in their general cultural characteristics, cannot reconcile their disagreements? Moreover, as time passes the separation between the two groups widens and the gap in understanding grows.

Throughout the history of Kipling-Békevár, jealousy, mutual mistrust, and hostility have plagued public life. This has resulted in church schism, severance of intergroup relations, and abandonment of joint actions for common causes—all solely on the grounds of a stubborn loyalty to distinct ancestral heritages. This division is much stronger than the tensions and stresses arising naturally from the acculturative process experienced by all American ethnic groups.[10] It seems unrelated to objective social disparities, nor can it be explained by the generation gap, linguistic conditions, or political, economic, and educational differences. The original reason for the split must be traced to the regional origins of the two groups who founded the colony and the circumstances of their settlement. In their subjective ethnic self-description, the Kipling Hungarians are oriented primarily toward the past; they conceive of their ancestral heritage in deeply religious terms as an emotional identification with the ever present, everlasting past. Although irrational and unrelated to current community issues, the loyalty to tradition—based on ancestral values—characterizes the ethnic dichotomy in Kipling-Békevár. In this case, representatives of two regional cultures settled side by side and built one community. Distinct cultural heritages inevitably developed, and were transformed, not only because cultural change continues naturally, but also because the two groups face each other as both audience and challenger. The stage of competition is the religious forum. Folklore expressions, revolving around and supporting religious belief, provide convincing examples of how regional ethnic tradition was maintained over time by continual reformulation of the original pattern, thereby satisfying the need for ethnic self-portrayal.

Each year Kipling-Békevár remembers its founding on July 20. On this day in 1975 the community celebrated its seventy-fifth anniversary. The commemoration and thanksgiving ritual was a great success: it drew a large audience from the province and brought officials as well as relatives from near and far to participate in the festivities. The whole town displayed a festive mood. Local stores sold souvenirs—spoons, plates, and tiles that bore the picture of the Békevár church, the symbol of the community and the source of pride for the descendants of the founding fathers. But the founding fathers belonged to the Highland clan.[11] For this and related reasons, the church is also the most frequent source of community discord. It was built as the principal place of worship in the center of old Békevár in 1910. The pioneers ordered the architect to make a miniature replica of the historic Calvinist church in Debrecen, the site of the Trans-Tisza episcopacy and the Mecca of all faithful Calvinists of the region in which their forebears lived. Although the attempt was unsuccessful, the similarity is taken for granted by the people who never saw the Debrecen church. When the town of Kipling took shape, the Highland clan wanted to move their cherished church building into its middle. However, the opposing faction, the rival Lowland clan, resisted. They wanted to build a modern American-style church and religious activities center.[12] Numerous stories provide dramatic details of how the Highlanders lost the struggle, how they were defeated, and why their sanctuary and the cemetery of their blessed ancestors is now defunct and in disrepair. Likewise, many stories tell of the stubborn backwardness and lack of common sense of the Highlanders, who were ready to bankrupt the community by moving the ramshackle structure to town.

The anniversary gave one last opportunity to make the defunct old Békevár church sparkle in its old colors. The cracks in the floor were superficially filled, the walls repainted for the service, and the weeds covering the founders' gravestones were mowed. But the Lowland party stayed away from the celebration because the church elders could not come to terms. Who should speak? In what language? And above all, who were the pioneers? The plan to erect a marble column with the names of the founding fathers had to be dropped because of passionate disagreement. Mrs. Steve Izsák, one of the local folk poets, wrote an elegy dedicated to the Békevár church, which was, as she had put it, "once the apple of the eye of the community":

> . . . your "welcome" gate is broken now
> as if to say don't be near around
> no one comes anymore anyway . . .
> Not far from you on the right hand side
> lay all the old pioneers who built you with pride
> they all loved you just as I do
> and someday I will be there too.

The original Highlanders were one large, enterprising extended family with a strong dedication to communalism. This group, which in 1900 first occupied the land, came from the village Bótrágy, Bereg County, in the northeasternmost part of Hungary (it is now in the Soviet Ukraine, close to the Hungarian border). Isolated by marshlands until the end of the nineteenth century, the population of that region developed a peculiarly self-contained practical and expressive culture, of which many features still maintain their symbolic significance in the minds of group members. The Protestant faith allowed the preservation of an archaic folk belief system in which shamanistic elements played an important role, and was liberal enough to tolerate the people's inclination toward religious fundamentalism and mysticism which became manifest in the formation of a small Baptist group in Bótrágy.[13]

Although the Highlanders retained only some of the characteristic legends about magic encounters and personages, visions, and the knowledge of magic healing, their mentality did not change over the decades. The imported traditions provided a solid base for the development in Canada of a new mysticism wrapped in rigid pietism. When the pastor, an extravagant person fresh from Hungary, introduced his new fascination with spiritualism to the people, they became deeply involved in the formation of a spiritualist association as early as 1908. They subsequently also founded a purely Hungarian Baptist congregation.[14] Furthermore, members of the Highland clan found new outlets for their need of magico-religious expressions by joining several American fundamentalist churches. Meanwhile, in order to maintain respectability as well as to remain faithful to ancestral tradition, they retained their membership in the main Calvinist-Hungarian church.

As a result of these conditions and the tendencies inherent in mysticism, a set of supernatural legends from the Hungarian folk tradition of the Bereg region were quite remarkably recast and fitted into the Békevár context of eclectic pietism. Gradually incidents that occurred during the short-lived spiritualist movement were incorporated into a set of traditional legends. Curiously, spiritualism thus remains a topic of daily conversation and is the focus of controversy within the Highland group and in its relationship with the Lowlanders. Moreover, the spiritualist experience justified the belief in visions, dreams, and spirit possession among the Highlanders, and opened the door for the acceptance of churches in which faith healing and trances are part of the service. In this way traditional folk beliefs infiltrated the Baptist church, despite its stiff, antifolkloric rules, and religion became the new refuge for the survival of ethnic forms. Later, after 1902 and as late as 1930, when new settlers from the same region (mainly Bereg and adjacent Szabolcs County) joined the colony, they reinforced the peculiar folk religion and related folkloric behavior that had developed in Kipling-Békevár.

The Highlanders continue to hold their ancestors in high esteem. Although they have never been in Bótrágy and first-hand information is unavailable because the pioneers are now all dead, the Highlanders perpetuate folk traditions about the old country and the occupation of the colony in multiple forms but set patterns. They enculturate their children by telling them the story of the origin and history of the colony and by showing them old photographs carefully preserved for posterity. The local high school welcomes projects on ethnic history by pupils, and grandfathers delight in furnishing information for such undertakings.

According to this self-styled history and mythology, the Bótrágy people were of noble origin, well-to-do, and well educated (a typical retrospective idealization of the lost home by peasant immigrants).[15] Their excellence was attributed, among other influences, to a prominent school teacher who taught pupils how to write poetry, a skill practiced and appreciated in Kipling. But the real hero of the genealogical Bótrágy myth is János Szabó, known as "Moses of Békevár." At twenty-three, according to the myth, Szabó was already known for his self-sacrificing work for the public welfare in his village and was nominated for the office of judge (*bíró*). But he lost the election because he was too young and ran away in embarrassment. After long wanderings and strenuous labor in the industrial plants of the United States, Szabó learned of a fabulous land in Canada where the able and virtuous could acquire 160 acres free of charge. The rest of the story tells how Szabó joined the good men of his clan, marched with them from Whitewood through the wilderness, and conquered the promised land, a "new Canaan." One of the several poetic immortalizations of the land taking is characteristic of the Highlander world-view:

> When the Magyars came to Canada
> they were very happy to come,
> hundreds and hundreds of miles of prairie land!
> One might ask, how can your feet take you that far?
> Bring plow, scythe, and harrow.
> Sing [hymns and songs] while you break up [the ground]
> to please the good Lord.
> So did the Magyar and when he started [to toil]
> he sent fervent prayers to his Lord.
> When he completed his mud house
> he moved his beloved family there.
> He broke the virgin soil with all the power he had;
> everybody struggled and struggled enough.
> Wherever Magyars lived,
> happiness and satisfaction dwelt with them.
> One farmer sang [hymns] and other sang [songs] ;
> the nightingale competed often with them.
> The good Lord blessed them
> with children and wealth.
> Be happy, my beloved Magyars,
> said the good Lord up high in heaven.[16]

The story then develops into a family saga in which helpers and villains appear. The episodes tell of feats and adventures of pioneer men and women and their offspring: how they fought the forces of nature and conquered the land, built their homes, planted, and harvested to the great pleasure of God. They also tell about family events: births, marriages, and deaths, and important community concerns. Because of the closeness of the group and its common interest in poetic formulation of past events, the epic and its parts appear in diverse forms. There are verse chronicles and auto-biographical diaries in written form to be passed on and read in family circles, and there are shorter verses written and repeated by inspired poets to a wider audience. The recitation of poems high-lights church services, patriotic feasts, family reunions, weddings, funerals, and other occasions honoring people and events. The epic is also transmitted in oral prose and might be told by anyone at any time. The most striking feature of the epic as a whole is its super-saturation with a religiosity in which farming, family success, and happiness are conceived as solely the reward and grace of God for obeying his command. The world is divided into bright white and threateningly black levels. There is reward and there is punishment: successes and distresses are interpreted in these terms. Later events, such as the Great Depression of the "dirty thirties," are described as punishment from God for the sins of the fathers.

Highlanders define their ethnicity in terms of loyalty to Bótrágy behavioral standards, which they believe worked well for the pio-neers. Any conversation among Highlanders will sooner or later refer to an example showing that they still accept the ancestral heritage as a source of inspiration in setting their rules of life. Farming, prayer, and poetry are the vehicles that convey these rules in terms of ethnic distinctiveness.

Highlanders claim that the Kipling-Békevár culture is their own creation. Nobody else could have turned a wilderness into a farmer's paradise but the Szabó clansmen, inspired by their leader's superior morality.[17] Friendly Bótrágy descendants are eager to welcome visitors and volunteer information about their history. Recognized community leaders act as public relations men and give the same general account of material and expressive aspects of their culture. Star informants usually advise the field worker whom to contact and where to go, and watch his moves to make sure he does not meet people who might contradict the traditional Highlander image. However, the hospitable and generous informants themselves very soon reveal the real situation. Highlanders usually contrast them-selves with the Lowlanders: "Our people do it this way, not like the Lowlanders . . . ," "The Lowlanders are snobs, hypocrites, . . ." "They are not serious about the Church like us, . . ." "They want power, not God's love like us . . . ," "Lowlanders are selling out to Canada. It is us who keep the Magyar heritage alive."

Who are the Lowlanders? They came from the Nagy-Kúnság, specifically from two large market towns, Karcag and Kisújszállás.

They are descendants of the Kúns (Cumans), a nomadic Turkish people who settled in Hungary in the 1200s. Only centuries later were they integrated into the main population. Free from serfdom, the Kúns enjoyed privileges from Hungarian kings and created a powerful peasant civilization on the Great Hungarian Plains. The first Lowlanders in Békevár did not come as paupers but as enterprising peasant-tradesmen with money and good social position who looked forward to transplanting their traditional skills in Canada, where more land was available than in their country of birth.[18] When the Lowlanders arrived in 1903 and 1904, the Bótrágy clan had already occupied the center of the Békevár colony and formed a solid neighborhood complex that forced the newcomers to occupy the lands on the perimeter. This was the point of departure for disagreement.

From the outset, the Lowlanders looked critically at their neighbors, essentially because of the cultural gulf between them. The Lowlanders were townspeople, experienced businessmen, sober and rational workers, without a rich body of traditional folklore. What they might have brought along to the New World had been consciously abandoned as useless and impractical. They replaced their traditional peasant wear with the "Canadian costume" and gave up traditional farming techniques for what "was required according to Canadian fashion." Lowlanders even relinquished their original dialect, switching to the standard Hungarian that they picked up by communicating with other Hungarian Canadians. Sometimes they reveal something of their traditional ways: "Kúns do not force their wives to work in the fields—woman's place is in their home, at the hearth." "The Karcag folk weren't that superstitious as far as I can remember. Not like in small villages where people were not that intelligent . . . ." The most prominent ethnic symbol of the Lowlanders appears to be their wastefully rich traditional cookery, feasting, and treating guests and then happily throwing the leftovers to the dogs. "The Bótrágy people did not know how to cook or how to make pastries. All what they know now of baking and cooking, Kún women taught them."

The general lack of concern for Old World folk traditions makes the cultural identity of Lowlanders less conspicuous than that of their opponents and closer to that of the provincial-urban Hungarian model. They reveal little of their Kún heritage in comparison to the Highlanders' active ethnicity display. Following the peasant-burgher behavioral pattern, Lowlanders are withdrawn, short-spoken, and hard-working. Most of the time they stay on their farms and appear in town only for important reasons. They come to town for the Sunday church service and drive up in their big, expensive cars with their families, except in the busy season. The men do the driving, as farm wives are not supposed to.

Very few retired Lowland farmers moved to Kipling. One of the most respected and wealthy leaders continues to live in the modest log house his father built fifty years ago. His weather-beaten home, which lacks running water, is surrounded by the modern farmhouses of his four sons.

In view of the cultural differences between the Highlanders and the Lowlanders, the events that stimulated and perpetuated the division between them are easily identified. The most decisive disagreement was caused by the Bótrágy people's religious mysticism as their main driving force and regulator of intellectual life: the metaphysical preoccupation that infuses their general community behavior. The Lowlanders label the Highlander's religiosity as "superstition," "heresy," "deviltry," and "idolatry." The first open conflict occurred in 1911, when the outraged and rational Lowlanders "terminated the devil worship" (i.e., spiritualistic seances) of the Highland clan by having the minister removed from the Békevár parish. To this day, the memory of that trauma lives on. It marked the beginning of all the ills that have plagued the community.

The Békevár church, as the main organizer of the religious as well as social and intellectual life of the people, became an open battlefield for the two factions. Who should be elected elder? Who should be the new minister? Who is not attending services and why? What should be the language of the services? These were the principal issues. Between 1911 and 1971 there were nineteen Hungarian pastors serving the community; none stayed longer than five years and some only for a few months. As Mrs. Sz. observed, "It has been predicted that we will not have a real dedicated minister for seventy years, after our pastor was dismissed. This is the Lord's punishment."

Since 1972 only visiting pastors have come to serve on high holidays. The last one was dismissed partly because "he had heavy, dark eyebrows and blue eyes and women feared his harming babies at baptism." The visiting pastors alternate between English- and Hungarian-language services because the elders cannot agree on the language issue. When the Highland clan lost its battle against moving the Békevár church to Kipling, it also lost the argument for the maintenance of Hungarian-language services. It came as a blow to the older generation that the younger Highlanders also opted for English. This turned sons against fathers, a fierce defiance of the traditional submission to paternal command according to Bótrágy kinship regulation. As a result, the authority of the church was undermined. A group of the most powerful families of the Highlanders called a Baptist minister from Transylvania and formed a separate Hungarian-Baptist congregation (rooted in the Bótrágy-Baptist tradition). This move by the Calvinist leaders prompted the question, Why give up? Why not fight for the cause? The answer was that "it had been in the Scriptures" that they had to act before God as they acted. I do not doubt that the dissidents believed that, some right at the start, while others became convinced later.

Thus, from the start the new Hungarian Baptist congregation's raison d'être was the maintenance of the ethnic heritage, whereas the congregation of Hungarian Calvinists, lacking strong and steady leadership, is crumbling. One of the most prestigious patriarchs and dedicated religious poets, Mr. Benjamin Szakács, wrote this:

> We are quite fortunate
> to hear the sermon in Hungarian.
> The young ministers of the Presbyterian Church
> are mostly offsprings of the Slavs
> and they decided because of envy
> that they will deprive us of Hungarian ministers.[19]
> Only a few days ago,
> Kennedy the moderator said
> that the Hungarians need a few years
> [until they are ready] to hear English sermons.
> But the young ministers did not wait
> but got rid of the Hungarian ministers.[20]
> So we had to leave our church,
> and make alliance with the Baptists.
> It is true, among the young Hungarians of Békevár
> there are many English [speakers]
> who scorn our language; [they]
> become the Judases of our nation.

The revitalization of Hungarian ethnicity through the new Baptist pastor, a newcomer from the old country who lacked any knowledge of English, was a success. Symbolizing Hungarian-ness in terms of piety, industry, and old-fashioned morality, he became not only the spiritual leader of the dissidents but also a friend and a humble servant of the needy. A tragic accident, however, took his life in autumn 1975 when a tractor he was driving overturned. It seemed as though the Hungarian Baptist church was doomed and that the fragile ethnic survival will soon fall victim to the power struggle raging in the Calvinist church. Many people, young and old, have joined more attractive churches and it is likely that the Lowland-Highland feud will eventually lead to the abandonment of the principles on which ethnic maintenance is based. At this time, however, the Baptist congregation continues to fight for its cause. Worship continues without their beloved pastor. Bible hours and prayer meetings continue. There is hardly a day in the week when the members do not meet for a pious sharing under the leadership of lay preachers and singers. Their desire for ethnic revitalization was so great that they appealed to the bishop of the Hungarian Baptists of America. The request for a new pastor for the Békevárians was directed to the Hungarian authorities through the World Federation of Hungarians.

The case of the Kipling-Békevár settlement, albeit peculiar in some respects, seems to be typical in many others. It suggests several hypothetical conclusions concerning the ethnic process.

First, orientation to past heritage (identification with ancestral values in ethnic self-portrayal) influences effectively the present and the future development of groups.

Second, the homogeneity of an ethnic group, even if reinforced by identical class conditions, religion, occupation, and other factors as in Kipling, can be eroded by seemingly insignificant, almost irrational, causes.

Third, religion (eclectic Protestant pietism in this case) can have enormous significance and assume a leading role in the formulation of ethnic group identity, supported and asserted by a set of testimonial narratives. If there is good reason to believe that "religion is more resistant to acculturation than ethnicity," which may or may not "serve to accelerate or retard the general acculturative process," in this case religion has shown itself to be identical with (or at least as the most prominent manifestation of) ethnicity.[21] Ethnic cohesion thus can be achieved and sustained through intensive participation in church-oriented religious activities by the majority of the membership.

Fourth, the passage of time may actually deepen the differences that separate groups that so define their ethnicity; it does not necessarily fill in or narrow the gulf between them. Regional representatives of the same national culture may oppose each other. Issues causing discord between them seem stronger than their common national origin. Under such conditions, ethnicity weakens and assimilation accelerates without outside pressure and despite a contrary endeavor on the part of concerned groups. Thus, loyalty to different regional identities rather than to the common national one can take over and perform efficiently the function of the melting pot where it was officially turned off or where it never existed.[22]

Notes

1. Wsevolod W. Isajev, "Definitions of Ethnicity," *Ethnicity* 1 (1974): 111-24; Carla Bianco, *The Two Rosetos* (Bloomington: Indiana University Press, 1974); Robert B. Klymasz, "From Immigrant to Ethnic Folklore: A Canadian View of Process and Transition," *Journal of the Folklore Institute* 10 (1973): 131-39; Linda Dégh, "The Study of Ethnicity in Modern European Ethnology," *Journal of the Folklore Institute* 12 (1975): 15-16.

2. Linda Dégh, "Survival and Revival of European Folk Cultures in America," *Ethnologia Europaea* 2-3 (1968/69): 103; George de Vos, "Ethnic Pluralism: Conflict and Accommodation," in *Ethnic Identity: Cultural Continuities and Change*, ed. George de Vos and Lola Romanucci-Ross (Palo Alto, Calif.: Mayfield Publishing Co., 1975), pp. 8, 13-15.

3. James B. Hedges, *Building the Canadian West: The Land and Colonization Policies of the Canadian Pacific Railways* (New York: Macmillan, 1939); Robert England, *The Colonization of Western Canada: A Study of Contemporary Land Settlement (1896-1934)* (London: King and Son, 1936).

4. So stated by an elder of the church.

5. Dezsö Ábrahám, "The Hungarian Reformed Churches in America," *Bethlen Almanac* (Ligonier: Hungarian Reformed Federation, 1960).

6. Oscar Handlin has observed that religion became a way of life for the peasants who had to make the transition from the system in which the church represented the Establishment to the one in which church membership was based on voluntary choice. Thus, their religious life grew rigid and they became "far more conservative than those of their fellows who had remained in Europe." See Oscar Handlin, *The Uprooted* (New York: Grosset and Dunlap, 1951), p. 142. See also Aladár Komjáthy, "The Hungarian Reformed Church in America: an Effort to Preserve a Denominational Heritage" (Ph.D. diss., Princeton Theological Seminary, 1962), pp. 230-31.

7. Gyula Izsák, the eyewitness chronicler of the settlement, gave an account of the name giving. First *Kenyérháza* (house of bread) was suggested, because the immigrants came for their bread; then *Békefalva* (peace village), because peace is so essential to happy life. Finally, the pioneers agreed on *Békevár* because of the double meaning of *vár* (as a noun it means fortress; as a verb, to expect). Thus the compound word designates the fortress in which everyone can expect to make and maintain peace. Gyula Izsák, *A Samaritánus·Igaz történet az elsö telepesek életéböl* (The Samaritan: A True Story from the Life of the First Settlers) (Toronto: 1954), p. 51.

8. Supported by the Canadian Centre for Folk Culture Studies (National

Museum of Man, Ottawa), I first did field work in Kipling in 1971. Later, when the Centre organized a Békevár Team Programme for a comprehensive ethnographical monograph, I joined the interdisciplinary team of ten researchers. The materials collected by the team during 1974 and 1975 are deposited in the archives of the Centre. See Renée Landry, "Archival Sources," *Ethnic Folklore in Canada* (special issue of *Canadian Ethnic Studies*, vol. 7 [1975], pp. 73–86. Publication of these materials is foreseen. According to the 1971 census, Greek, German, Dutch, Polish, Scandinavian (*sic*), French, Ukrainian, and Asian ethnics constitute the rest of the population, 275 persons altogether.

9. "The Church was familiar to the peasant's day-to-day existence. Its outward forms and ceremonies were established in the round of the year . . . each festival had a seasonal connotation. . . . All the acts of worship were embedded in a setting, in which the landscape, the weather, and the sight of the heavens all were aspects." This description by Handlin, *The Uprooted*, pp. 120–21, applies to the outlook of modern-day Kipling farmers; see also Linda Dégh, "Two Hungarian-American Stereotypes," *New York Folklore Quarterly* 28 (March 1972): 11–12.

10. Tamotsou Shibutani and Kian M. Kwan, *Ethnic Stratification* (New York: Macmillan, 1965), pp. 116–34, 473–501; Milton N. Gordon, *Assimilation in American Life: The Role of Race, Religion and National Origins* (New York: Oxford University Press, 1964); Leonard Dinnerstein and David M. Reimers, *Ethnic Americans: A History of Immigration and Assimilation* (New York: Harper and Row, 1975).

11. This seems evident from the twenty-six-page pamphlet (*1900–1950: Golden Jubilee of Békévar*) honoring the fiftieth anniversary of the foundation of Békevár as symbolized by the church. The accounts given therein highlight the personal deeds of Highlander pioneers and their later feats without even mentioning others.

12. It is well known that the reconstruction of their home town church was crucial for peasant immigrants in general. "These people were anxious that religion do and mean . . . all that it had back there. . . . There were differences among the various groups in the ways this goal was reached, but the problem was always the same: how to transplant a way of religious life to a new environment" (Handlin, *The Uprooted*, pp. 121, 124). Specifically, "Protestants were the most energetic organizers, the Calvinists and other Reformed churches being the most strongly inspired by national-historical traditions. The very fact that the liturgies of these denominations were read in the mother tongue rendered it more imperative to organize the settlers within the ethnic framework" (Julia Puskás, "The Background and Its Role in Shaping Magyar Communities in the USA, 1880–1914," paper read at Symposium on East European Ethnicity, Bellagio, Italy, 1977). Komjáthy points out that Hungarians, just like other new immigrant church members, preferred brick buildings and that church-oriented social affairs became an integral part of their lives, substituting for the lost village way of life (Komjáthy, "Hungarian Reformed Church," pp. 23–24).

13. Vilmos Diószegi, *A sámánhit emlékei a magyar népi műveltségben*

(Shamanistic Remains in Hungarian Folk Culture) (Budapest: Akadémiai Kiadó, 1958).

14. Gyula Izsák, the folk poet and chronicler, was a leading member of the spiritualist circle and described in his book its activities in great detail. See *A Szamaritánus*. The early Baptist church building, the congregation, and Sunday school children are pictured in Jenő Ruzsa, *A kanadai magyarság története* (The History of Hungarians in Canada) (Toronto: privately published, 1940).

15. The well-established complex epic of many episodes had been passed on through oral transmission for more than seven decades. The oral versions were paralleled and standardized by longer and shorter written forms, created by inspired Highlanders enraptured with the glorious past. The longest literary version is perhaps that of Gyula Izsák (*A Szamaritánus*). Both those printed accounts published in Ruzsa, *A kanadai magyarság története*, pp. 124–30 and *Golden Jubilee*, not to mention numerous others, conform to the orally circulated prose and verse stories.

16. The original Hungarian script of this and the following poem contains many misspellings and lacks proper punctuation. My translation is as literal as possible, but in the interest of clarity I have added some punctuation.

17. The image of the farmer as "peculiarly favorable to virtue," living in "rustic plenty, remote from the contagion of popular vices," and as the owner of the soil and its cultivator "thus rendered honorable and independent," was proudly accepted by Highlanders. Henry Nash Smith, *Virgin Land: The American West as Symbol and Myth* (Cambridge: Harvard University Press, 1950), pp. 170–72.

18. Emigration of craftsmen, merchants, and small businessmen, according to Puskás, preceded the mass exodus of agricultural laborers from Hungary. See Julia Puskás, "Emigration from Hungary to the United States Before 1914," *Studia Historica* (Budapest: Akadémiai Kiadó, 1975), pp. 7–8.

19. Suspicion and mistrust of the minorities of the pre–World War I Kingdom of Hungary continues in general among Magyar immigrants in America.

20. This refers to the belief that young Canadian-born Presbyterian ministers (suspected of being of Slovak origin and therefore of arch-enemy ancestry), conspired to have the "pure and true" Hungarian ministers of the Kipling Presbyterian Church removed from office and replaced.

21. Melford E. Spiro, "The Acculturation of American Ethnic Groups," in *The USA as Anthropologists See It*, ed. Margaret Lantis (special issue of *American Anthropologist*, vol. 57 [1955], p. 1245.

22. The ideas developed in this study resulted from my research "The Image of the Old Country: Ethnicity of Hungarian-Americans as Expressed in Their Orientation to the Ancestral Heritage," conducted during 1977 and 1978 with a grant from the Social Science Research Council and the American Council of Learned Societies (ACLS). As a participant in the Symposium on East European Ethnicity (Bellagio, Italy, June, 1977), sponsored by ACLS, I presented the case of ethnicity as basis for social conflict and cleavage.

Czech-American Freethinkers
on the Great Plains, 1871–1914

Bruce M. Garver

The history of immigrants from continental Europe on the Great
Plains is beginning to receive from American historians the attention
that it deserves.[1] Of those immigrants, the Czechs were among the
most numerous and influential in Nebraska, Texas, Kansas, Oklahoma, and the Dakotas. In 1910 more than 125,000, or almost one
in every four American Czechs, resided in those states. These Czechs
were not only the first Slavs to settle in the region, but continued to
outnumber all other Slavic settlers by more than two to one.

Most Czechs came to the United States in search of individual
freedom and greater economic opportunity. Among all the nationalities that emigrated from Austria-Hungary, they ranked highest in the
percentage of skilled laborers and of literate adults—98.5 percent—
and perhaps most strongly resented authoritarian Habsburg rule. Of
the one in three Czechs who settled west of the Mississippi, approximately half became farmers, many on land obtained under terms of
the Homestead Act of 1862. Others became skilled laborers or businessmen or entered journalism or the professions. Most maintained
strong family ties, perhaps in part because Czech women immigrated
in numbers almost equal to those of men. In all of these and other
respects, Czechs resembled Scandinavians and Germans, the only
continental European immigrants who outnumbered them in the
Great Plains states and in Iowa.[2]

Czech farmers, workers, and intellectuals brought to America
more than intelligence, ambition, and a capacity for hard work. They
also brought a suspicion of duly constituted authority and a tradition of political radicalism, including varieties of socialism as well
as freethought and strongly civil libertarian views. This and the many
ideological conflicts within the Czech community are at times for-
gotten, perhaps in some cases deliberately, but more likely because
of the stability and conservatism that has characterized much of
Czech-American society during the past two generations.

147

What most distinguished Czechs from other immigrant groups in America was their having been the only group among whom a majority became freethinkers and severed all formal ties with organized religion. In the United States before 1914, approximately 40–45 percent of Czech immigrants remained practicing Roman Catholics. A slight majority, perhaps as many as 55 percent, called themselves freethinkers and stood apart from all churches, especially the Roman Catholic Church, to which most had once, if only nominally, belonged. Of this majority, at least one in six advocated some form of socialism.[3] Czech socialists became a powerful force in Chicago, Cleveland, and New York, the three cities where Czech workers settled in largest numbers, but exercised virtually no influence west of the Mississippi, not even in Omaha, the fourth among large American cities in numbers of Czech-speaking citizens.[4] One may largely discount the importance of Omaha's Czech Socialist Section "Karel Havlíček Borovský" as well as that of the few Czechs in North Dakota and Minnesota who drifted into farmer-labor politics. Czech Protestants, a minority of roughly 5 percent, were not numerous enough to have any moderating influence upon the conflict between freethinkers and Catholics and were themselves divided between Presbyterianism, Congregationalism, Methodism, the Moravian Church, and a group of wholly independent congregations.[5]

The history of Czech freethought, or for that matter Czech Catholicism or Protestantism, in the Great Plains states cannot be thoroughly or objectively written without studying the abundant Czech-language materials and without referring to Czechs elsewhere in the United States and in the Czech lands of Bohemia and Moravia. Not only did all ideological and social conflicts among Czech Americans obtain nation-wide, but most fraternal associations were organized on a national basis and maintained ties with compatriots abroad.

This article surveys the ideas, activities, and organizations of Czech freethinkers in the six Great Plains states during the heyday of freethought from 1871 to 1914. The former date marks the beginning of mass Czech immigration into these states and the founding of the first freethinking Czech-language weekly west of the Missouri, the *Pokrok západu* (Progress of the West) in Omaha. After 1914, enthusiasm for propagating freethought declined among American Czechs as many turned to the more pressing task of aiding the wartime struggle for Czechoslovak independence.

One must distinguish between a militant minority within Czech-American freethought and the broader movement of which it was a part, that is, between a militantly agnostic and sometimes atheistic minority, organized in local Free Communities from 1870 and after 1907 in a nation-wide Freethought Union, on the one hand, and a resolutely secular but generally tolerant majority on the other, whose adherents predominated in the Sokol and in fraternal and benevolent organizations. The militants thought that organized religion had no place in a free country, whereas the moderates worked primarily to maintain complete separation of church and state. The latter were resolutely anticlerical, whereas the former were antireligious as well. Both shared the liberal and anticlerical outlook characteristic of middle-class and agrarian Czech political parties in the Czech lands during the years 1860–1914.[6] In the United States, both movements sought to advance the material, intellectual, and physical welfare of Czech Americans and to encourage the use of Czech as well as the learning of English. As a rule, the moderate majority of freethinkers took an interest in ethical questions and were tolerant in matters of religion and willing to live and let live so far as Czech Catholics were concerned.

The intellectual origins of Czech freethought in Europe and America may be found in the European Enlightenment. Less powerful influences came later from French positivism, German materialism, and the theories of Charles Darwin. To reveal the varieties and subtleties of Czech freethought and its views of man, mind, and cosmos would require a broader paper of a different sort. Suffice it to say that freethinkers generally believed in human progress and expected reason and scientific inquiry to supplant belief in a supreme being. Their political objectives, first well expressed by Karel Havlíček and Vojta Náprstek, dated from the Revolution of 1848 in the Czech lands and included extension of civil liberties, absolute separation of church and state, introduction of universal suffrage, and gradual emancipation of women.[7] The popularity of freethought among Czechs in Europe and America owed as much to its advocacy of such programs as it did to Czech resentment of Roman Catholicism for having supported authoritarian Habsburg rule and having earlier helped crush Czech efforts at religious reform from John Hus through the Reformation.[8] The presence of many former Catholic seminarians or of priests like Ladimir Klácel (1802–82) among Czech apostles of freethought in America is in large part explained by their opposition to the reactionary policies of Pope Pius IX.

On the Great Plains and western prairies, the freethinking Czech-language press helped to serve as the mind and conscience of Czech America and to maintain some sense of solidarity and common purpose among Czechs residing in widely scattered communities. With Czechs as with other American pioneers, the establishment of local newspapers often preceded mass migration into a frontier area, as in the case of the *Pokrok západu*, founded in 1871 as the first Czech newspaper in Nebraska by Edward Rosewater, a Czech Jew and leading citizen of Omaha. Initially the Union Pacific and Burlington railways subsidized this paper by advertisements that urged Czech families to take up farming along or near rail lines west. Jan Rosický (1847–1910) edited the paper for Rosewater before buying it in 1877 and transforming it into a freethinking weekly. He subsequently built his National Printing Company (Národní tiskarna) into the largest Czech-language publishing house west of Chicago and won recognition as the leading Czech freethinker in the western United States.[9]

The rapid growth of the Czech-language press in the United States from 1860 to 1910 well illustrates the Czechs' desire to maintain their native tongue as well as to engage in vigorous political and intellectual debate. From 1900 through 1920, the circulation per issue of all Czech-language publications in the United States roughly equaled the American Czech population of one-half million. This press overwhelmingly endorsed freethought, with seven freethinking dailies as opposed to one Roman Catholic daily circulating by 1910. Chicago remained the greatest center of freethought publication from the establishment there of the daily *Svornost* in 1875 by František Zdrůbek (1842–1910) and August Geringer (1842–1930). Thanks largely to Rosický's National Printing Company, Omaha soon became the leading Czech-language publishing and intellectual center for western Iowa and Minnesota as well as the plains states north of Texas. Among the many newspapers published by National Printing were the fourteen that it distributed exclusively outside of Nebraska. Each carried articles written in Omaha as well as in the town or city from which that paper ostensibly came. To a greater extent than freethinking publishers in Chicago and New York, Rosický emphasized the publication of books and newspapers on practical subjects. His weekly *Hospodář* (The Husbandman) reached a circulation of almost thirty thousand, thereby becoming the world's largest Czech-language newspaper devoted primarily to agriculture.[10]

In the Great Plains states, as elsewhere in Czech America, the freethinking Czech press advanced hand in hand with business enterprise and the various Czech fraternal and benevolent associations. Owners or editors of freethinking Czech journals, like Omahans Jan

Rosický and Stanislav Šerpán, were often prosperous businessmen as well as leaders in their city and Czech community. Like former Omahan Tomáš Čapek, lawyer and founder-president of the Bank of Europe in New York, leading Czech-American publishers and civic leaders prided themselves on being self-made men. This perhaps best reveals the compatibility between the aspirations of Czech freethinkers and those of middle-class Americans of the same era.

On the prairies and Great Plains of America, Czechs, like other immigrants, were impressed by the abundance of free and fertile land, the sensation of almost infinite space, and the severity of the weather. West of the 99th meridian, Czech farmers had to adopt dry-farming methods, but nothing suggests that having done so in any way affected their political or religious views. Pioneer Czech settlers told of the joys and hardships of making a new home in the New World while Czech-American writers portrayed the distinctive beauty of the western prairies in different times and places. Foremost among such works are *Rodina Petra Běla*, Václav Alois Jung's novel about Nebraska farm life, and the collection of poems *Z prerie* by Jan Štěpán Brož, a Catholic priest in Nebraska and author of books on American Indian life. Perhaps the best-known poem on Czech pioneers west of the Missouri is that by Bartoš Bittner (1861–1912), freethinking Czech American satirist and editor of the magazine *Šotek* (The Imp) in Chicago:

> Brave pioneers, view now what was that wilderness
> Into which you came homesick and with empty hands!
> From "Father of Waters" to the Rockies' cloudy crest,
> Prosperity, like sweet streams, flows over prairie lands.
>
> Success so crowns your harsh, back-breaking labor there
> That none begrudge your having viewed with joyful pride
> How skillful hands gave works a countenance quite fair.
> Thus we wish you well: may success with you abide![11]

One may properly speak of large concentrations of Czech Americans in the Great Plains states but not in the Great Plains proper. In 1910, the 5,308 Czech residents of Montana, Wyoming, Colorado, and New Mexico constituted less than 1 percent of the American Czech population. In the six Great Plains states to the east, no more than 10,000, or 8 percent, of all Czechs lived west of the 100th meridian and most of these lived in fourteen counties in the five states north of Texas.[12]

The six Great Plains states in 1920 held 141,742, or 22.8 percent, of the Czech-speaking population of the United States, compared to 125,140, or 23.6 percent, in 1910. Of the latter, 40.3 percent lived in Nebraska, 32.5 percent in Texas, and 27.2 percent in the other four states. Omaha, with 11,416 Czech inhabitants in 1920, was the fifth largest Czech city in the United States and the third largest outside of metropolitan Chicago. Elsewhere in the Great Plains states, Czechs lived almost exclusively on farms or in small towns, with no more than 700 Czechs residing in any city over 25,000 except Omaha. After the turn of the century, more than 53 percent of all Czechs in the five states north of Texas were concentrated in twelve counties, all but one of which were prodominantly rural. And almost three-quarters of the Czech settlers in Texas inhabited the east-central part of the state within a triangular area marked by Waco, Beeville, and Galveston.

In Nebraska, more than 55 percent of all Czechs lived in the five eastern counties of Douglas, Saunders, Butler, Colfax, and Saline. The latter three counties had a higher percentage of Czech inhabitants than any other counties in the United States, with Czechs comprising half the total population in Colfax County and more than one-third in Butler and Saline counties. In these five counties and adjacent Fillmore County, some towns like Wilber, Milligan, Clarkson, Prague, Bruno, Dwight, and Abie have remained almost entirely Czech.[13] In all but Saunders County, Czech freethinkers outnumbered Czech Roman Catholics; and in each of the six counties, Czech Protestants maintained at least one congregation. Large numbers of Czech Jews settled only in Omaha.[14]

Half of the 10,000 Czechs residing in Kansas after the turn of the century lived in Republic and Ellsworth counties. Roughly another quarter lived in the four northern counties of Brown, Marshall, Washington, and Decatur, which, like Republic County, lay along the Nebraska state line. Freethinking Czechs outnumbered Czech Roman Catholics throughout Kansas, especially in Ellsworth and Wilson counties. Narka, in the latter county, had no church whatsoever as late as 1910; and in Caldwell, near the Oklahoma line, militant freethinkers organized the only Free Community in the state.[15]

The majority of Czechs living in the Dakotas after the turn of the century were likewise concentrated in a few counties. Ninety percent of the 9,831 Czechs of South Dakota in 1910 lived in five counties in the southeastern part of the state—Yankton, Bon Homme, Charles Mix, Gregory, and Brule, with 60 percent in the first two alone. Among these Czechs, freethinkers almost equaled Roman Catholics in number and looked primarily to nearby Omaha for intellectual leadership. North Dakota and Texas were the only Great Plains states in which Czech Roman Catholics outnumbered Czech freethinkers and Protestants combined. Of the 7,167 Czechs in North Dakota in 1910, more than two-thirds embraced Catholicism and roughly one-third lived in Walsh County in the northeastern corner of the state.[16]

Oklahoma was the only state at the turn of the century to which more Czechs came from other American states than from Bohemia or Moravia. Czechs, numbering 5,581 by 1910, had first settled after 1889 in the central part of the state, west of what was until 1907 Indian Territory. The majority, who came from freethinking communities elsewhere, promptly established fraternal and benevolent societies in places like Perry and Oklahoma City.[17]

Czech freethought in the Great Plains states differed not at all in theory or in practice from that elsewhere in the United States but was proportionally stronger in Nebraska, Kansas, Oklahoma, and South Dakota than anywhere else except Illinois, New York, and Iowa. In its organization, freethought in Nebraska, Kansas, Oklahoma, and the Dakotas was identical to that in Iowa and Minnesota, primarily because in these states after 1897 the Western Bohemian Fraternal Association (WBFA) was the principal Czech fraternal and benevolent society. Texas differed from the five states to the north not only in its greater numbers of Moravian Czech and Czech Roman Catholic inhabitants but in its largely autonomous freethought organization founded in 1898, the Slavic Benevolent Order of the State of Texas.[18] Its lodges, like those of the Western Bohemian Fraternal Association, had seceded from the parent Czecho-Slavonic Benevolent Society in order to obtain lower life insurance premiums and admit women equally with men. The establishment of the order and of regional Roman Catholic Czech organizations in Texas may in part be explained by the prevalence there of Moravian as opposed to Bohemian Czechs and in part by its distance from Chicago and eastern Nebraska, the nearest large centers of Czech population.

As one would expect in a predominantly agricultural region, roughly half of all rank-and-file freethinkers lived on farms. In fact as many as one-third of all members and one-half of all male members of the Western Bohemian Fraternal Association appear to have been farmers at the turn of the century. This is revealed by a survey of the occupations of the 718 members who died during the five years ending July 6, 1917. Below are listed all the occupations pursued by more than one percent of the deceased members, most of whom were immigrants from Bohemia. Among the ninety-two whose forty occupations can be identified, one finds two doctors, one banker, one editor, and three professional musicians.

Occupations of Deceased Members of the WBFA, July 1912–July 1917[19]

Number	Occupation	Percent of Total
233	Farmers	32.5
226	Housewives	31.5
67	Workers	9.3
43	Self-employed businessmen	6.0
20	Saloonkeepers	2.8
11	Carpenters and joiners	1.5
9	Tailors	1.3
8	Teamsters	1.1
92	Forty different occupations	12.3
9	Occupation unidentified	1.3
718		100.0

The division between Czech freethinkers and Catholics on the Great Plains and western prairies, as elsewhere in the United States, cut across class and occupational lines. The European experience appears to have most determined the ideological outlook of Czech immigrants because most adults arrived either devoutly Catholic or with a predilection for freethought. Such division resembled that among other immigrant groups such as the Germans, among whom Catholics, Lutherans, Calvinists, Methodists, and a few freethinkers differed markedly.

The division between Czech freethinkers and Czech Roman Catholics appears to have little affected allegiance to political parties among Czech Americans. Like most American Catholics, Czechs of that faith more often supported Democratic than Republican candidates. Virtually all Czechs opposed avowedly prohibitionist candidates. East of the Mississippi and north of Democratic Texas and Oklahoma, Czech freethinkers appear to have supported Republican and Democratic candidates in approximately equal numbers and backed third parties at times when many other Americans did so, clearly indicating that most Czech Americans tried to advance their own interests without pledging firm allegiance to either of the two large parties. From 1870 to 1890, freethinking Nebraska Czechs usually endorsed the Republican party, largely because it had championed civil liberties and public schools and subsidized the *Pokrok západu* and other freethinking Czech-language newspapers. Beginning in the 1890s in Omaha and as early as the 1880s in the larger Czech settlements of Saline, Saunders, and Butler counties, Czech free-thinkers voted Democratic almost as often as they voted Republican and in some areas ran candidates on Populist or independent slates. In 1890, Tomáš Čapek of Omaha became the first Czech freethinker to win election as a Democrat to the Nebraska House of Representatives and in doing so defeated a Republican endorsed by his colleague and former employer Jan Rosický. Shifts in party allegiance often corresponded to state or local trends and appear to have been based more often on political or economic issues than on personal rivalry, indicating that the initial inclination of freethought toward Republicanism diminished once Czech Americans discovered how to make the two-party system work to their own advantage.[20]

Most Czech-American freethinkers of the period 1871–1914 were conscious of belonging to a like-minded nation-wide community. Many also looked at important questions of the day in an international context and communicated regularly with friends and relatives in the homelands of Bohemia and Moravia. Not only did ideas and the printed word circulate rapidly but leading freethinkers moved about frequently. For example, among those who had worked in Omaha but made their greatest reputation elsewhere were Tomáš Čapek in New York, František Zdrůbek in Chicago, and Václav A. Jung in Prague. Of course, Czech Roman Catholic and Protestant clergymen in America likewise participated in the national and to a lesser extent international undertakings of their churches.[21]

Czech-American freethinkers in the Great Plains states and elsewhere established many voluntary associations that, much like immigrant churches or American fraternal orders, provided fellowship and mutual protection from childhood to the grave. These Czech associations differed from those of other immigrants primarily in the extent to which they endorsed freethought as opposed to some form of organized religion. All were resolutely secular and sought to maintain Czech language and culture while helping members become productive and prosperous American citizens. These associations were of five basic types: educational and cultural societies, the Sokol organization, fraternal and benevolent orders, cemetery associations, and, finally, the Free Congregations (Svobodné obce) for outspoken atheists and agnostics that in 1907 helped organize the national Freethought Union (Svaz svoʋodomyslných). The first four types represented broadly based and generally tolerant freethought, whereas the fifth constituted the militant wing of that movement. Since each type of association assumed specific tasks, the same people often served several associations as leaders or members. In 1920, the national membership in all freethought associations, excluding Free Congregations, totaled 112,881, more than twice that in comparable Roman Catholic organizations. An almost identical ratio obtained in the central Great Plains states, with Nebraska, for example, in 1926 having 10,380 members in freethinking societies, excluding cemetery associations, as opposed to 5,420 in the corresponding Catholic institutions. All organizations, except fraternal and benevolent orders that addressed specifically American circumstances, had exact or similar counterparts among those associations that Czechs had established in Bohemia and Moravia upon the advent of constitutional rule in 1860.[22]

Among the most important freethinking educational and cultural societies were the Czech-language Free Schools (Svobodné školy) that supplemented the public school curriculum. The number of these schools in Nebraska alone reached sixteen after the turn of the century, the first having been established at Crete in 1873. Free School teachers, for the most part unpaid or poorly paid volunteers, taught Czech language, history, and literature to all grades and tried, especially among advanced students, to develop critical minds and rational judgment. Free Congregations in Nebraska and South Dakota and elsewhere helped subsidize the publication in Chicago of the monthly *Svobodná škola* (The Free School), "an illustrated magazine for educating Czech youth in the spirit of freethought." Typical issues that circulated in up to five thousand copies presented everything from nursery rhymes to selections from Czech literary classics and included articles on national heroes like Hus and Komenský and on advances in science and technology. Editorials compared religion unfavorably with freethought, as did the polemical poem "Nature or God" of May 1902. The extent to which this magazine helped perpetuate freethought in small communities on the Great Plains and western prairies may best be gauged by noting that 38.5 percent of its correspondents reported from five Great Plains states.[23]

As a rule, every Free School in the Great Plains states received some support from the nearest lodge of the Western Bohemian Fraternal Association and presented courses designed to supplement the American public school curriculum, which all freethinkers preferred to that of parochial schools of any faith. The fact that organizations like the YMCA and YWCA as well as extracurricular public school activities attracted Czech youth nonetheless gave some freethinkers cause for alarm, primarily because they believed such attractions to be so thoroughly permeated by Protestant ideals and practices that freethought among Czech youth might be impaired: "In the old country, we fought a pure and simple fight against Roman Catholicism. In the United States, we must struggle against all sorts of churches, many of which do not enunciate their goals and policies so straightforwardly as do the Catholics. The dangers to Freethought are thus less readily apparent."[24]

Of all the associations organized by Czech freethinkers, the Sokol with its colorful uniforms and mass gymnastics demonstrations provided the most impressive display of Czech discipline and solidarity. After its founding in Prague in 1862, this patriotic and gymnastics society became the most popular association among Czechs in the Czech lands. The Sokol encouraged intellectual as well as physical fitness and the development of a "sound mind in a sound body" in accordance with the wishes of its founder, Miroslav Tyrš, a classicist, art critic, and Czech patriot.

Sokol ideas and organization spread swiftly among Czechs in America as well as in Europe.[25] Within three years of the Sokol's advent in Prague, Czechs in St. Louis established the first Sokol unit in the United States. In 1874, Czechs in Crete, Nebraska, set up the first unit west of the Missouri River. Sokol Omaha became in 1877 the thirteenth unit of a national Sokol network that would by 1919 grow to 120 units and 10,302 members. Women's auxiliaries soon appeared, with the Women's Sokol Unit of Omaha in 1889 being one of the first. In 1897, a nation-wide split developed between units adhering to the parent National Sokol Union and those seceding to establish the District Fügner-Tyrš. The two groups reunited in 1917 to form the present American Sokol Organization. Within it, Omaha became the administrative center of the Western Sokol Organization, which has included units in Nebraska, Kansas, Iowa, Minnesota, and the Dakotas and whose goals and programs have differed little from those of other American Sokol units. Efforts by the Roman Catholic Church to promote its own Catholic Sokol by way of competition met with no more success than did attempts by Czech workingmen to maintain independent workers' Sokol organizations before the turn of the century. West of the Missouri, no workers' Sokol and few branches of the Catholic Sokol ever appeared.

Omaha freethinkers František Jelen, Šimon Rokůsek, and Josef Mík were by all accounts among the outstanding Sokol leaders in the Great Plains states around the turn of the century. Jelen took the lead in founding Sokol Omaha in 1877, Rokůsek in building it up, while Mík became "the best-known Czech in America" because as stationmaster of the Burlington depot in Omaha he had for decades met most arriving and departing passengers and greeted virtually every Czech visitor to the city.[26]

Voluntary fraternal and benevolent associations were the backbone of Czech freethought on the Great Plains and western prairies as elsewhere in the United States. As their name implies, they provided mutual life and health insurance of various types. More important, they provided many benefits to Czechs that church-related organizations provided to immigrants, like Scandinavians or Germans, who were of a more religious frame of mind. Fellowship, entertainment, and opportunities for community service were as important to Czechs as to other pioneer settlers west of the Missouri in overcoming physical and psychological isolation and advancing business or professional interests. Some organization and solidarity among Czechs was essential if the Czech language and culture were to survive in America and if Czechs were to prosper and establish some degree of fiscal independence. Surplus funds saved by the associations financed charitable and educational activities, including drama and operas in Czech. In the Great Plains states, such events customarily took place in halls of local WBFA lodges, which, especially in smaller towns, often provided a meeting place for any local Free School, Sokol, or cemetery association.

Since a majority of Czech adults in many such small towns belonged to the local WBFA lodge, it often served as the base from which Czechs organized to participate in municipal, county, and state politics. Lodge activities helped prepare many Czechs for participation in American public life, with popular leaders of local lodges at times winning nomination to municipal, county, or state office. The fact that the association and its lodges encouraged self-help and individual initiative as well as group solidarity undoubtedly accelerated the entry of Czech Americans into positions of responsibility in American society.

All freethinking Czech fraternal and benevolent societies grew out of the Czecho-Slavonic Benevolent Society (Česko-Slovanský Podpourjící Spolek), founded in St. Louis in 1854 and the first organization of its type in the United States.[27] Czechs established lodges of this society throughout America, including the Great Plains states after 1870. Czech Catholics and Czech socialists ultimately established comparable benevolent organizations that attracted, respectively, about two-fifths and one-sixth as many members.

Czech Protestants, too few in number to support an autonomous society of the same type, either joined those of Czech freethought or of American Protestant denominations.

Within a generation, dissident Czech freethinkers set up three types of associations that competed directly with the Czecho-Slavonic Benevolent Society: those organized by men to complement or challenge the society, those founded by and for women, and the two formed by seceding western lodges of the society in 1897 and 1898—respectively, the Western Bohemian Fraternal Association and the Slavonic Benevolent Order of the State of Texas. The first type included four small competitors of the Czecho-Slavonic Benevolent Society that arose during the later nineteenth century and merged with the society in 1933 to form the still active Czechoslovak Society of America—the Unity of Taborites (1880), the Czecho-Slavonic Fraternal Benevolent Union (1884), the Czech-American Foresters (1892), and the Czecho-Slavonic Union (1899). Neither these nor the small Czech-American Union of 1910 ever acquired much influence in the Great Plains states.

Freethinking Czech women began in the 1870s to establish their own benevolent orders, primarily because the Czecho-Slavonic Benevolent Society discriminated against women by admitting to membership only the wives of members and then by limiting the amount of insurance any wife might buy. The number and variety of such orders testifies to the imagination and resourcefulness of freethinking women and to the fact that the society had abridged in practice much of what freethought represented in theory. The first and largest women's order was the Unity of Czech Women (Jednota Českých Dam), established in Chicago in 1870. It organized lodges throughout Czech-speaking America, with the first west of the Missouri coming to Wilber, Nebraska, in 1885. Represented at the Eighth National Congress of the Unity in August 1913 were 142 lodges with a total of some 23,000 members.[28] The Sisterly Benevolent Society (Sesterská Podporující Jednota), founded in Cleveland in 1890, exercised little influence west of Chicago, exceptions being two lodges in Omaha and one in Wilber. Its membership peaked at 12,000 in the early 1920s. Three small orders of slight importance in the West and whose combined membership seldom exceeded 9,000 were the Union of Patriotic Czech Women (Jednota Českých Vlastenek), the Association of Czech-American Women (Sdružení Česko-Amerických Dam), and the Czecho-Slavonic Benevolent Societies for Women (Česko-Slovanské Podporující Dámské Spolky).

The secession of western lodges of the Czecho-Slavonic Benevolent Society in 1897 and 1898 followed disputes over preferential insurance rates and whether or not to admit women on the same basis as men. The western lodges favored such admission and the establishment of a large contingency fund and wanted to obtain lower rates for younger than for older members and for western than for eastern lodges, given the generally better health of the predominantly rural western members. After the Benevolent Society at its St. Paul convention of 1896 rejected reform despite western threats of secession, a vast majority of the western lodges, led by Jan Rosický, decided to go it alone. On February 9–11, 1897, in Omaha, representatives from forty-nine lodges representing 1,259 members in twelve western states decided to establish themselves on July 4 of that year as the wholly independent Western Bohemian Fraternal Association (Západní Česká Bratrská Jednota). Jan Rosický served as the first editor of its journal, *Bratrský věstník* (The Fraternal Herald), until he died in 1910. Two years later Stanislav Šerpán succeeded F. J. Kvíták, Rosický's successor, and remained editor until his death in 1940. The Western Bohemian Fraternal Association had 7,085 members in Nebraska by 1926 and a national membership that grew from 21,149 in November 1918 to 39,280 in 381 lodges by 1938.[29] Representatives from the Texas lodges of the Czecho-Slavonic Benevolent Society met at La Grange, Texas, in June of 1898 to set up the Slavonic Benevolent Order of the State of Texas (Slovanská Podporující Jednota státu Texas), an organization analogous in most respects to the Western Association except in its later giving only lukewarm support to the Freethought Union and tardy support to the cause of Czechoslovak independence.

Freethinking Czechs in most towns and cities organized and managed their own Czech national cemeteries. In Chicago in 1877, freethinkers founded the largest if not the first of these, the Bohemian National Cemetery. The larger Czech Catholic parishes established cemeteries of their own, as did several of the few Czech Protestant congregations. By 1920, in Nebraska alone, Czech freethinkers maintained thirty cemeteries, Czech Catholics twenty-two, and Czech Protestants three. Few freethinkers believed in the immortality of the soul, and the care that they lavished on their many cemeteries may in part have reflected this. Their view of death is well expressed by the inscription above the main gate to the Czecho-Slavonic National Cemetery in Wilber, Nebraska: "What you are, we were—what we are, you shall be." Freethinkers in Chicago, who strongly advocated cremation, founded in 1886 the Society for the

Cremation of the Dead (Společnost pro spalování mrtvol) and built by 1914 through public subscription the first Czech crematorium in the world. This fad aroused little support among Czech-American freethinkers elsewhere, primarily because smaller Czech communities, like most of those in the Great Plains states, could not afford to build anything so expensive as a crematorium.

The popularity of freethought among Czech Americans in the Great Plains and upper Middle West was best indicated by the fact that next to Chicago Czechs they were the principal supporters of the national Freethought Union from its founding in Chicago in June 1907 until 1917. Its leaders included Jan Rosický and his daughters from Omaha and Anna Kovandová from Table Rock, Nebraska. Widespread rural support for militant freethought was revealed by the presence of Czechs from the agrarian upper Missouri and Mississippi valleys among the twenty Free Congregations represented at the First Freethought Congress of June 1907. Fourteen of the twenty, or 70 percent of those represented, came from states where the Western Bohemian Fraternal Association was the principal benevolent society; one other Free Congregation came from Texas. Comparable figures for the lodges of fraternal and benevolent societies represented at the Congress are 28.4 percent and 2 percent, respectively, and for the monetary value of individual contributions a total of 52.1 and 10.4 percent.[30]

Czech-American freethinkers in the early twentieth century established national representative organizations of two sorts. The first aimed to advance freethought and facilitate cooperation among the Free Communities and like-minded associations. The second sought to mobilize the press and fraternal and benevolent societies with a view to publicizing and aiding Czech national and liberal parties in Bohemia and Moravia. In each case, freethinking Czechs, including many from the Great Plains states, succeeded after earlier attempts had failed. In the first instance, the Freethought Union fulfilled all of its objectives from 1907 until the outbreak of World War I.

The National Committee of American Czechs (Národní výbor Čechů amerických), established in Chicago in 1891, was the first of three attempts at making a national organization of the second sort. Executives of the Czecho-Slavonic Benevolent Society and prominent freethinkers like Karel Jonáš and Tomáš Čapek led in founding the National Committee and electing Lev J. Palda, a moderate socialist, as its first president and Jan Rosický of Omaha as its second. Before disbanding in 1895, the committee initiated lasting ties between prominent freethinking Czech Americans and leaders of the liberal Young Czech party in Prague shortly after that party's landslide victory in the 1891 Reichsrat elections. This is reflected in letters from Palda and Rosický to the party's chairman, Emanuel Engel.[31] In September 1892, at its new Omaha headquarters, the committee began publishing the *Bohemian Voice*, the first periodical in English published by Czechs for native-born Americans. Until its demise in November 1894, its editors, Tomáš Čapek and J. J. Kral, informed American readers of the aims and problems of Czechs in Austria-Hungary, thus providing a prototype two decades later for English-language propaganda advocating Czechoslovak independence.[32]

The committee, despite its short life, revealed shortcomings that were overcome by two successive and successful Czech-American national organizations of the early twentieth century. The first of these, the Czech-American Press Bureau (Českoamerická tisková kancelář), founded in Chicago in December 1909 at the behest of August Geringer, Jan Rosický, and Jaroslav E. S. Vojan, encouraged not only cooperation among freethinking editors in America but the establishment of closer commercial and cultural ties between Czech Americans and Czechs abroad. Its successor, the Bohemian National Alliance (Česká Národní Sdružení), was founded by freethinkers and socialists in Chicago on September 25, 1914, and in 1915 began to coordinate all Czech-American efforts on behalf of the struggle for Czechoslovak independence led by T. G. Masaryk and the Czechoslovak National Council (Československá národní rada) in western Europe. The National Alliance expanded to over 350 branches within four years, enlisting the support of most Czech American freethinkers, socialists, and Protestants almost immediately, that of Czechs from Texas and Cleveland by 1916, and that of most Czech-American Catholics after July 4, 1917. The National Alliance helped British intelligence from 1915 on and after April 16, 1917, enthusiastically supported the American war effort, recognizing that the American national interest as well as the achievement of Czechoslovak independence required the defeat of the Central Powers.[33]

Freethinking Czechs in the five northern Great Plains states were among the first and most loyal supporters of the Bohemian National Alliance. In fact, Czechs in Omaha, led by Jan Janák and Stanislav Šerpán, initiated on September 12, 1914, the first public subscription of funds to support any attempt Czechs in Bohemia and Moravia might make to overthrow the Hapsburgs.[34] How Czechs west of the

Missouri gave generously of time and money to help achieve Czechoslovak independence is well chronicled and beyond the scope of this paper.

The mainline organizations and press of Czech-American freethought took pride in their contribution to the Allied victory and to the winning of Czechoslovak independence. Unlike them, the militant freethought of "believing unbelievers" did not long survive the World War as an important force in Czech-American life. By the early twenties, Free Congregations had disbanded in the Great Plains states for the same reasons that membership in congregations elsewhere declined precipitously. Jaroslav E. S. Vojan lamented this development in addressing the Seventh Congress of the Freethought Union in Chicago on May 8–10, 1926: "Nebraska, the historic stamping ground of Jan Rosický, has today not even the tiniest Freethought movement. All is quiet in Omaha, Wilber, Schuyler, and Clarkson. . . . Oklahoma is silent. . . . Thus can one proceed from state to state, to Connecticut, Michigan, Minnesota, Missouri, Kansas, and both Dakotas."[35]

Foremost among the causes of this decline appears to have been the growing acculturation of American Czechs during the 1920s, a process in part attributable to the immigration law of 1925, which drastically reduced what had been an annual influx of three thousand to five thousand Czechs. Militant freethinkers also had the dubious satisfaction of seeing participation in Free Congregations diminish for the same reasons that church attendance was declining. New amusements like cinema and automobiles proved more attractive to youth than did serious intellectual discussion of the sort that Free Congregations liked to provide. A young woman attending one of Vojan's lectures on Darwinism well expressed this attitude when she impatiently asked, "When is he going to stop talking about all those monkeys?"[36] As youth withdrew to other pleasures and fewer immigrant youth arrived, the average age in Free Congregations climbed rapidly, with the result that freethought became even less attractive to younger persons.

The changing intellectual atmosphere of the postwar era also retarded the spread of freethought among the educated. Quantum theory and the theory of relativity in physics as well as Freudian psychology had helped undermine the authority of the scientific premises upon which much of freethought had been based. Reason no longer appeared to be all-powerful, and positivism was long dead as an intellectual force.

In opposing nativist efforts to restrict immigration, some Czech-American leaders deliberately downplayed Czech radical and free-thinking traditions in order to present the most "American" face possible to lawmakers and the general public. American-born Czechs who joined American fraternal orders like the Elks or the Odd Fellows discovered that outspoken freethinkers were given the cold shoulder. Attempts by Chicago freethinkers to take on Protestantism as well as Roman Catholicism proved to be increasingly unproductive. That Czech-American Protestants had long been disturbed by the deportment of unchurched freethinkers is evident in remarks by the pastor of Omaha's Czech Presbyterian Church in 1900: "Here the majority of Czechs are indifferent to religion or are nonbelievers. Above all, they believe in formal dancing, picnics, and inordinate drinking. Even the youngsters of such folk are being introduced to a life whose only pleasures are dancing and alcoholic beverages. We will have to bear witness here a long time before our fellow countrymen learn that it is better to serve the Lord than in indulge in worldly delights."[37]

Czech-American freethought had grown primarily out of conditions of authoritarian government and a state church in Bohemia and Moravia. Conditions in the homelands improved markedly after 1918 with the advent of a democratic Czechoslovak Republic, social and land reform, and a separation of church and state ultimately accepted by the Vatican. Under such circumstances, relationships between Czech-American freethinkers and Catholics were bound to improve, especially since most of the latter had in the summer of 1917 endorsed Czechoslovak independence.

Meanwhile, both the Free Congregation of Chicago and the Free-thought Union emerged from the World War with their reputation for Czech patriotism somewhat tarnished. František Iška, Zdrůbek's successor as speaker of the Congregation and chairman of the Union, had after 1914 in the journal *Vesmír* (Universe) taken a pro-Habsburg line and denounced the leaders and goals of the struggle for Czechoslovak independence. After the *Providence Journal* and *Chicago Record Herald* in February 1916 revealed him to be a paid agent of the Austro-Hungarian government, he was forced to resign his offices. Although spokesmen of the Union like Jaroslav E. S. Vojan loyally served the Bohemian National Alliance, Iška's sellout did irreparable damage to militant freethought.[38]

Moreover, President-Liberator T. G. Masaryk, hero to Czechs and Czech Americans alike, had long perspicaciously criticized militant freethought from a moral perspective, and reached a wide audience not only in public lectures in Boston and Chicago in 1907 but in a 1902 article based on his travels in America.[39] Similar views appeared in his private correspondence, including this statement of September 1, 1913, to Dr. Henry J. John of Cleveland: "Our people are lacking the essential element of life—spirituality. They have cast off religion and church organization but seek no substitute for these in new forms of religion or even in moral endeavors. They have economic interests and some interest in politics, though nothing very profound—and that's all. Only our socialists have tenacity and discipline, whereas our liberals—'freethinkers'—are without principles. We must get them to realize this so that they begin searching for something."[40]

Czech freethinkers helped build up the economy and society of the Great Plains states during the late nineteenth and early twentieth centuries while powerfully influencing the development of Czech-American society generally. That a majority of Czechs on the Great Plains and western prairies adhered to freethought instead of to some organized religion was the most important difference between Czechs and other continental European immigrants in the area and undoubtedly facilitated Czech participation in public life.

That most Czech freethinkers, regardless of class or ideological orientation, so long maintained their native language and distinctive fraternal organizations is one of several examples of how men, institutions, and ideas more profoundly shaped the society of the Great Plains states than did the mere physical environment. So does the fact that the acculturation of Czech Americans proceeded rapidly in part because they voluntarily participated in all aspects of American life. Moreover, the story of the Czech freethinkers lends weight to the argument that the Great Plains states cannot be well understood apart from the rest of the United States and that their history since 1865 is very much that of those continental European immigrants who came to account for almost half of the inhabitants of these states.

Notes

1. Frederick C. Luebke, "Ethnic Group Settlement on the Great Plains," *Western Historical Quarterly* 8, no. 4 (October 1977): 405–30, surveys the topic and pertinent literature. For critically evaluating an earlier draft of this chapter I am indebted to my colleagues Karel Bicha, Harl Dalstrom, and Joseph Svoboda.

I thank the following persons for the loan of materials otherwise unavailable: Mrs. Donald Bucknam, Sister Marilyn Graskowiak, Professor Victor Greene, Mr. Lad E. Kostel, and Mrs. Edgar Thompson.

2. The best general surveys are Tomáš Čapek, *The Čechs [Bohemians] in America* (Boston: Houghton Mifflin, 1920), and his more critical and complete *Naše Amerika* (Prague: Orbis, 1926). Others include Francis Dvornik, *Czech Contributions to the Growth of the United States* (Cleveland: Benedictine Press, 1957); Jan Habenicht, *Dějiny Čechů amerických* (St. Louis: "Hlas," 1910), from a Catholic perspective; and essays in Miloslav Rechcigl, Jr., ed., *The Czechoslovak Contribution to World Culture* (The Hague: Mouton, 1964), pp. 493–554; and Vlasta Vraz, ed., *Panorama: A Historical Review of Czechs and Slovaks in the United States of America* (Cicero, Ill.: Czechoslovak National Council, 1970). The best work on one state is Růžena Rosická, *Dějiny Čechů v Nebrasce* (Omaha: Czech Historical Club of Nebraska, 1928), or its English version, Rose Rosický, *A History of the Czechs [Bohemians] in Nebraska* (Omaha: Czech Historical Club of Nebraska, 1929). On religion among Czech immigrants, especially those from working-class families in Chicago, see Josef J. Barton, "Religion and Cultural Change in Czech Immigrant Communities, 1850–1920," in *Immigrants and Religion in Urban America*, ed. Randall Miller and Thomas Marzik (Philadelphia: Temple University Press, 1977), pp. 3–24.

3. Estimates are based on Stanislav Klíma, *Čechové a Slováci za hranicemi* (Prague: J. Otto, 1925), pp. 214–16; and Čapek, *The Čechs*, pp. 263–64.

4. Works on Czech socialism in America include Josef Polišenský, ed., *Začiatky českej a slovenskij emigrácie do USA v obdobi I. internacionály* (Bratislava: V.S.A.V., 1970); František Soukup, *Amerika: řada obrazů amerického života* (Prague: "Právo Lidu," 1912); Vraz, *Panorama*, pp. 85–89; and Joseph Chada, "A Survey of Radicalism in the Bohemian-American Community," MS, 1954, University of Chicago Library.

5. The most complete survey of Czech-American Protestantism is Vilém Šiller, Václav Průcha, et al., *Památník Českých Evanjelických církví ve Spojených Státech* (Chicago: "Křesťanský Posel," 1900).

6. On the Czech lands, see Bruce M. Garver, *The Young Czech Party, 1874–1901: The Emergence of a Multi-Party System* (New Haven, Conn.: Yale University Press, 1978).

7. On Havlíček and Náprstek, see T. G. Masaryk, *Americké přednášky*, 2d ed. (Prague: Čin, 1929), pp. 9–23; and Čapek, *Naše Amerika*, pp. 251–53.

8. Josef Falta, *Sto let Svobodné obce v Chicagu* (Cicero, Ill.: Svobodná obec, 1970); Karel Bicha, "Settling Accounts with an Old Adversary: The Decatholicization of Czech Immigrants in America," *Social History* 4, no. 8 (November 1972), pp. 45–60; Joseph Svoboda, "Czechs: The Love of Liberty," in Paul A. Olson, et al., *Broken Hoops and Plains People* (Lincoln: Nebraska Curriculum Development Center, 1976), pp. 153–91 and an unpublished paper of 1977, "Religion and the Czechs on the Great Plains."

9. Tomáš Čapek, *Moje Amerika* (Prague: F. Borový, 1934), pp. 84–85; and Rosická, *Dějiny Čechů*, pp. 21–22.

10. The best survey of this press remains Tomáš Čapek's encyclopedic and analytical *Padesat let českého tisku v Americe* (New York: Bank of Europe, 1911).

Later developments are covered by František Štědronský, *Zahraniční krajanské noviny, časopisy a kalendáře do roku 1958* (Prague: Národní Knihovná, 1958), and Vojtěch Nevlud-Duben, *The Czech and Slovak Periodical Press outside Czechoslovakia* (Washington, D.C.: S.V.U., 1962).

11. My translation from Rosická, *Dějiny Čechů*, p. 24.

12. All data in this section, unless otherwise indicated, are from the *1920 U.S. Census*, vol. 2, tables 11 and 14, pp. 1006, 1030–31; Čapek, *Naše Amerika*, pp. 625–36; and Habenicht, *Dějiny*, pp. 129, 375–88.

13. On Milligan, see Robert I. Kutak, *The Story of a Bohemian-American Village* (Louisville, Ky.: Standard Printing Co., 1933).

14. The best source on Nebraska remains Rosická, *Dějiny Čechů*, or its English translation. See also Vladimír Kučera and Alfréd Nováček, eds., *Czech Contributions to the Progress of Nebraska* (Ord, Nebr.: n.p., 1976).

15. Habenicht, *Dějiny*, pp. 307–24; and F. J. Swehla, "Bohemians in Central Kansas," *Kansas Historical Collections* 13 (1913–14), pp. 469–512.

16. Josef A. Dvořák, ed., *Dějiny Čechův ve Státu South Dakota* (Tabor, S.Dak: n.p., 1920), is the best source on that state. On North Dakota, see Habenicht, *Dějiny*, pp. 383–88. On the distribution of small Czech settlements in the western part of that state, see William Sherman, "Ethnic Distribution in Western North Dakota," *North Dakota History* 46 (Winter 1979): 4–12.

17. "Nové vzrůstající osady," *Amerikán* (1911), pp. 266–68; R. W. Lynch, *Czech Farmers in Oklahoma*, Department of Geography Bulletin (Stillwater: Oklahoma A&M, 1942); and Vraz, *Panorama*, pp. 58–62.

18. On Texas, see Rechcigl, *Czechoslovak Contribution*, pp. 510–15; Vraz, *Panorama*, pp. 35–39; and Estelle Houston and Henry R. Maresh, *Czech Pioneers of the Southwest* (Dallas: South-West Press, 1934).

19. From *Zpráva úřadníků Hlavní Úřadovny Z.Č.B.J. pátemu sjezdu Jednoty* (Cedar Rapids: Z.Č.B.J., 1917), pp. 26–31.

20. See Čapek, *Moje Amerika*, pp. 98–99; and Rosická, *Dějiny Čechů*, pp. 281–341, 365–70, 415–23, for the data on which my conclusions are based.

21. Tomáš Čapek, *Navštěvníci z Čech a Moravy v Americe v letech 1848–1939* (Chicago: Color Printing Co., 1940), best surveys international contact. On Czech-American Catholicism, see Joseph Cada, *Czech-American Catholics, 1850–1920* (Lisle, Ill.: Benedictine Abbey Press, 1964); and Peter Mizera, *Czech Benedictines in America, 1877–1901* (Lisle, Ill.: Benedictine Abbey Press, 1969).

22. Rosická, *Dějiny Čechů*, pp. 349–56; Garver, *Young Czech Party*, pp. 88–120.

23. Typical issues include *Svobodná škola* 6, no. 5 (May 1902); 8, no. 6 (June 1904); and no. 9 (September 1904).

24. "Referát o českém svobodomyslném školství," in *Jednání, Usnesení a Resoluce přijaté na VII. Řadném Sjezdu Svazu Svobodomyslných . . . května 1926*, ed. J. J. Jeliník (Chicago: Svaz Svobodomyslných, 1926), pp. 41–42.

25. *Sokol* means "falcon." On the organization, see Josef Scheiner, *Sokolská výprava do Ameriky r. 1909* (Prague: Ed. Grégr, 1910); Čapek, *The Čechs*, pp. 264 ff.; Rosická, *Dějiny Čechů*, p. 347; and Vraz, *Panorama*, pp. 133-44.

26. "Josef Mík z Omahy: Nejznámnější Čech v Americe," *Amerikán* (1914), pp. 278-82.

27. On the history of the society (ČSPS), see the 100th anniversary issue of *Orgán Československých spolků v Americe* 62 (March 1, 1954), "Jubileum století Č.S.A."

28. Ludmila Veselská, "Osmý sjezd Jednoty českých dam v St. Louis," *Amerikán* (1915), p. 32.

29. On the founding of the WBFA (ZČBJ), see *Protokol Sjezdu západních řádů Č.S.P.S. . . . února 1897 v Omaha* (Omaha: Z.Č.B.J., 1897), and *Protokol Prvního Sjezdu Z.Č.B.J. . . . února 1899 v Nové Praze* (New Prague, Minn.: Z.Č.B.J., 1899). For histories of individual lodges, see *Památník Československého Dne a státního sjezdu řádů Z. Č.B.J. v Nebrasce* (Omaha: National Printing Co., 1937).

30. *Jednání, usnešení a resoluce přijaté na Sjezdu Svobodomyslných v zasedání dne 13., 14., a 15. června, roku 1907* (Chicago: Národní Tiskárna, 1907), pp. 81-82, 186-87, 193-97.

31. Lev J. Palda to Emanuel Engel, February 23 and September 18, 1892, and Bohemian National Committee, Omaha, Nebraska, R. V. Miškovský, secretary, Jan Rosický, chairman, and Tomáš Čapek, editor, *Bohemian Voice*, to Emanuel Engel, March 25 and October 18, 1893. Literary Archive of the Památník Národního Písemnictví, Prague, Czechoslovakia, Emanuel Engel Papers, 6S82, envelope "Dopisování do novin anglo-amerických, dopisy amerických krajanům do Englovi, 1892-93."

32. For example, *Bohemian Voice* 1, no. 8 (April 1893); 2, no. 12 (August 1894); and 3, no. 2 (October 1894), all front pages.

33. On Czech-American participation in the struggle for Czechoslovak independence, see Vojta Beneš, *Československá Amerika v obdobi*, vol. 1, *Od června 1914 do srpna 1915* (Prague: "Pokrok," 1931), for the first year; František Šindelář, *Z boje za svobodu otčiny* (Chicago: Nárochí Svaz Českých Katolíků, 1924), for contributions by Catholics; and Vojta Beneš, *Vojáci zapomenuté fronty* (Prague: Památník odboje, 1923) for speeches and documents. Charles Pergler, *America in the Struggle for Czechoslovak Independence* (Philadelphia: Dorrance, 1926), is sketchy. Victor S. Mamatey, *The United States and East Central Europe 1914-1918* (Princeton, N.J.: Princeton University Press, 1957), shows events in historical perspective.

34. Beneš, *Československá Amerika*, 1:130-36, "Omaha v čele." An outstanding event was the Omaha charity bazaar that netted $65,109.20 in September 1918. See *Květy Americké* (Omaha) 26, no. 2 (September 4, 1918): 16, and 26, no. 3 (September 11, 1918): 16.

35. Jelínek, *Jednání a Resoluce 1926*, p. 21.

36. Ibid., p. 22.

37. Šiller et al., *Památník církví*, p. 85.

38. On Iška, see Beneš, *Československá Amerika*, 1:195-207; and Falta, *100 let*, pp. 3-4.

39. T. G. Masaryk, *Americké přednášky*, for lectures, and "Svobodomyslní Čechové v America," *Naše doba* 10, no. 1 (October 1902): pp. 1-7.

40. Masaryk's letter in Czech is from the Dr. Henry J. John Collection, University of Nebraska Archives–Special Collections. I thank Joseph Svoboda for calling it to my attention.

Agricultural Change among Nebraska Immigrants, 1880–1900

Bradley H. Baltensperger

A central concern of studies of immigrants in American society is the degree to which cultural traits of migrants are retained, modified, or eliminated after settlement. The process of acculturation of immigrants is a function of many factors, not the least of which include the disruptive effects of migration, exposure to a new culture, the isolation of immigrants from one another, and the interaction of immigrants with a new physical environment and a different set of economic forces.

Many studies have stressed certain European patterns that have been retained in spite of overwhelming pressures favoring accultura-tion.[1] In numerous other cases, however, the distinctiveness of immigrants has been shown to be more apparent than substantive. European farmers in many areas of the United States were virtually indistinguishable from their American neighbors in mobility, scale of operations, cropping systems, and propensity to settle in sparsely populated areas.[2] Yet, cultural distinctiveness certainly did not dis-appear immediately upon the immigrants' arrival. Some traits may have been quickly discarded, but others were introduced and tried, only to be abandoned after several years or decades. Certain other practices survived for a long period, in some cases to the present, while a few traits were apparently abandoned for a short period after settlement, only to reappear several years later. For the most part, it is reasonable to assume that acculturation was a temporal process in which the convergence of two or more cultural groups increased with time.

Because the ethnic variety of the plains has often been ignored, the acculturation of European immigrants in the region has not been adequately studied.[3] Scholars have examined the agricultural prac-tices of Norwegians in Wisconsin, Irish in Canada, and Germans in Texas, Pennsylvania, the Midwest, and the Ozarks.[4] Presumably the processes of assimilation were somewhat different on the Great

Plains, at least in part because of a different physical environment, the importance of railroads in settlement, and the rapidity with which settlement occurred. This study of the agricultural adjustments of plains ethnic groups seeks to discover which traits persisted among immigrant farmers in Nebraska, as well as the rates at which other immigrant practices came to resemble those of American-born farmers.

Any study of the acculturation of migrant groups must account for differences in the physical environment and the influence of length of residence. The first may be accomplished through the selection of small, internally homogeneous areas, thereby reducing the effect of variations in soil, climate, or terrain on differences in group agricultural practices. The effect of spatial factors such as market accessibility is also thus reduced.

The second factor—the length of time immigrants have been in their new locations—must be considered because acculturation is a product of exposure to the host culture. Comparisons of immigrant farmers with their American-born equivalents can be deceptive if one group consists of established settlers, while members of the other group have arrived only recently. Differences due to variations in experience are easily attributed to cultural background.[5]

The most common solution to this problem—comparison of farmers whose names appear for the first time in a census—is unworkable on the Great Plains, where only one or two censuses are available from the settlement period of a county. This procedure also allows for wide variability within a group, since it combines farmers who have just arrived with those who have been in the area nine years. These problems can be minimized by determining the approximate year of arrival of each settler through examination of the ages and birthplaces of the children in the family. Farmers are then classified as having settled in a specific period with little error and their agricultural operations can be compared with those of other groups that arrived in the same period.[6]

This method selects only those farmers with younger children born in Nebraska and older children born elsewhere. All others are excluded. This limitation, along with the selection of a small study area, sometimes so reduces the size of the samples that comparisons and conclusions based on them are misleading.

Two study areas on the eastern edge of the Great Plains in Nebraska were selected for analysis (fig. 1). Each was settled by a large number of immigrants; assessment records are available for both. The first is located in Madison and Pierce counties, a district

NEBRASKA- STUDY AREA

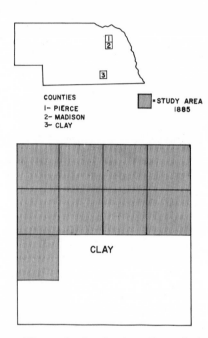

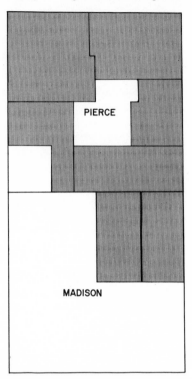

COUNTIES
1- PIERCE
2- MADISON
3- CLAY

STUDY AREA
1885

Figure 1. Study Area Boundaries in 1885. All of Pierce County was examined for 1880. For both 1880 and 1885 a one-third sample of Americans in the five western Clay County townships was taken, along with a complete sample of European-born farmers. For 1889, 1892, and 1896, only areas in Madison and Clay counties were studied. Data for the two north-central precincts in Clay County were missing for 1892.

first settled in the late 1860s by a group of Germans, chiefly Prussians, who relocated from Wisconsin. They were joined by farmers born in Ohio, Pennsylvania, and New York, who came to Nebraska from the Midwest, primarily Iowa and Illinois. Later German settlers migrated either directly from Europe or from intermediate locations in Iowa. Some of the townships in Pierce County were inhabited almost completely by German Americans by 1880, while others were settled principally by Americans.

The second study area, located in Clay County, was first settled in the early 1870s by four distinct groups consisting of persons born in the United States, Germany, and Sweden, along with Germans born in Russia. Most of the native Americans were born in Ohio, Pennsylvania, New York, or Illinois, but migrated from homes in Illinois or Iowa. The Germans, who settled principally in the northwestern townships, were chiefly Prussians from Illinois. The Russian Germans arrived directly from Russia and settled in the northeastern townships of the county. The Swedes, included for purposes of comparison, began farming in several north-central townships. About half moved directly to Nebraska from Sweden. The others came from homes in Illinois or Iowa.

The agricultural background of these four groups is of considerable importance in their behavior as farmers in Nebraska, especially in the first years after settlement. The Americans had gained most of their farming experience in the Midwest, where the dominant farming system included raising corn to be fed to cattle and hogs. Oats were commonly grown on a small scale and wheat was of considerably less importance in most of the Midwest than was corn. Barley, rye, and flax were raised only occasionally, except in a few restricted areas, and sheep were uncommon.[7]

While agriculture in Germany varied considerably from region to region, certain common elements distinguished German practices and emphases from those of Americans. German farms were typically smaller and the farming more intensive and diversified than in the American Midwest. Various small grains, rather than corn and cattle, dominated the agricultural landscape. Sheep and swine were the most important livestock, with one or the other more numerous, depending upon the region within Germany. Dairy cattle, poultry, and potatoes were important elements of agriculture in certain areas. Like the Germans, the Russian Germans were heavily dependent upon a variety of small grains, but they were accustomed to more extensive forms of production than were the Germans.[8]

All groups modified their farming practices when they settled on the Great Plains. The changing operations of these farmers of varied background will be followed during the last two decades of the nineteenth century. Examination of the federal and state censuses of 1880 and 1885, respectively, along with county assessment records from 1889, 1892, and 1896, provides the data needed to compare the rate and extent of acculturation as measured by agricultural practices.

Major Crops

Corn was by far the most important crop for farmers in all groups throughout the late nineteenth century. The rapid acceptance of corn by Europeans with little experience in its cultivation was dramatic in both study areas (table 1). In fact, as early as 1880 Clay County Germans and Russian Germans were even more likely to raise corn than were Americans. Nearly equal, but modest, acreages were reported by all four ethnic groups in that year, with even newly arrived settlers likely to be raising corn on nearly the same scale as established farmers. In Madison and Pierce counties the earliest settlers reported greater acreage than newcomers in 1880, but throughout the study period there were only minor differences in corn acreage between native-American and German-born farmers who had been in Nebraska the same length of time.

In Clay County, however, Germans and Russian Germans raised more corn than the Americans after 1885. Corn acreage and its share of total cropland increased among all four groups during the study period, as wheat rapidly lost importance. By 1896 only the Russian Germans devoted less than half their improved acreage to corn.

The most important small grain from 1880 to 1900 was wheat, which was more common on immigrant farms than on those of their American neighbors. During the 1880s the average wheat acreage of Germans in the northern area was double that of the American-born farmers, and a greater proportion of Germans than Americans raised wheat (table 2).

In Clay County wheat acreage was approximately equal among the four groups in 1880, except that the Russian Germans grew more wheat than did the others. After 1880 the average wheat acreage and percentage of farmers reporting wheat fell for all groups, but the Russian Germans and Germans were most resistant to this trend. In 1885 Russian Germans, both established and new, still raised more wheat than corn and even when the Clay County wheat acreage dipped to its lowest point in 1889, a majority of both groups continued to report some wheat. Nevertheless, wheat acreage was minuscule compared to corn acreage. The ratio of corn to wheat acreage in 1889 was 26:1 among native Americans, and 47:1 among Swedes. Russian Germans and Germans in Clay County reported five and six acres of corn to every acre of wheat, while among Madison County Germans the ratio was 3:1. By the late 1880s wheat had nearly disappeared from the American cropping system, but remained a viable component of the German selection of crops.

TABLE 1

Average Corn Acreage per Farm[a]

Year	Clay County												Madison and Pierce Counties					
	A1	G1	R1	S1	A2	G2	R2	S2	A	G	R	S	A1	G1	A2	G2	A	G
1880	25 (19)	26 (17)	28 (12)	19 (13)	21 (18)	17 (17)	18 (14)	16 (12)	23 (19)	29 (16)	21 (14)	18 (13)	29 (50)	23 (37)	9 (29)	10 (24)	20 (45)	21 (36)
1885	48 (31)	52 (37)	46 (20)	52 (36)	50 (40)	61 (45)	26 (27)	34 (37)	49 (36)	58 (42)	38 (22)	44 (37)	33 (25)	33 (16)	25 (29)	19 (23)	28 (28)	29 (18)
1889	58 (46)	84 (45)	83 (39)	62 (57)	58 (44)	89 (51)	b	52 (66)	58 (45)	87 (48)	75 (38)	59 (60)	57 (42)	41 (50)	46 (52)	b	52 (46)	40 (49)
1892	61 (40)	94 (37)	143 (46)	69 (50)	93 (47)	116 (46)	b	62 (44)	73 (43)	106 (42)	132 (46)	66 (46)	57 (49)	53 (43)	46 (58)	b	51 (53)	52 (43)
1896	90 (51)	121 (45)	114 (46)	104 (55)	111 (57)	167 (58)	b	76 (61)	99 (54)	142 (51)	101 (43)	93 (57)	71 (33)	54 (43)	60 (51)	b	65 (40)	51 (40)

Sources: Calculated from manuscript enumeration sheets of the 1880 U.S. census and the 1885 census of Nebraska; 1889, 1892, and 1896 assessment records of Clay and Madison counties, Nebraska. Assessment records for Pierce County are not available.

[a]Figures in parentheses indicate corn acreage as a percentage of improved acreage. For this and succeeding tables, A = American-born, G = German, R = Russian German, S = Swedish; 1 = those who moved to Nebraska before 1878 (before 1875, for 1880 data); 2 = those who moved between 1878 and 1885 (between 1875 and 1880, for 1880 data).

[b]Fewer than twelve farmers sampled.

TABLE 2

Average Wheat Acreage per Farm[a]

Year	Clay County				Madison and Pierce Counties	
	U.S.	Germany	Russia	Sweden	U.S.	Germany
1880	51 (93)	46 (87)	67 (97)	47 (92)	10 (59)	20 (68)
1885	25 (80)	35 (89)	45 (84)	28 (85)	6 (44)	16 (80)
1889	2 (17)	14 (58)	14 (62)	1 (14)	2 (21)	13 (57)
1892	13 (47)	23 (77)	49 (94)	3 (19)	7 (52)	15 (79)
1896	10 (43)	19 (65)	24 (83)	13 (64)	27 (78)	16 (78)

Sources: Calculated by author. See table 1.

[a]Figures in parentheses indicate percentage of farmers reporting.

In the 1890s the Russian Germans increased wheat production, perhaps as a drought adjustment, and nearly all farmers in this group reported the crop, averaging forty-seven acres per farm. Germans in both areas also reported significant acreage and participation rate increases, while Americans and Swedes showed only moderate increases. By the end of the study period, only Russian Germans and Germans were major wheat producers in Clay County, but American participation in wheat culture in Madison County equaled that of the Germans, and their acreage was greater. There appeared to be little difference between new and established farmers.

A majority of farmers in each category raised oats, with Germans and Russian Germans reporting somewhat greater acreages than Swedes and Americans in Clay County, especially after 1885. In the northern area differences between Americans and Germans were minimal.

The lesser small grains were distinctly more favored by Germans and Russian Germans than by other groups. The near equality of emphasis on barley among the four groups in Clay County in 1885 disappeared by 1889, when Germans were the principal cultivators of the crop (table 3). By 1892 more than half the Germans and one-third of the Russians grew barley, but few Swedes and Americans

TABLE 3

Average Barley Acreage per Farm[a]

Year	Clay County				Madison and Pierce Counties	
	U.S.	Germany	Russia	Sweden	U.S.	Germany
1880	8 (53)	9 (56)	11 (78)	2 (35)	.2 (5)	.5 (11)
1885	12 (55)	12 (65)	10 (53)	6 (58)	.8 (14)	3 (39)
1889	3 (11)	8 (31)	0 (0)	1 (3)	.1 (4)	1 (7)
1892	5 (19)	16 (53)	6 (31)	2 (9)	.4 (7)	1 (21)
1896	2 (8)	3 (12)	1 (4)	0 (0)	.8 (11)	2 (26)

Source: Calculated by author. See table 1.

[a]Figures in parentheses indicate percentage of farmers reporting.

raised the crop. German dominance was evident by 1885 in the northern counties, but by the end of the study period very few farmers produced any barley.

In all years the proportion of farmers reporting rye was low (table 4). Newcomers were especially likely to ignore the crop, even among the principal cultivators of rye—Germans in Madison and Pierce counties and Russian Germans in Clay County. While German production of rye declined rapidly after 1885, the number of Russian Germans growing rye rose. Even though they had not produced it in their first years in the state, many Russian Germans began planting the crop after becoming established in Nebraska. This resurgence of interest in the 1890s did not occur in any other group. Even among the Russian Germans, however, rye acreage never approached the scale of corn, wheat, or oats.

Beginning in 1885 a substantial number of Clay County farmers reported flax. The Russian Germans, particularly the earliest settlers, were most heavily involved in its production (table 5). By 1889 flax acreage was second only to corn among Russian Germans, indicating that although flax might not be grown by new settlers, once Russian Germans were beyond the difficult initial years, they often included flax in their cropping system. The cultivation of flax diffused from several established Russian Germans to the non-

TABLE 4
Percentage of Farmers Reporting Rye

Year	Clay County												Madison and Pierce Counties					
	A1	G1	R1	S1	A2	G2	R2	S2	A	G	R	S	A1	G1	A2	G2	A	G
1880	23	25	22	15	9	4	6	8	15	10	10	10	5	35	0	18	2	32
1885	15	5	30	20	16	11	29	12	15	9	30	16	19	51	7	37	11	47
1889	0	11	13	13	0	0	a	8	0	6	14	11	7	7	0	a	4	7
1892	9	8	46	17	14	6	a	0	11	7	44	9	0	0	6	a	3	0
1896	4	11	35	10	0	6	a	8	3	9	39	9	17	8	27	a	22	11

Source: Calculated by author. See table 1.
aFewer than twelve farmers sampled.

TABLE 5

Percentage of Clay County Farmers Reporting Flax[a]

Year	A1	G1	R1	S1	A2	G2	R2	S2	A	G	R	S
1880	2	0	17	0	0	0	2	0	1 (1)	0 (0)	6 (1)	0 (0)
1885	17	0	55	10	11	11	20	8	13 (3)	7 (2)	44 (10)	9 (1)
1889	19	21	91	21	9	12	b	0	15 (7)	17 (4)	90 (49)	14 (3)
1892	14	15	77	44	14	29	b	29	14 (5)	23 (8)	75 (31)	38 (10)
1896	0	0	0	0	0	0	b	0	0 (0)	0 (0)	0 (0)	0 (0)

Source: Calculated by author. See table 1.

[a]Figures in parentheses indicate average flax acreage per arm.

[b]Fewer than twelve farmers sampled.

Russian-German communities in the mid and late 1880s. The absence of flax acreage in 1896 was possibly due to the assessor's failure to report the crop.

Diversity

The diversified cropping systems of Russian Germans and German farmers distinguished them from their American neighbors in both areas. In each year studied, Clay County Russian Germans reported more crops per farm than did any other group, and the difference was often substantial (table 6). In 1892 the average Russian German raised more than four crops. The Germans were second in diversity, averaging three. In Pierce and Madison counties Germans operated more diversified systems than Americans until 1889, when the declining importance of rye and barley produced similar levels of diversification between the two groups.

To some extent greater crop diversity among Clay County Germans and Russian Germans was related to their larger operations. In all years the correlation between the number of crops raised and the number of improved acres was positive (+.31 to +.47), yet there was a small, but significant, inverse relationship between total acreage and corn acreage as a proportion of total acreage (-.16:-.27). Larger farmers were thus likely to devote a somewhat smaller share of

TABLE 6
Average Number of Major Crops per Farm

Year	Clay County												Madison and Pierce Counties					
	A1	G1	R1	S1	A2	G2	R2	S2	A	G	R	S	A1	G1	A2	G2	A	G
1880	3.3	3.8	3.9	3.2	2.8	2.5	3.2	2.5	3.0	2.9	3.4	2.7	2.6	3.1	1.4	2.4	2.1	3.0
1885	3.4	3.2	4.2	3.6	3.3	3.1	2.8	3.0	3.3	3.5	3.6	3.3	3.1	3.9	2.1	3.0	2.5	3.6
1889	2.3	3.2	3.5	2.1	2.0	2.8	a	2.1	2.2	3.0	3.5	2.1	1.8	2.2	1.8	a	1.8	2.2
1892	2.7	3.1	3.2	2.5	2.1	2.6	a	2.4	2.7	3.4	4.3	2.6	2.4	2.6	2.3	a	2.3	2.6
1896	2.4	3.1	3.2	2.5	2.1	2.6	a	2.4	2.3	2.9	3.1	2.5	3.2	2.8	2.9	a	3.0	2.7

Source: Calculated by author. See table 1.
aFewer than twelve farmers sampled.

their land to corn production, but their operations were still slightly more diverse than those with fewer acres. No pattern emerged for the northern area.

Diversity apparently developed only after several years in Nebraska. Farmers who settled in the state in the late 1870s and early 1880s relied on fewer crops than those who arrived in the early 1870s. Among the Russian Germans this distinction between diversified early arrivers and less diversified newcomers was especially pronounced. Old World crop preferences were being reasserted after several years of absence during the frontiering process, a phenomenon Jordan has labeled "cultural rebound."[9]

Minor Crops

Small grains such as buckwheat and sorghum were seldom produced in the two study areas, but most established farmers reported potatoes. Cultural differences were minimal. A number of residents also reported small orchards, usually of apple or peach trees. Naturally, established farmers were most likely to raise fruit. In the early years Americans held a significant lead over immigrants, but by 1889 Clay County immigrants reported fruit as frequently as the American-born. Madison County Germans reported orchards less often than Americans, but the gap narrowed by 1896.

Livestock

Differences among the groups in livestock production, while less striking than crop differences, were significant in many cases. Nearly every farmer reported horses, with averages ranging from four per farm in 1880 to seven by the end of the century. Cultural differences were minimal, except that the Russian Germans raised more horses than other groups. The earliest settlers of all four groups reported more horses than later arrivals, a pattern particularly evident among the Russian Germans. Generally no more than 30 percent of any group owned mules, but the proportion of Russian Germans and Madison County Germans with mules never exceeded 10 percent. In this sense they remained distinctive.

Cattle were an important element of most farm operations. Nearly every farmer had a few dairy cows, usually two to six head per family. In the northern counties farmers also reported sizable numbers of beef cattle, with the earliest settlers owning the largest herds. Before 1889 more Germans than American-born farmers reported cattle, but herd sizes were about equal. Cultural differences in cattle production disappeared after that time. Herds in Clay County were smaller (about seven head per farm in 1885) than in the northern counties. The percentage of farmers reporting cattle was usually greatest among the early settlers; however, herd sizes did not vary according to time of migration or cultural background.

Poultry was raised by nearly all established farmers and most new farmers in both 1880 and 1885, though the earlier arrivals usually owned more. Cultural differences in flock size were negligible in Clay County, but more Russian Germans owned poultry than did members of other groups. In the northern study area Germans owned about twice as many birds as the Americans.

Swine were reported by nearly all European-born farmers, but more than 10 percent of the Americans in Clay County owned none. While this difference is not great, it is statistically significant for most years and was especially pronounced by the end of the period. The earliest settlers in both study areas owned more head than later arrivals, particularly among the immigrants.

In sheep production certain ethnic groups were clearly different from the American-born farmers. In the northern area Germans were more likely to raise sheep than were Americans, and they maintained larger flocks (table 7). The average flock size among the Germans

TABLE 7

Average Number of Sheep per Farm[a]

Year	Clay County				Madison and Pierce Counties	
	U.S.	Germany	Russia	Sweden	U.S.	Germany
1880	.3 (1)	5 (2)	23 (13)	.2 (2)	.5 (6)	12 (64)
1885	6 (6)	.1 (2)	45 (9)	.3 (5)	7 (10)	7 (44)
1889	0 (0)	.1 (2)	0 (0)	.1 (3)	.9 (9)	3 (39)
1892	0 (0)	.3 (12)	.6 (12)	0 (0)	0 (0)	3 (33)
1896	0 (0)	0 (0)	.5 (15)	0 (0)	.1 (8)	2 (38)

Source: Calculated by author. See table 1.

[a]Percentage of farmers reporting sheep in parentheses.

declined throughout the period, as did the proportion reporting sheep, but at least one-third of the Germans reported some sheep each year. Newcomers owned fewer head than did established farmers.

In Clay County only the Russian Germans were important sheep producers, but their flocks, impressive in size, were owned by fewer than ten farmers, one of whom reported 1,325 head in the 1885 census. No more than 20 percent of the Russian Germans ever reported sheep.

Scale of Operations

In spite of backgrounds in more intensive, smaller-scale agriculture, Germans and Swedes established farms that were comparable in size and value to those of Americans and Russian Germans in 1880. Within a few years major changes in farm scale occurred. In Madison and Pierce counties German Americans reported 60 percent more improved land than American-born farmers (table 8) and the value of German farms was 45 percent higher than the American figure (table 9). Clay County Germans equaled Americans in improved acreage and value in 1885, but Russian-German operations were consistently larger than those of any other group in the county.

The effect of experience on farm scale was especially pronounced in Clay County. Among the earliest settlers, Russian Germans owned 50 percent more improved land than the Americans and cash farm value was higher. After 1885 German farms were also larger and more valuable than those of American-born farmers who had settled in Clay County in the 1870s, even though overall figures indicate only minor differences among the four groups. In the northern area the German farm value was consistently higher than the American value, but improved acreage fluctuated considerably.

Recently arrived Americans and Germans had larger, more valuable farms than did pioneering Russian Germans or Swedes, particularly in 1885. In that year Russian-German farms were among the smallest and were worth less than those of other groups who had recently settled. In Madison and Pierce counties the farms of newer Germans and Americans were of nearly equal scale and value.

The relationship between farm scale and years of plains experience differed from one group to another. In 1880 and 1885 the size of operations among Clay County Americans, Germans, and Swedes was only loosely related to experience, but for both groups in the northern area, and especially for the Russian Germans in Clay County, increasing experience meant considerably larger, more

TABLE 8
Number of Improved Acres per Farm

Year	Clay County												Madison and Pierce Counties					
	A1	G1	R1	S1	A2	G2	R2	S2	A	G	R	S	A1	G1	A2	G2	A	G
1880	131	154	231	149	115	102	126	131	123	117	154	136	58	63	31	41	44	58
1885	154	139	228	143	126	136	98	93	137	137	173	120	132	202	86	83	100	159
1889	126	188	212	109	132	175	a	79	128	182	196	98	136	82	89	a	113	82
1892	153	256	314	138	196	251	a	146	169	253	288	142	117	124	80	a	96	120
1896	175	267	250	189	194	286	a	124	183	276	233	163	217	127	117	a	162	126

Source: Calculated by author. See table 1.

aFewer than twelve farmers sampled.

TABLE 9

Cash Farm Value, 1880 and 1885, and Value of Land, 1889, 1892, and 1896

Year	Clay County												Madison and Pierce Counties					
	A1	G1	R1	S1	A2	G2	R2	S2	A	G	R	S	A1	G1	A2	G2	A	G
1880	2381	2267	3068	1845	1852	1453	1544	1645	2094	1691	1948	1695	1619	1426	617	642	1048	1272
1885	4083	4358	6127	4083	3653	3504	2725	2948	3821	3857	4695	3567	3489	4975	2665	2961	2926	4252
1889	667	835	998	643	643	768	a	451	657	804	910	576	523	636	427	a	482	618
1892	700	1133	1603	786	898	1056	a	560	777	1089	1470	687	589	615	383	a	475	604
1896	597	882	827	700	672	912	a	721	628	896	735	709	904	1176	540	a	708	1128

Source: Calculated by author. See table 1.

aFewer than twelve farmers sampled.

valuable farms. While Russian Germans reported large acreages of great value, this clearly reflected the influence of the earliest settlers. Recent arrivals began on a much smaller scale.

Tenure and Labor

The more established farmers were less likely to be renters in both study areas, and the proportion of owners increased nearly every year. Cultural differences in tenure were expressed in high tenancy levels among the most recent Russian-German immigrants. In both 1880 and 1885 farmers in this group were more likely to rent than to own. More than half were owners by 1889, but the proportion of owners grew more slowly than it did among other groups. This high level of tenancy was somewhat related to farmer persistence. Four years after the 1885 census, only about half of the Russian Germans remained in the study area, but American farmers in Clay County and both groups in the northern study area were also quite mobile, in spite of lower tenancy rates.

Few farmers relied on outside labor. Only about one-fourth of the farmers in Madison and Pierce counties reported hiring laborers, while Clay County farmers were somewhat more likely to tap the farm labor market. Established farmers were more frequently employers, paying an average of about sixty dollars per Clay County farm in 1879 and over one hundred dollars in 1884. Russian Germans spent more than other groups. In spite of the sod-breaking needs of new farmers, they seldom hired labor, averaging less than thirty dollars per farm. Newly arrived Americans were more likely to hire labor than were recent immigrants. With time, immigrants came to rely on outside labor as much as or more than American farmers.

Conclusions: Convergence, Rebound, and Retention

Examination of the trends in crops, livestock, and scale of operations among the cultural groups of Clay, Madison, and Pierce counties indicates that important changes were occurring in immigrant agriculture. Many differences between the several European agricultural forms and American practices disappeared, while other traits were less subject to modification. As a result the agricultural operations of immigrant farmers reflected a blend of adopted and retained traits.[10]

At least four overlapping processes were molding the agricultural practices of immigrant farmers in the last two decades of the nineteenth century. In many instances they rapidly adopted American cropping and livestock practices. The most dramatic example was the almost immediate acceptance of corn as the staple crop by all three immigrant groups. Among the Swedes rapid convergence was also expressed in the production of all grains and livestock. They retained few distinctive traits after 1885. Germans were somewhat more slowly acculturated, but convergence was rapid in oats, rye, and flax production, as well as most livestock. The rate of tenancy and the use of hired labor differed little from the American pattern. Among the Russian Germans, livestock numbers were similar to those of Americans, but cropping systems remained relatively distinct. Russian-German and German farm size and value equaled or exceeded those of Americans soon after settlement.

A second set of immigrant practices became less distinguishable from those of Americans within one or two decades. These traits included barley production and crop diversity among the Madison County Germans, as well as fruit production by all immigrant groups. Some of the differences which persisted after settlement were retained until near the end of the century. These included wheat production and crop diversity among Madison County Germans and the production of barley by Russian Germans in Clay County.

A third group of distinctive features of European agriculture disappeared in the first few years of settlement, but later reappeared among the immigrants through the process of "cultural rebound."[11] Many crops familiar to the Russian Germans and Germans were unimportant in the first years of settlement. After these farmers became established they placed renewed emphasis on crop diversity, a system to which they had been accustomed before migration, but recently arrived immigrants remained more dependent on corn. Cultural rebound seems to be indicated by the increased attention of Clay County Germans to wheat production and crop diversity. Rebound was also likely among Russian-German farmers in rye and flax production, as well as crop diversity. In each case German and Russian-German distinctiveness persisted through the end of the century.

A final process in immigrant agriculture was the retention of cultural features. Russian production of wheat and the emphasis on sheep by Madison County Germans were apparently so deeply ingrained in the cultures that they were transferred to the plains without a frontier lull in production. Both practices, along with those which underwent cultural rebound, continued to distinguish the two groups at the turn of the century.

By the end of the study period much of the agricultural distinctiveness of the ethnic groups in the two areas had disappeared. Nevertheless, the Germans, and particularly the Germans born in

Russia, retained some degree of uniqueness. Even though one might expect European farmers not to be noticeable in an area settled primarily by midwesterners, both groups remained distinctive in their attention to small grains, crop diversity, and scale of operations. The extension of this and similar studies into the twentieth century will provide further understanding of the retention of agricultural traits of immigrants, as well as the processes that produce cultural convergence and assimilation.

Notes

1. See, for example, Russel L. Gerlach, *Immigrants in the Ozarks: A Study in Ethnic Geography* (Columbia: University of Missouri Press, 1976); Walter M. Kollmorgen, *The German Settlement in Cullman County, Alabama: An Agricultural Island in the Cotton Belt* (Washington, D.C.: U.S. Department of Agriculture, Bureau of Agricultural Economics, 1941); Russell W. Lynch, "Czech Farmers in Oklahoma," *Economic Geography* 20 (January 1944): 9-13.

2. Allan G. Bogue, *From Prairie to Corn Belt* (Chicago: University of Chicago Press, 1963); Merle Curti et al., *The Making of an American Community* (Stanford, Calif.: Stanford University Press, 1959).

3. Frederick C. Luebke, "Ethnic Group Settlement on the Great Plains," *Western Historical Quarterly* 8 (October 1977): 405-30; Lynch, "Czech Farmers"; D. Aidan McQuillan, "Adaptation of Three Immigrant Groups to Farming in Central Kansas, 1875-1925" (Ph.D. diss., University of Wisconsin, 1975).

4. Terry G. Jordan, *German Seed in Texas Soil: Immigrant Farmers in Nineteenth-Century Texas* (Austin: University of Texas Press, 1966); John G. Gagliardo, "Germans and Agriculture in Colonial Pennsylvania," *Pennsylvania Magazine of History and Biography* 83 (1959): 192-218; Curti, *American Community*; Gerlach, *Immigrants in the Ozarks*; Richard H. Shryock, "British versus German Traditions in Colonial Agriculture," *Mississippi Valley Historical Review* 26 (1939): 39-54; John J. Mannion, *Irish Settlements in Eastern Canada: A Study of Cultural Transfer and Adaptation*, University of Toronto Department of Geography Research Publication no. 12 (Toronto, 1974).

5. Curti, *American Community*, p. 178.

6. The method allows a deviation of approximately two years in determining time of settlement. For example, if a farmer listed in the 1885 census had an eight-year-old child born in Wisconsin and a five-year-old born in Nebraska, he entered the state sometime between 1877 and 1880. It is reasonable to conclude that he arrived in 1878 or later. If his children were ten and four, the range of possible entry dates is so great that he is eliminated from the sample.

7. Percy W. Bidwell and John I. Falconer, *History of Agriculture in the Northern United States, 1620-1860* (New York: Peter Smith, 1941).

8. Jordan, *German Seed*, pp. 33-38; Fred C. Koch, *The Volga Germans in Russia and the Americas from 1763 to the Present* (University Park: Pennsylvania State University Press, 1977); Hattie Plum Williams, *The Czar's Germans,*

with Particular Reference to the Volga Germans (Lincoln, Nebr.: American Historical Society of Germans from Russia, 1975).

   9. Jordan, *German Seed*, pp. 199-200.

   10. Ibid., 192.

   11. Ibid., pp. 199-200. Jordan argues that while the evidence is usually indirect, cultural rebound would be an understandable reaction of immigrant settlers who had to rely for information about farming their new lands on their American neighbors and on guidebooks, sources which were presumably better informed about the most appropriate farming techniques and crops. After the initial years of frontier hardship had passed, immigrant farmers might be well enough established to experiment with crops and techniques that were untested in the new environment. Oscar F. Hoffman, "Cultural Changes in a Rural Wisconsin Ethnic Island," *Rural Sociology* 14 (March 1949): 39-50, found that Germans in eastern Wisconsin returned to a diversified economy after having emphasized cash crops for twenty years.

Land, Labor, and Community in Nueces: Czech Farmers and Mexican Laborers in South Texas, 1880–1930

Josef J. Barton

Nueces County is part of a barbarously large country, alternately drab and dazzling, spectral and remote. South of San Antonio, the plain veers to the southeast, driving the timber line to the Gulf of Mexico at Matagorda Bay. Here, in a diamond-shaped territory bounded by that bay, by the mouth of the Rio Grande, by Laredo, and by San Antonio, lay all the requirements of ranching: Texas grasslands, Spanish stock, Indian horses, and American cowboys. Hungry cities and eager railroads assured markets, northern capital and Texas management spurred expansion. Between the end of the Civil War and 1885, while an astonishing swarming of cattle covered the Great Plains, the Nueces country was the seat of the cattle kingdom.[1]

Toward the end of the nineteenth century, as the pull of market demand raised the value of produce and so of land, an agrarian transformation swept this corner of the Great Plains. Production of sheep and cattle for cash drove the first engine of change. The number and value of sheep reached a peak between 1874 and 1876, that of cattle between 1882 and 1889. Values of land first lagged behind, then caught the tempo of stock raising; prices doubled between 1876 and 1879, again between 1881 and 1884. Accompanying the steep rise in value was enclosure, begun on small scale around 1870 and accomplished by 1885, by means of which big ranchers secured their hold over the most productive land. The Nueces countryside came under a regime of agrarian capitalism: a consolidation of private control over land, and the consequent ease of its conversion from one use to another and of its movement into the hands of owners eager to extract a maximum of revenue.[2]

Cotton drove the second engine of change. The extension of railroads throughout Texas in the late 1870s opened new territory; cotton acreage rose from two to seven million acres between 1879 and 1899. In an already specialized economy, cotton farming worked another transformation of south Texas. While ranching remained the dominant activity in Nueces County until the early twentieth century, cotton patches appeared on marginal lands in the 1880s. A decade later, 120 farms, on which farmers produced five hundred bales in a good year, dotted the county. Clearing began in earnest in 1899; gangs of Mexican and black laborers changed stretches of land from mesquite clumps to vast open fields. The major part of the country remained in enormous ranches of 100,000 to 200,000 acres in 1910, but now divided into hundreds of cleared farms of 20 to 200 acres. Simple statistics illustrate these dramatic changes: between 1910 and 1930, the number of holdings grew from 945 to 1,947; the proportion of cultivated land rose from 3.5 percent to 76 percent, the proportion of arable land in cotton from 6.6 percent to 88 percent. In 1929, Nueces led the counties of Texas in cotton production, in 1930, the counties of the entire United States.[3]

The drive to raise production sprang partly from new farmers' notions of the good life, more from habits of enterprise and risk taking. A large proportion of the cotton farmers came from east and central Texas, Louisiana, Arkansas, and Mississippi; of two samples of twenty new farmers with 600 or more acres, in each of two five-year periods (1910–15 and 1920–25), fifteen came from counties in which cotton accounted for more than half the farm acreage. Like two Louisiana farmers who arrived in Nueces in 1911, J. B. Womack and W. T. Munne, they routinely committed three-quarters of their improved acreage to cotton and, when opportunity came, leased great tracts from old landed families and made ranches into cotton lands. New landowners quickly married into old families as they gained the best lands and so gave new life to what passed for an old social structure. Everywhere in the cotton fields appeared the signs of the new planters' presence: machinery, white-suited purchasing agents for southern mills, Missionary Baptist and Southern Methodist churches.[4] A new elite had, by the end of World War I, worked a revolution on this bleak, flat land.

A new force of labor emerged as King Cotton overthrew the stock regime. Ranching had fitfully drawn upon herders and hands from ranches and farms on the periphery of the great holdings. A small proportion of the rural population worked steadily on the ranches in herding and fencing. During times of more intense demand, from April to August, big ranchers hired men from the two hundred tiny ranches in the county, but even then few worked for stretches longer than three weeks. Cotton demanded a new formation of the rural labor force, a complex pattern of farmers, tenants, and laborers. Immigrant farmers on less than 50 acres, half of them Czech, operated a third of the cotton farms in 1910. A regiment of tenants, at first largely Mexican and later mostly southern black and white, carved out small farms of 20 to 80 acres; they accounted for one-third of all farms in 1910, three-fourths in 1930. Alongside tenants, during the sixty days of peak demand from mid-July to mid-September, worked an army of laborers; almost wholly of Mexican origin, this rural proletariat made up a third of the population in 1919. On farms of 600 acres, where ten laborers ordinarily worked, the labor of chopping and picking required forty. This fourfold increase in demand drew hundreds of families to Nueces and created a reserve of mobile labor. A sudden spurt of growth created a characteristic formation of rural labor which, by the mid-1930s, accompanied large-scale agriculture not only in the cotton Southwest, but also in the cotton and sugar South, on the sugar operations of Puerto Rico and Cuba, and in the factories in the fields of southern California.[5]

Three related themes—the origins, development, and maturation of ethnic communities in a modernizing rural society—concern me here. I take up each of these themes and bring my considerations to bear on a question, Why did Czechs and Mexicans choose to be *Czech* farmers and *Mexican* laborers and not just farmers and laborers? If the term *ethnicity* is to be given palpable meaning and its social and cultural implications uncovered, the connection between ethnic identity and such developments as capitalist forms of agricultural organization, the growth of voluntary associations, the emergence of new classes, and a whole host of other social realities must be discovered. My contribution to this large task depends upon an entrance into the landscape and history of a place, and upon my sense of connection with two farming populations, their cultures and their interests. What I seek are the particulars of a situation, for an exploration of context and choice in ethnic allegiance winds through a thicket of observations.

The twentieth century arrival of immigrant peoples in Nueces marked the last stages of two movements. In the 1760s the Spanish had pushed north to the Nueces River, where they claimed great landholdings until the Texas War of Independence. Spanish grantees abandoned their lands during the war and, between 1840 and 1848, transferred seven of fifteen original grants to Anglo-Americans. The sale of the last Spanish grant to an Anglo-American in 1883 left only patches of land in Mexican hands. The resurgence of Mexican movement into south Texas in the mid-1870s came as Anglo-American ranchers consolidated their control of the land. The migration of Mexican ranch hands and their families proceeded through Laredo and then into rural areas around Zapata and San Ygnacio, northward to San José and Concepción, finally to San Diego and so to

Nueces. A steady stream flowed from the northern Mexican states of Tamaulipas and Nuevo León around the hundreds of islands of Mexican families in the ranching country between the Rio Grande and Nueces Rivers.[6]

Czech immigrants began a southward movement from central Texas during the same years. Latecomers to the cotton counties, they found them already crowded. German farmers had established agricultural colonies in the 1830s and 1840s, then spread southward after the Civil War in a segmentary belt of settlement through the cotton counties. These communities matured in the 1870s, whereupon the second generation again scattered southward deeper into the coastal plain. Polish farmers also moved southward from their settlements near San Antonio into coastal counties, where they established dispersed cotton farms in the 1880s and 1890s. When Czech farmers shifted south and west, from the mid-century settlements of Praha and Dubina, on to the 1870s settlements of Frydek and Wied, and to the turn-of-the-century settlements of Siller and Panna Maria, they followed well-worn paths.[7]

Newcomers to Nueces were a mix of first- and second-generation immigrants. Mexicans entering the county between 1900 and 1920, so far as I can learn from a sample of two hundred people, were three-fifths of them born in Mexico, two-fifths in Texas. Their Mexican origins lay in the agglomerations of laborers on haciendas in the states of Tamaulipas, Nuevo León, and Coahuila, from which 95 percent of them came. The rapid development of large-scale agriculture in the North, and the consequent shortage of labor, created a mobile rural proletariat. Caught in fitful cycles of development, families sought employment in both Mexican and Texas agriculture. Already in motion when Villa's revolution burned over the North, great numbers streamed northward into Texas.[8]

Czech peasants left an old countryside in transition. A third of Czech newcomers, in a sample of seventy-seven, were born abroad, in two clusters of southern Bohemian and eastern Moravian villages. Although living in mountainous areas to which agrarian transformation came late, these peasants nonetheless became in the 1860s part laborers and part cultivators. Expanding local markets, stimulated by the industrialization of Bohemia, drove agricultural productivity forward in the latter part of the century. In these villages—Nová Ves, Dolní Kralovice, and Zahrádka, near Havlíčkův Brod in southern Bohemia; Hovězi, Jablůnka, and Polánka, near Vsetín in eastern Moravia—a system of wage work gained ascendency, the use of machines began, and an old organization of work gave way to new forms of capitalist management. In response to their displacement,

young men and women sought work in highly commercialized agricultural areas of Bohemia and Poland, then whole familes started out
for Texas.[9]

Czech farmers quickly acquired land in Texas, learned to plant
cotton, and established households. There followed a characteristic
development of parishes, mutual benefit societies, and farmers'
unions—in short, of communities. But in the early twentieth century,
the lands of central Texas were already crowded, with little room
left for the continuing stream of newcomers; in 1906, for example,
three of every five Czech families in Williamson County were sharecroppers. Hence began another exodus, of whole families, from
Williamson County in particular and central Texas in general.[10]

Mexican laborers moved north, gathering in the catch basins of
small ranches and farms around the great estates of south Texas,
alternately herding their own sheep and cattle and working on big
ranches. Households clumped around rural Catholic chapels where
families assembled once or twice yearly for confession, baptism, first
communion, marriage, and requiem. Never was theirs a settled life,
for families moved constantly in search of work and shelter; and so
they arrived in Nueces County.[11]

After lives of extraordinary transiency, Czech and Mexican
newcomers reached Nueces. Their constant movements, first from
changing homelands and then from Texas settlements, made them
uprooted peoples. Yet if we follow their movements long enough, we
find prior ties of locale and kinship among the migrants. All the
foreign-born Czechs in my sample (one-third of the newcomers)
came from six villages, one wholly Catholic cluster in Bohemia,
another wholly Protestant in Moravia. Among second-generation
Czechs (two-thirds of the arrivals), two of three came from Williamson County, of families whose parents had left the same six Bohemian and Moravian villages a generation earlier. Three-quarters
of the Czech newcomers, then, belonged to moving communities.
What bound them was more than memories of place, for two-thirds
of the newcomers belonged to vertically extended families of three
generations.[12] At first glance an uprooted people, the Czech immigrants are seen on closer examination to be bound together by common origins and kinship.

The Mexican families also shared ties of locale and kinship.
Three-quarters of the Mexican-born newcomers (two-thirds of the
newcomers to Nueces) came from five contiguous haciendas south
of Bustamante, in Tamaulipas, and from three neighboring haciendas
near Cadereyta Jiménez, in Nuevo León. Of the Texas-born (one-
third of the newcomers), 60 percent came from a string of six
ranches south of San Diego. More than origins bound them: a third

of the newcomers moved in the company of brothers and sisters, another third with other kindred.[13] Both origins and kinship, then, linked Mexican families on the move.

What strikes the observer of both Czech and Mexican immigrants is the durable bonds of place and blood. The persistence and proliferation of personal relations, among the members of two groups in which we expect disruption and insecurity, require further comment. In the case of the Czechs, what initially linked newcomers was lineal families of three generations' depth, a kind of segmentation of kinfolk into lineal units. In the case of the Mexicans, what early bound was a web of crosscutting relationships among kinfolk. Czech immigrants, in short, allied themselves in families of three generations, Mexican newcomers in families of lateral kindred. This fundamental difference in patterns of initial bonds had cardinal importance in the subsequent development of the two communities. The locus of membership and alliance in the Czech community was the lineal unit of the family; for the Mexican community, the armature of belonging and association was the lateral network of kindred.[14] In order to grasp the character and consequences of this difference, we look now at the agrarian realities of the peoples' lives.

The fortunes of the Czech and Mexican newcomers stand out in bare summary. As both groups moved into the county around 1910, the take-off of cotton production made places for them. But what different locations! Of the ninety-nine Mexican families resident for three decades, only Juan Saldaña was able to scratch together a thousand dollars to buy a twenty-acre patch. Another sixteen families bought small lots in Robstown and Bishop. Of the sample, 80 percent were landless, without title to farm, garden, or lot. Eight families among the propertyless secured sharecropping rights to farms or gardens for short times, but not one climbed the agricultural ladder. The great part of the Mexican families—three-quarters—entered and endured lives of agricultural labor.

The steady drift of Mexican families into Nueces before the massive migration of 1907-17 provided tenant farmers for the young county. On their tiny plots of ten or twenty acres they picked four or five bales of cotton. The Sánchez family, for instance, entered a sharecropping arrangement with W. B. Croft and W. W. Meek in 1900, cultivated five acres of cotton, and expanded their farm to one hundred acres by 1903. Two brothers, Paulino and Rafael Cadena, jointly worked fifty acres of cotton under a crop lien to Croft and Meek in 1903. Tenancies, however, rarely led to ownership. Occasionally a family like that of León Galván acquired a planter, middle buster, cultivator, and harrow, but its hold on such machinery was precarious. Moreover, the rapid influx of southern tenants at the end of World War I forced Mexican tenants off the most productive farms and onto marginal lands. By the early 1920s, all eight Mexican tenants in my sample had lost access to land, their places taken by black and white southerners.[15]

That left for three of every four Mexican families only agricultural labor. July's surge of workers, come to chop and to pick, left behind new families at September's ebb. Every large cotton farm provided seasonal work for two or three families. Laborers' shacks thickened the countryside and eventually raised whole towns on the plain. The movement into towns marked the maturation of a landless, wage-earning, store-buying, rural proletariat. The Mexican community now formed a mobile labor force whose major problem was to survive the dead times. "I'm going to Pennsylvania to escape the vagrant's lot," ran a famous *corrido* of south Texas; "Farewell, Texas, with your planted fields, I'm going to Pennsylvania so I won't have to pick cotton." So rapid a proletarianization threw families into an unending struggle to get through slack months and eventually to join great seasonal migrations to other areas of large-scale farming.[16]

The contrast of Czech with Mexican families leaps to the eye. Of the thirty-five families in my sample that remained three decades, two-thirds acquired farms. The holdings were modest, the median size barely exceeding eighty acres. The remainder of the families held long-term cash leases from family or relatives.

Czech families secured land largely because they had their own reserves of labor. Six families, five of whom came as families of three generations, with a little capital, a knowledge of cotton, and, most important, abundant labor, initially held 160 acres or more. All six endured into the second generation. Families starting out with 120 acres or less commonly lacked generational extension: ten of these sixteen families were young, lacked capital, and commanded only the husband's and wife's labor. The outcome of such beginnings was brutal: among the nine families with tiny farms of 20 to 40 acres, five lost everything before ten years passed, four clung to their farms by means of heavy mortgages. The successful establishment of a household depended upon a large labor force and upon the slow consolidation of resources over the cycle of a family's life. Only by fully exploiting their reserve of labor did families survive for two generations upon the land.[17]

The consequences of familial strategies over the long run show up in the passage from generation to generation. Now the first generation sorted sons and daughters into heirs and disinherited, into advantaged and disadvantaged. The eleven families that had come with mature children succeeded in ten cases in establishing at least one son. Like the family of Stanislav Procháska, by purchase, by gift, by will, they settled a new generation upon the land. Procháska moved to Nueces in 1909, when his family already counted two sons of fourteen and seventeen; Vlasta Mrázek bore him three more sons and a daughter. Procháska and his two eldest sons, Emil and Frank, worked a tenant farm of 80 acres between 1909 and 1921, then bought a farm of 160 acres in 1922; Ladislav and Anton settled on a new farm of 160 acres in 1926; Timothy, the youngest, briefly farmed 80 acres in 1929, then left this farm to his father. In his will, Procháska left the big farm to Emil and Frank and divided his farm equipment between them; each, in turn, chose one of his sons as major heir. Contrast Procháska with Anton Krušinsky, who came with his wife and one son in 1923, purchased 79 acres of cotton land, and conveyed 40 acres by deed of gift to his son in 1930. Often forced to enter chattel mortgages for operating expenses, Krušinsky and his family worked 39 acres for three decades, until at his death he divided his patch into five equal portions and gave them to his five children. Within a few months all but Rosa had sold their lands; she kept the old house and grew onions on her 8 acres. Like the Krušinskys, nine of the eleven families in similar circumstances were extinguished as farming families.[18]

Czechs came to Nueces to keep a customary way of farming and to maintain their united families and the kind of future they wanted for their families. They wanted to escape the changing agriculture of central Texas, so they moved on to another frontier where they hoped to renovate old forms of security. The families of this little community possessed several resources, of which the most significant was a labor force. Those families that realized their aim of assuring another generation's livelihood arrived in the county just as their children one after another reached maturity and provided a rising curve of labor. But those families without such working capacity largely disappeared from farming within ten years. And so was set in motion yet another migration, of the sons and daughters of extinguished farmers, now toward the cities.[19]

Immigrant families formed a complex pattern of farmers, tenants, and laborers. Czech farmers settled on the land; some held on to farms for at least two generations and thereby established a lineage in a situation of considerable uncertainty. Each successful family was a little community of labor and land. Although the accumulation and inheritance of land appears a wholly domestic affair, it had a crucial public dimension, for it created the conditions for the recruitment of a core population and hence maintained a Czech community. Mexican families met with extraordinary changes in these few years, for as tenants they were members of a little community of families, while as laborers they were as much participants in the wider society as members of a local community. They lost even their access to tenancies, hence their landlessness was no longer concealed. Mexican laborers, like Czech farmers, could not make things happen except collectively, though, unlike the farmers', the Mexican laborers' experience of labor demonstrated every day that they must act collectively or not at all.[20]

One thing becomes clear from the realities of the Czech and Mexican immigrants' lives. The departures from old situations and arrival in new rendered the past problematic. The past of Mexican haciendas and Czech villages ceased to be the soil in which these peoples had their roots and from which they drew life. At least they no longer did so in the matter-of-course manner of old. With special reference to their need for continuity, for stability—in a word, for culture—the fit between the world the immigrants lived in and life as they lived it, on the one hand, and the forms and institutions that their ancestors had used to order it and make it meaningful, on the other, had gone.

In order to grasp the distinctive attempts of Czech and Mexican newcomers to place their new worlds in some frame, we must seize upon the particular ways in which they used old forms in confrontation with altered conditions of life and how, out of that confrontation, came ethnic cultures that shaped and sustained their lives and communities. "For most individuals," Sidney Mintz and Richard Price remind us in their recent discussion of Afro-American cultures, "a commitment to, and an engagement in, a new social world must have taken precedence rather quickly over what would have become before long largely a nostalgia for their homelands." People ordinarily long, not for an abstract heritage, but for immediately experienced personal relationships, evolved in specific cultural and social settings, that any deracination such as migration may destroy. Hence a culture, in this sense, becomes closely linked to the social contexts in which ties of kinship and friendship are experienced.[21] I have trained my analysis thus far on the realities of economics and stratification by which the newcomers were restricted, and on the particular frameworks within which their new lives were fabricated. I turn now to a brief consideration of the manner in which cooperative efforts became institutions, of the ways in which religion became a bond of community, and, finally, of the means by which men and women transformed ritual associations into resources for collective action.

The Czech and Mexican families endured and, having endured,

reached beyond their households to bind themselves in little communities. Some shreds of evidence suggest that Mexican immigrants entered cooperative efforts soon after their arrival in Nueces County. Gang laborers on clearance projects formed a mutual benefit society in the mid-1880s; tenant farmers organized three similar societies between 1897 and 1905. Such voluntary networks of mutual aid widened after 1907 to include rural laborers; in the two following decades at least seventeen laborers' societies appeared. Formed sometimes among families already linked by kinship, more often among households in burgeoning rural settlements, mutual benefit societies translated private relations of trust into public cooperation. And in so doing, Mexican laborers made kinship and friendship, ritual and ceremonial—dimensions of old communities they had left—into passageways toward new communities.[22]

Czech families entered similarly reciprocal relationships. The springs of such cooperative acts were, in the case of Roman Catholics, the saints' societies of native villages, in which expectations of mutuality took visible form. From Williamson County eight families carried an image of St. Joseph that their parents had brought from the homeland; other allied families gathered under the patronage of St. Isadore. By the mid-1920s, eleven such societies, each numbering nine or ten families, pulled the Czech Catholics of Nueces into a round of organized life. Protestants also created societies of mutual aid, often as their first cooperative act. Among the Protestant heads of households were five men who had founded benefit societies upon their arrival in Texas, and now in Nueces their first response was establishment of a lodge of Podporná jednota (Mutual Aid Society). Wider than the circle of kindred but drawing upon the obligatory mutuality of kinship, such societies practiced the rituals of reciprocity without which a community cannot long endure. Such artificial families became the cores of both Czech and Mexican communities.[23]

The weave of small decisions of family and association also formed patterns of religious life. Institutional development flowed from the choices of many ordinary families as they reached beyond their own households for aid and support and, in so doing, forged some sense of the ordering of their world. "In the morning," noted an itinerant priest during a month's journey through the Mexican communities of Nueces in 1876, "Mass at about 7. Then on horseback to the next ranch, in the evening after supper Catechism, Rosary, a little instruction to the people, next day the same as the day before." In the two decades following, the dispersed communities of the region built chapels with such names as Concepción, Jesús María, Santo Tomás, Dolores, San Juan, Los Reyes, Las Ánimas.

Priests visited these missions sometimes once a year, most often once every six months.[24] The religious life of Mexican parishes, then, was a life of lay confraternities and sodalities in which the priest's role was sporadic and peripheral.

The Catholicism of rural communities responded to the needs of Mexican families in that it made a ritual statement about social relationships and obligations. My scraps of evidence indicate early lay initiative in the establishment of confraternities and sodalities, and a subsequent development of a complex and integrated religious framework. The proliferation of saints' societies, each encompassing families already bound by kinship, marked the emergence of community life, for now such families became associated in enactments of the Catholic calendar. In the parish of San José, for instance, newly arrived Mexican sharecroppers founded three saints' societies in 1898; gang laborers from a hacienda in Tamaulipas established a confraternity in honor of their patron saint in 1904; rural laborers created many such societies in 1914 and 1915. Such associations, set within networks of ongoing social relations, became the heart of parishes. At La Cejita, sixty families of rural laborers living within a few minutes' walk of each other formed six sodalities and confraternities between 1907 and 1916. They petitioned their bishop for a chapel in 1917, "in order better to manifest our good will and to secure our children's good, to practice more regularly our Catholic religion, and to receive proper instruction." The maturing communities of laborers built their own religious institutions, which the bishop and clergy served to sanction, not to control. The families' sense of making institutions on their own was expressed in the 1920s in petition after petition to their bishops in which hundreds of men and women resisted the efforts of clergy to exercise control over lay societies. Nowhere was this sense more urgently expressed than in a new parish of some two hundred laboring families in which members of several saints' societies successfully thwarted their priests' authority for five years. In practicing the ceremonials of togetherness in this world and procuring the salvation of their members in the next, saints' societies created a ritual method of living rich in human relationships.[25]

While Mexican Catholicism was expressive of concentric circles of social relations, Czech religious life formalized tangential circles of familial relationships. Czech Catholics quickly formed saints' societies, but with an important difference from Mexican societies; the charter members of Czech societies, in every case for which documentation survives, restricted membership to lineal and affinal kin, and thus created closed corporate groups. Such associations were the linchpins of parochial life, for their marches, vigils, and feasts drew families into representations of solidarity. The saints' day, customarily celebrated in the household of the oldest family in the society, periodically enacted the little dramas of Catholic life.[26]

Czech Protestants of the Jednota bratrska (Unity of the Brethren) created a similar framework for religious life. The heads of large families were the heart of the church; "Grant thy peace to this household and its heirs," prayed the pastor at the funerals of men, "even as Thou takest this thy son to thine own house." In such households the itinerant pastor administered ceremonies of baptism and confirmation, of marriage and burial, rites of personal and familial passage. Within this congregation were articulated relationships among members of the Czech Protestant community: the Elders, whose task was the maintenance of good order; the Christian Sisters, whose charge was charitable acts; and the Sunday school class, whose preparation was for passage through confirmation into adulthood.[27]

Out of the exigencies of lives predominantly hard and unendowed, Czech and Mexican immigrants evolved an unexpectedly mature pattern of sanctions and responsibilities. An assessment of the transition of peasants and laborers to modern agriculture depends upon a firm knowledge of ordinary peoples' lives, of the interaction of family, farm, and community, of older and new attitudes, and of particular places. Czech and Mexican families entered an unsettled rural world with distinctive cultures, but those cultures were more than backgrounds. Their cultures had their own meanings, expectations, definitions of purpose; they had their own rituals of reciprocity and rites of passage. After other impressions fade, this one remains: along with the loss of any felt cohesion in these communities, Czech farmers and Mexican laborers built for themselves new domestic and familial ties, new cooperative relationships, and new religious institutions.[28]

The achievement of contrasting solidarities—of a lineal order of familial and associational alliances among Czechs, of a concentric order of alliances among Mexicans—shaped different forms of collective action. In the Czech settlement, families fastened upon farmers' unions, which were gatherings of the heads of households, as a means of communal control of resources. The advantaged families—the landed core—found in this union sources of credit, cooperative arrangements for the purchase of equipment, and mutual aid in times of drought and low prices. A communal form of collective action, the Czech unions succeeded only sporadically in making alliances beyond the local circles of families.[29] Yet the union, a kind of local brotherhood, was the effective expression of Czech farmers' aspirations, for it assured continuity of lineage and property.

In the urgency of their needs, Mexican laborers reached beyond households, beyond mutual aid and religious associations, outward to solidary unions. The early stage of the movement was defensive and consisted of leagues of laborers bound together in opposition to landlords and foremen. Such defensive associations soon claimed not merely old but new rights, the most important of which was the right to organize. Agricultural laborers on one great Nueces cotton farm organized a defensive league in 1911; two years later they refused to work without a contract for wages and hours. The ferment of action and organization was alive in the county: gang laborers on clearance projects struck in 1907; teamsters walked off their jobs in 1910; rural laborers organized several locals between 1926 and 1937 and tried to form an agricultural workers' union in south Texas in 1937.[30] The failure of Mexican laborers to provide a centralized expression of their resistance should not obscure the importance of their constant stirrings; in opposition to their labor and their masters, rural laborers drew upon the resources of their communities to give political expression to their needs and aspirations.

To return to my initial question, Why did Czechs and Mexicans choose to be *Czech* farmers and *Mexican* laborers, and not just farmers and laborers? In their new world of modernized agriculture, these immigrants pursued two mingled yet distinct ends, the one a search for identity, the other a pursuit of decent and secure lives. Both demands led families beyond their households into communal association and, in the case of Mexican laborers, into labor organization. Ethnicity was, then, an expression of primary but extrafamilial identity, and a protean resource for collective action. Yet these contrary impulses produced ironic consequences. The little community of Czech farmers endured from generation to generation by securing the continuity upon the land of a few children and by disinheriting the others, hence the greater part of each generation had to find livelihood elsewhere. The community of Mexican laborers achieved a measure of solidarity, yet the maturation of that solidarity required alliance with other working-class organizations. Thus was set in motion processes of integration whose implications for these rural communities are still unfolding.[31]

Notes

1. Walter Prescott Webb, *The Great Plains* (Boston: Ginn and Co., 1931), pp. 207–10, 215, 224–25.

2. Data based on assessments in *Reports* of the Comptroller of Texas, 1871–1930. See A. W. Spaight, *The Resources, Soil, and Climate of Texas* (Galveston, 1882), p. 240; Paul S. Taylor, *An American-Mexican Frontier: Nueces*

County, Texas (Chapel Hill: University of North Carolina Press, 1934), pp. 71-85; Samuel L. Evans, "Texas Agriculture, 1880-1930" (Ph.D. diss., University of Texas, 1960), pp. 269, 272-73; Klaus Schroeder, *Agrarlandschaftsstudien in südlichsten Texas* (Frankfurt am Main: W. Kramer, 1962), pp. 40-46, 134-36. Cf. William N. Parker's "Introduction" to *European Peasants and Their Markets: Essays in Agrarian Economic History*, ed. William N. Parker and Eric L. Jones (Princeton, N.J.: Princeton University Press, 1975); and Pasquale Villani, *Feudalità, riforme, capitalismo agrario* (Bari, Italy: Laterza, 1968), pp. 159-60.

3. *Cotton and Cottonseed: Acreage, Yield, Production, Disposition, Price, Value: By States, 1866-1952*, U.S. Department of Agriculture, Statistical Bulletin 164 (1955), p. 18; John S. Spratt, *The Road to Spindletop: Economic Change in Texas, 1875-1901* (Dallas: Southern Methodist University Press, 1955), pp. 61-67, 70, 82-83; Texas, Department of Agriculture, *Eighth Annual Report . . . 1894*, pp. 202-3; John Willacy to James C. Fulton, January 8, 1900, George W. and James Fulton Papers, University of Texas Archives, Austin (hereafter cited as UTA); A. W. Mangum and H. L. Westover, "Soil Survey of Corpus Christi Area, Texas," U.S. Department of Agriculture, *Field Operations of the Bureau of Soils, 1908* (1911), pp. 901-2, 905, 909-10; U.S. Congress, Senate, *Commission on Industrial Relations*, 64th Cong., 1st sess., pt. 10 (1916), 9222-23; U.S. Bureau of the Census, *Thirteenth Census, 1910*, vol. 7, *Agriculture*, p. 648; *Fourteenth Census, 1920*, vol. 6, pt. 2, *Agriculture*, p. 731; *Fifteenth Census, 1930*, vol. 3, pt. 2, *Agriculture, Type of Farm, the Southern States*, p. 963.

4. Nueces County, Chattel Mortgage Record, H:111-12, 126-28, L:74-75; Harry Crawford to W. S. Crawford, August 4, 1907, October 27, 1909, Eli J. Capell Papers, Louisiana State University, Department of Archives, Baton Rouge; Tom Field to Donald Comer, January 11, 1923, James Comer Papers, Birmingham Public Library, Tutwiler Collection; Nueces County, Deeds, 121: 405-6, 206:7-8; Taylor, *American-Mexican Frontier*, pp. 91, 302, 305, 308. My construction of this material borrows from Richard Herr's essay, "Spain," in *European Landed Elites in the Nineteenth Century*, ed. David Spring (Baltimore: Johns Hopkins University Press, 1977), pp. 104-5, 110-11.

5. Joseph Almond Diary, August 1, 3, 9, 13, 15, 17, 1875, La Retama Library, Corpus Christi; Claude Jaullet Diary, 1876, pp. 15-16, Diocese of Corpus Christi Archives (hereafter cited as DCCA); Plum Creek Ranch Daybook, 1882, p. 105, Shelton Clark Dowell Ranch Records, UTA; Daybook, 1882-85, p. 259; Account Book, 1884-87, pp. 107, 109, 114, 117, 119, 124; Account Book 1886-89, pp. 300, 313, Fulton Papers, UTA; Census reports cited above, n. 3. The occupational and ethnic data from the countryside are based on a sample of males (N = 239), aged eighteen to thirty-five, drawn from draft records prepared in 1918-19 (Texas War Records Collection, UTA). *Commission on Industrial Relations*, pt. 10, pp. 9214-15; U.S. Congress, House, Immigration and Naturalization Committee, *Temporary Admission of Illiterate Mexican Laborers*, 66th Cong., 2d sess., H. J. Res. 271 (January 26-February 2, 1920), pp. 30-31, 48-49, 106, 133-34, 203-5; U.S. Congress, House, Immigration and Naturalization Committee, *Seasonal Agricultural Laborers from Mexico*, 69th Cong., 1st sess., H. R. 6741, 7559, 9036 (January 28-February 23, 1926), pp. 41-42; U.S. Congress, Senate, Committee on Education and Labor, *Violations of Free*

204 Czech Farmers and Mexican Laborers in South Texas

Speech and Rights of Labor, 76th Cong., 2d sess., pt. 47 (1939), pp. 17270-74. Cf. Vernon A. Briggs, Jr., Walter Fogel, and Fred H. Schmitt, *The Chicano Worker* (Austin: University of Texas Press, 1977), pp. 80-81.

6. David J. Weber, ed., *Foreigners in Their Native Land: Historical Roots of the Mexican Americans* (Albuquerque: University of New Mexico Press, 1973), pp. 145-47, 155-56; Rodman W. Paul, "The Spanish-Americans in the Southwest, 1848-1900," in *The Frontier Challenge: Responses to the Trans-Mississippi West,* ed. John G. Clark (Lawrence: University Press of Kansas, 1971), pp. 50-52; Taylor, *American-Mexican Frontier,* pp. 9-13, 179-88; Claude Jaillet to "Monsier le Directeur," August 20, 1886, DCCA; *El eco liberal* (San Diego, Tex.), January 25, 1891; *La fé católica* (San Antonio), March 26, 1898; Pierre F. Parisot, *The Reminiscences of a Texas Missionary* (San Antonio, 1899), pp. 120-33; Victor S. Clark, *Mexican Labor in the United States,* U.S. Bureau of Labor, Bulletin 78 (1908), pp. 468, 470-71, 514-15.

7. Terry G. Jordan, *German Seed in Texas Soil: Immigrant Farmers in Nineteenth-Century Texas* (Austin: University of Texas Press, 1966), pp. 31-59; F. H. Lohmann, *Comfort, ein kurzer Überblicht über das Leben and Treiben* (Comfort, Tex., 1904), pp. 32-36, 43-50; *Übersichtliche Darstellung über die Gründung, Entwicklung, und das Wirten der Neu Braunfelser . . . Unterstützungs-Verein . . . 1876-1901* (n.p., [1901]), pp. 8-10; *Kurze Geschichte des Suedlich-Deutschen Konfernz zum 50-jaehringen Jubilaeum . . . 1872-1922* (n.p., [1922]), pp. 72-87; *Festschrift zum 75-jähringen Jubiläum der St. Marien-Gemeinde zu Friedrichsburg, Texas, 1849-1921* (n.p. [1921]), pp. 61-65; *Schutze's Jahrbuch für Texas, Hermanns-Sohn Kalender für 1925* (San Antonio), pp. 49-52; Andrezj Brożek, *Ślązacy w Teksasie* (Warsaw: Pánstwowe Wydawn. Naukowe, 1972), pp. 23-38, 93, 95, 98, 100-1, 106-8, 122-24, 169-72; U.S. Congress, Senate, *Reports of the Immigration Commission,* 61st Cong., 2d sess., pt. 24, fasc. 2 (1911), pp. 383-86; *Svoboda* (La Grange, Tex.), March 8, 17, April 1, May 7, 1886; *Křest'anské listy* (Omaha) 4 (March 1902): 73-74, 91-92, 95-96; *Texan* (Houston), November 23, 1933.

8. Moisés Gonzáles Navarro, *El Porfiriato: La vida social,* vol. 4 of *Historia moderna de México,* ed. Daniel Cosío Villegas (Mexico City and Buenos Aires: Hermes, 1957), pp. 198-99, 213; Jan Bazant, *Cinco haciendas mexicanas: Tres siglos de vida rural en San Luis Potosí* (Mexico City: Colegio de México, 1975), pp. 152-54, 160, 174-75, 178-79; Friedrich Katz, "Labor Conditions on Haciendas in Porfirian Mexico: Some Trends and Tendencies," *Hispanic American Historical Review* 54 (February 1974): 34-37; idem, "Agrarian Changes in Northern Mexico in the Period of *Villista* Rule, 1913-1915," in *Contemporary Mexico: Papers of the IV International Congress of Mexican History,* ed. James W. Wilkie, Michael C. Meyer, and Edna Monzón de Wilkie (Berkeley: University of California Press, 1976), pp. 266-68, 273; Arthur F. Corwin, "Causes of Mexican Emigration to the United States: A Summary View," *Perspectives in American History* 7 (1973): 564.

The reconstitution of Mexican (N = 99) and Czech (N = 35) families from parochial and civil records forms the basis of Sections II and III. Since the number is small, I do not attach much importance to any single distribution; I have sought, rather, to reconstruct patterns of migration, family formation and maturation, and agricultural activity over two generations.

9. Bedřich Šindelář, "K bojinu moravského selského lidu proti kapitalismu za posledních sto let," Matica moravská, *Sborník* 72 (1953): 80–128; Zdenek Salzmann and Vladimír Scheufler, *Komárov: A Czech Farming Village* (New York: Holt, Rinehart, & Winston, 1974), pp. 44–47, 64–67; Jaroslava Hoffmannová, *Vystěhovalectví z Polně do Severní Ameriky ve druhé polovině XIX. století* (Havlíčkův Brod: G. Jihlava, 1969), pp. 10–20, 34–39; Ludmila Kárníková, *Vyvoj obyvatelstva v českých zemích, 1754–1914* (Prague: Nakl. Československé Akademie Věd, 1965), pp. 133–36.

10. U.S. Bureau of the Census, *Tenth Census, 1880,* vol. 5, *Report on Cotton Production in the United States,* pt. 1, 102–3, 130–32; Národní Svaz Českých Katolíků v Texas, *Naše dějiny* (Granger, Tex.: Našinec, 1939), pp. 68–69, 194–201, 437–41; *Památník českých evanjelických církví ve Spojených Státech* (Chicago: Vilem Šiller, 1900), pp. 148–50, 157–58, 160; *Svoboda,* April 25, May 16, 1895; *Bratrské listy* (La Grange, Tex.) 1 (May 1902): 35–36. Cf. Oscar Lewis, *On the Edge of the Black Waxy* (St. Louis: Washington University, 1948), pp. 74–75, 104. Immigration Commission, *Reports,* pt. 24, fasc. pp. 389, 393; cf. *Svoboda,* November 19, 1900, January 26, 1905; *Obzor* (Hallettsville, Tex.) 15 (1905–1906): 265; J. T. Sanders, *Farm Ownership and Tenancy in the Black Prairie of Texas,* U.S. Department of Agriculture, Bulletin 1068 (1922), pp. 5–7, 16–17, 31–33.

11. Jaillet Diary, 1876, pp. 16–17, DCCA; Dominic Manucy to "Monsieur le Directeur," January 17, 1880, and J. P. Bard to Claude Jaillet, June 15, 1912, DCCA; Paul S. Taylor, *Mexican Labor in the United States,* 2 vols. (Berkeley: University of California Press, 1928–32), 1:299, 304–5; idem, *American-Mexican Frontier,* pp. 113–15; *Adelante* (San Antonio) 1 (January 1920): 12. Cf. Charles H. Harris's discussion of chapels and hacienda laborers in *A Mexican Family Empire: The Latifundo of the Sánchez Navarros, 1765–1867* (Austin: University of Texas Press, 1975), pp. 219–21.

12. Cf. the remarkable letter from a settlement of families from Režnová (Moravia) near Floresville, in *Našinec* (Hallettsville, Tex.), February 2, 1916.

13. Paul Taylor's sample of 1,078 Mexican nationals registered at the Mexican Consulate, Corpus Christi, 1928–29, shows three-quarters from the northern states of Nuevo León, Tamaulipas, San Luis Potosí, and Coahuila (*American-Mexican Frontier,* p. 95). See Alberto Montemayor's description of his and his brother's families' movements about south Texas, in *El demócrata fronterizo* (Laredo), September 2, 1905. The following accounts convey a sense of the remarkable resiliency of family bonds among migrant Mexican families: Ruth A. Allen, *The Labor of Women in the Production of Cotton* (Austin: University of Texas Press, 1931), pp. 225–27; U.S. Congress, House, *Hearings . . . Select Committee to Investigate the Interstate Migration of Destitute Citizens,* 76th Cong., 3d sess., pt. 3 (1940), pp. 1310–12; Amber A. Warburton, Helen Wood, and Marian M. Crane, *The Work and Welfare of Agricultural Laborers in Hidalgo County, Texas,* U.S. Department of Labor, Children's Bureau Publication 298 (1943), pp. 53, 69–70.

14. Cf. Eric R. Wolf, "Cultural Dissonance in the Italian Alps," *Comparative Studies in Society and History* 5 (October 1962): 9-11; Julian Pitt-Rivers, *The Fate of Schechem: Essays in the Anthropology of the Mediterranean* (Cambridge: Cambridge University Press, 1977), p. 91; Charles Tilly and C. Harold Brown, "On Uprooting, Kinship, and the Auspices of Migration," in *An Urban World*, ed. Charles Tilly (Boston: Little, Brown, 1974), pp. 111-14, 127-28, 130.

15. Nueces County, Chattel Mortgage Record, B:28, 69, 78-79, 84, 90; H:97, 111-12, 126-28, L:74-75, 104, 1:86-87. A survey of vols. 1-4 (1923-24) of Chattel Mortgage Record confirms the disappearance of Mexican tenants. Cf. the reports of the displacement of Mexican tenants by black and white southerners in *Commission on Industrial Relations*, pt. 10, pp. 9282-85; Peter Verdaguer to S. R. Dyer, September 11, 1915, DCCA; *La prensa* (San Antonio), May 24, 1922.

16. *El demócrata fronterizo*, October 14, 1905; *La crónica* (Laredo), February 5, December 17, 1910, January 26, 1911; John Toujas to Paul Nussbaum, September 15, 1914, DCCA; *La prensa*, May 24, 1922. Cf. Clark, *Mexican Labor*, pp. 482-83; *Commission on Industrial Relations*, pt. 10, p. 9083; Taylor, *American-Mexican Frontier*, pp. 98-99, 118, 121, 189. Américo Paredes, *A Texas-Mexican Cancionero: Folksongs of the Lower Border* (Urbana: University of Illinois Press, 1976), p. 56; U.S. Congress, House, Immigration and Naturalization Committee, *Immigration from Countries of the Western Hemisphere*, 70th Cong., 1st sess., H. R. 6495, 7358, 10955, 11687 (February 21-April 5, 1928), pp. 578; Migration Committee, *Hearings*, pt. 5 (1940), pp. 1875-77, 1888-95. Sidney W. Mintz's *Worker in the Cane* (New Haven, Conn.: Yale University Press, 1960), pp. 131-39, 173-76, 206-7, and his *Caribbean Transformations* (Chicago: Aldine, 1974), p. 125, inform my understanding of the emergence of a rural proletariat.

17. Czech farmers reveal in their letters a full awareness of this crucial aspect of family farming; see, e.g., *Svoboda*, December 15, 1904, June 12, 1906, May 9, July 15, 1910, September 16, 1920; *Obzor* 15 (1905-1906): 267; *Nový domov* (Hallettsville, Tex.), February 5, August 2, 1925; *Našinec*, May 14, 1925. Plats of Bohemian Colony Lands and Agua Dulce Farm Lots reveal characteristic patterns of succession (Nueces County, Plat Records, A:48, 76). On labor allocation in family farming, see Theodore W. Schultz, *Transforming Traditional Agriculture* (New Haven, Conn.: Yale University Press, 1964), pp. 30-31, 39, 48.

18. My treatment owes much to Emmanuel Le Roy Ladurie, *Le Territoire de l'historien* (Paris: Gallimard, 1973), pp. 224-25, 249-50; and to Lutz K. Berkner and Franklin F. Mendels, "Inheritance Systems, Family Structure, and Demographic Patterns in Western Europe, 1700-1900," in *Historical Studies of Changing Fertility*, ed. Charles Tilly (Princeton, N.J.: Princeton University Press, 1978), pp. 213-14. Nueces County, Deeds, 138:227-30, 144:133-35, 165: 568-69, 199:193-94; Nueces County Clerk, Probate Record, 73:119-21, 127, 134:599-603, 143:274-79, 188:576-77; Nueces County, Chattel Mortgage Record, 1:88.

19. Cf. Lutz K. Berkner, "The Stem Family and the Developmental Cycle of the Peasant Household: An Eighteenth-Century Austrian Example," *American Historical Review* 77 (April 1972): 414, 418. *Svoboda*, January 26, 1905; *Nový domov*, September 3, October 5, 1925; *Našinec* (Granger, Tex.), February 3, 1950.

20. Cf. John W. Cole and Eric R. Wolf, *The Hidden Frontier: Ecology and Ethnicity in an Alpine Valley* (New York: Academic Press, 1974), pp. 181, 202-4; Sidney W. Mintz, "The Rural Proletariat and the Problem of Rural Proletarian Consciousness," *Journal of Peasant Studies* 1 (April 1974): 308-11.

21. My sense of relationships between context and culture draws on the work of Clifford Geertz, especially on *Islam Observed: Religious Development in Morocco and Indonesia* (New Haven, Conn.: Yale University Press, 1968), pp. 20-21. Sidney W. Mintz and Richard Price, *An Anthropological Approach to the Afro-American Past: A Caribbean Perspective*, ISHI Occasional Papers in Social Change, no. 2 (Philadelphia: Institute for the Study of Human Issues, 1976), p. 24. Cf. Orlando Patterson, "Context and Choice in Ethnic Allegiance: A Theoretical Framework and Caribbean Case Study," in *Ethnicity: Theory and Experience*, ed. Nathan Glazer and Daniel P. Moynihan (Cambridge, Mass.: Harvard University Press, 1975), pp. 308-9.

22. *El horizonte* (Laredo), October 11, 1884; Nueces County, Deeds, 1:494-95, 15:640, 116:455-57; *La fé católica*, May 15, December 4, 1897; *El demócrata fronterizo*, May 6, 1905. Cf. Weber, *Foreigners in Their Native Land*, pp. 216-19. *El demócrata fronterizo*, June 20, 1908, May 10, 1913; *La crónica*, April 2, 30, July 9, 1910, July 27, 1911; Nueces County, Deeds, 116:607-8; Leonard Cunningham to Paul Nussbaum, November 22, 1915; E. M. De Bruyn to Emmanuel Ledvina, [1923]; Joseph Leben to Ledvina, June 14, 1928, all in DCCA; *El progreso* (Corpus Christi), July 7, 1939. Cf. Taylor, *American-Mexican Frontier*, pp. 173-74. See Eric R. Wolf, "Kinship, Friendship, and Patron-Client Relations in Complex Societies," in *The Social Anthropology of Complex Societies*, ed. Michael Banton (London: Tavistock, 1966), pp. 9-15; Abner Cohen, "Introduction: The Lesson of Ethnicity," in *Urban Ethnicity*, ed. Abner Cohen (London: Tavistock, 1974), p. xvii.

23. *Svoboda*, February 5, 1900, February 9, July 6, 1905, June 12, 1906; *Obzor* 15 (1905-1906): 46, 56; *Našinec*, March 24, May 5, September 6, 1951; Nueces County, Deeds, 244:118-19; *Památník devacetipěti-letého trvání Podpůrné Jednoty Česko-Moravských Bratří . . . 6. a 7. čer'ce. 1930* (Granger, Tex.: Bratrské Listy, 1932), pp. 3-4, 7-8, 12-13, 19; *Bratrské listy* 4 (September 1905): 382-86, 7 (July 1908): 741-43, 12 (April 1913): 13; Josef Barton, notebook labeled "Jihozápad, 1933-39," entry for June 30, 1939 (in possession of Josef A. Barton). Cf. Gabriel Le Bras's discussion of confraternities in *Etudes de sociologie religieuse*, 2 vols. (Paris: Presses Universitaires de France, 1955-56), 2:423.

24. Jaillet Diary, 1876, p. 15, DCCA; Peter Verdaguer to Felipe Caballero, September 4, 1892, Verdaguer Letterbook, DCCA; *La fé católica*, June 11, 1898; *A Parish Remembers . . . Fifty Years of Oblate Endeavour in the Valley of the Rio Grande (1909-1959)* (Mercedes, Tex., 1959), pp. 7-9.

25. *La fè catòlica*, January 8, 1898; *El demòcrata fronterizo*, October 29, 1904; *Southern Messenger* (New Orleans), March 12, October 22, 1914, April 1, 22, June 24, 1915; "Al Ilmô Señor Paul Nussbaum, Obispo de Corpus Christi," June 23, 1917, DCCA; Francisco Rodríguez et al. to Emmanuel Ledvina, April 6, 1924; Bernardino García et al. to Ledvina, June 1928; Mateo Bôsquez et al. to Ledvina, June 1928; cf. "A su Ilustrísima el Señor Obispo Pablo Juan," March 29, 1916; T. J. Connoly to Ledvina, October 21, 1924, December 30, 1926, all in DCCA; *El progreso*, September 15, 1939. On Mexican Catholicism as both product of and response to social life, see Jean Meyer, *La cristiada*, 3 vols. (Mexico City: Siglo Veintiuno, 1973-74), 3:304-7.

26. Národní Svaz, *Naše dějiny*, pp. 30-31, 78-80, 370-71; *Našinec* (Taylor, Tex.), February 14, 1919; Joseph Klobouk to Emmanuel Ledvina, November 18, 1921; Ledvina to Valentin Kohlbeck, December 4, 1923, both in DCCA; *Našinec*, February 16, March 16, June 4, 18, 1925; *Nový domov*, February 15, 1926.

27. *Agenda čili způsoby církevního přisluhování pro reformované sbory v Čechách a na Moravě . . . 1877* (Vienna, 1881), p. 228; *Bratrské listy* 12 (January 1913): 4-5, 13 (May 1914): 6-7, 14 (November 1915): 10; Josef Barton, notebook labeled "Robstown, Kingsville Diaspora," entry for November 23, 1924; idem, "Jihozápad," November 25, 1934, January 27, 1935 (both in possession of Josef A. Barton).

28. See, on these themes, Herbert G. Gutman, *Work, Culture, and Society in Industrializing America* (New York: Knopf, 1976), pp. 74-75; E. P. Thompson, "On History, Sociology, and Historical Relevance," *British Journal of Sociology* 27 (September 1976): 399-400; Timothy L. Smith, "Religion and Ethnicity in America," *American Historical Review* 83 (December 1978): 1178-79.

29. *Svoboda*, August 3, 1905, May 17, 1907, April 21, 1908; *Našinec*, September 6, 1915; *Minutes . . . Eleventh Annual Meeting . . . Farmers' Educational and Cooperative Union of Texas . . . August 5-9, 1913*, pp. 17, 58.

30. O. Douglas Weeks, "The Texas-Mexicans and the Politics of South Texas," *American Political Science Quarterly* 24 (1930): 620, 626-27; *El aldeano* (Uribeño, Tex.), September 27, 1908; *Commission on Industrial Relations*, pt. 10, pp. 9200-9205; *La crônica*, July 6, September 28, 1911; *La prensa*, July 30, 1914, November 17, 1922; *The Rebel* (Hallettsville, Tex.), November 25, 1911, July 12, 1913; *El defensor del obrero* (Laredo), 1 (1906-1907): 160; *Houston Labor Journal*, June 4, 1910; Agricultural Workers' Union minutes, January 23, 1937, Labor Movement in Texas Collection, UTA; *El progreso*, June 21, 1939.

31. Clifford Geertz, *The Interpretation of Cultures* (New York: Basic Books, 1973), pp. 258, 268-69, 308-9, gives a thoughtful account of these linked, different meanings of ethnicity. Cf. E. J. Hobsbawm's reflections on newcomers to modern industrial society, in *Primitive Rebels*, 3d ed. (Manchester: Manchester University Press, 1971), pp. 10, 108. John Higham, *Send*

These to Me: Jews and Other Immigrants in Urban America (New York: Atheneum, 1975), pp. 22-28, 232-33, provides an illuminating context for these last considerations.

Ethnic Assimilation and Pluralism in Nebraska

*J. Allen Williams, Jr., David R. Johnson,
and Miguel A. Carranza*

Empirical studies dealing with ethnic identity and assimilation in the United States were first conducted in the early part of this century as immigration from southern and eastern Europe and Asia increased (Thomas and Znaniecki's *The Polish Peasant in Europe and America* and Louis Wirth's *The Ghetto* are outstanding examples). However, interest in nationality groups appears to have declined with the cessation of large-scale immigration after 1929. Beginning in the 1930s, sociologists and psychologists working in the field of race and ethnic relations tended to concentrate most of their efforts on studying either racial minorities, especially black Americans, or on trying to discover the origins of prejudice and discrimination. The plight of racial minorities was no doubt perceived as a most pressing issue, and the focusing of research on solving race-related problems is understandable in that light. But study of other ethnic groups did not cease entirely. For example, anti-Semitism prompted research; the "Yankee City Series" devoted a volume to an examination of ethnic communities; and several studies of specific ethnic groups were carried out. Nevertheless, comparative, empirical research on the importance of nationality identifications and whether these identifications have been changing over time has generally been neglected. In fact, Nathan Glazer and Daniel Moynihan's *Beyond the Melting Pot*, published in 1963, was the first major comparative study of American ethnic groups since R. J. R. Kennedy's analysis of ethnic intermarriage in 1944, and both of those studies were limited to single northeastern cities.[1]

The past tendency to focus on specific groups rather than conduct comparative studies, the restricted geographical coverage of past studies, and the dearth of research on nationality groups in general explains why there is little consensus among scholars regarding the current importance of ethnicity in American society. On the one hand, Robin Williams, in his *American Society: A Sociological*

Interpretation, states that "nationality and ethnic identifications and sociocultural characteristics persist as important influences in present day American life." Milton Gordon has stated the "essential thesis" of his *Assimilation in American Life* to be that "the sense of ethnicity has proved to be hardy." He goes on to place nation of origin, "the nation which our ancestors who first came to this country came *from*," at the heart of self-identity. Leonard Dinnerstein and David Reimers, on the other hand, maintain that "the old immigrants, those coming in large numbers between 1840 and 1890 from northern and western Europe, have largely assimilated and lost much of their original culture." They suggest that immigrants from southern and eastern Europe retain some aspects of their original culture, but "believe that we are on the threshold of the disappearance of the European ethnic minorities."[2]

The purpose of this paper is to report findings from a 1977 survey that asked a random sample of 1,867 adult Nebraskans about their ethnic background and its importance to them.[3] The study is state-wide and compares the degree of assimilation among seventeen different ethnic groups. Our primary goals were to determine whether some groups are more assimilated than others and, if so, why.

Ethnic Assimilation: The Dependent Variable

Although assimilation has been defined in a variety of ways, a central notion is the merger of groups. We find it useful to distinguish among three types of assimilation: cultural, social, and psychological.[4] *Cultural assimilation*, or acculturation, is the process whereby the cultures of two or more groups are fused into a common culture shared by the groups. *Social assimilation* occurs when the social organizations of two or more groups merge into an integrated social system. *Psychological assimilation* results when two or more groups move toward sharing a single ethnic self-concept or sense of peoplehood. Each of these refers to a process that permits one to speak of degrees of assimilation. Furthermore, each can vary in the extent of "balance." That is, the cultures of the groups may be blended into a new culture (following the "melting pot" theory), or a group may lose its culture while taking on the culture of another group. Within the context of the United States, the latter type of assimilation has been referred to as Americanization and as Anglo-conformity. To the extent that the original cultures are not merged, we have *cultural pluralism*, or an "ethnic federation."[5]

To measure ethnicity we asked respondents, "From what countries or part of the world did your ancestors come?" If they gave the name of a single country or did not know, we coded the response and went on to the next question. If they mentioned two or more countries, we asked them which they felt closest to. In addition to measuring ethnic background, this question gives us a first approximation of assimilation, in that persons who do not know their national origins would seem to be rather thoroughly merged into the American social system and its culture and to have lost any other sense of ethnic identity. Persons who named two or more countries and could not choose one they felt closest to would also appear to be far along the path to assimilation. Of course it is possible to name a single country or to choose one from among two or more and still feel little, if any, psychological identification with the country named. Consequently, our second question was, "Is thinking of yourself as of (Country Named) descent very important, somewhat important, or not very important to you?" Those who answered "not very important" are assumed to be the most psychologically assimilated.

A measure of social and cultural assimilation was developed by computing the proportion of each ethnic group stating that their ancestors came from two or more countries. Ethnic intermarriage requires crossing social-system lines and merging the social organizations of the groups through the extended family. At least the married couples and the children of these interethnic unions, and probably others as well, are exposed to both cultural heritages.

Ethnic Assimilation in Nebraska and the United States

The findings in response to the questions discussed above are presented in table 1 for both Nebraska and the United States.[6] We believe that an understanding of ethnicity and ethnic assimilation in this Great Plains state is enhanced through a comparison with the national population. These data suggest that knowledge of one's ethnic background is a widely shared form of information. Only 8.7 percent of Nebraskans and 11.8 percent of the national sample were unable to name a country of origin. However, combining these respondents with those who mentioned two or more nations of origin but could not choose one they felt closest to, we have a minimum of 18.7 percent of Nebraskans and 22.7 percent of all Americans who express no identity with a nation other than the United States.

TABLE 1

Ability to Name National Origins,
Nebraskans and All Americans, 1977

	Nebraska		United States	
	Number	Percent	Number	Percent
Named one country of origin	1,053	57.0	842	55.4
Named two or more countries, chose one	449	24.3	334	22.0
Named two or more countries, could not choose one	185	10.0	166	10.9
Could not name a country of origin	160	8.7	179	11.8
Total	1,847	100.0	1,521	100.0

Table 2 shows the national origins of both the Nebraska and the United States population. As can be seen, among those who named a single country or were able to indicate one they felt closest to, Nebraska exceeds the national average in persons whose ancestors came from Czechoslovakia, Denmark, Germany, and Sweden. On the other hand, Nebraska has proportionally smaller populations with ancestors from Africa, Italy, and the various smaller groups combined in the category "Other." Persons of German descent constitute by far the largest group, 39.9 percent. The next largest group, 13.8 percent, trace their ancestry to England or Wales. If those who have ancestors from the three Scandinavian countries of Denmark, Norway, and Sweden are combined, they make up the third-largest segment of the population, 12.2 percent. About 11.3 percent named Ireland and 5.3 percent have ancestors from Czechoslovakia. Together, these groups make up 82.5 percent of Nebraska's ethnic population.

As noted above, we asked people in our second question if their national origin was important to them. The same question was asked of a national sample in 1973.[7] About half, 50.2 percent, of Nebraskans told us that it was not very important, while 67.9 percent of all Americans responded that way. This information, along with the data on persons who either could not name a country from which their ancestors came or who could not choose one they felt

TABLE 2

National Origins of Nebraskans and All Americans, 1977

| | Nebraska | | United States* | |
Country	Number	Percent	Number	Percent
Africa	20	1.3	516	7.2
Czechoslovakia	79	5.3	104	1.5
Denmark	59	3.9	74	1.0
England and Wales	208	13.8	1,071	15.0
France	13	0.9	174	2.4
Germany	600	39.9	1,419	19.9
Ireland	170	11.3	852	11.9
Italy	23	1.5	446	6.2
Mexico	11	0.7	169	2.4
Netherlands	16	1.1	140	2.0
Norway	24	1.6	158	2.2
Poland	33	2.2	248	3.5
Russia (USSR)	22	1.5	154	2.2
Scotland	33	2.2	237	3.3
Sweden	101	6.7	132	1.9
Switzerland	17	1.1	40	0.6
Other	60	4.0	1,008	14.1
American Indian	15	1.0	203	2.8
Totals	1,504	100.0	7,145	100.0

*Aggregated data, 1972–77.

closest to, suggests that a majority of Americans are very near to total psychological assimilation. This type of assimilation, however, appears to be less prevalent in Nebraska than in the nation as a whole.

Table 3 gives the percentages of persons identifying their national origin who stated that it was not very important, ranked by ethnic group for Nebraska and the United States as a whole. With the exception of Scotland, all of the percentages for nationality groups in Nebraska are smaller than those for the total population. Some of the differences, however, are much greater than others. For example, the difference between Nebraskans who trace their ancestry to the Netherlands and their counterparts in the national sample is 43.4 percent, while the two Danish groups differ by only 2.3 percent.

TABLE 3

Persons Responding That National Origin Was Not Important, Nebraska, 1977, and the United States, 1973

Country	Nebraska			United States		
	Number	Percent	Rank	Number	Percent	Rank
Scotland	33	72.3	1	117	65.2	10
Russia (USSR)	22	66.6	2	75	85.5	1
Switzerland	17	64.1	3	13	73.8	6
Denmark	59	62.7	4	17	65.0	11
England and Wales	208	57.8	5	459	81.3	2
France	13	56.3	6	76	76.2	5
Germany	594	55.8	7	553	77.6	4
Ireland	170	45.6	8	362	68.0	8
Poland	24	39.8	9	107	53.9	13
Sweden	101	37.3	10	54	70.4	7
Norway	24	36.5	11	39	56.1	12
American Indian	14	35.9	12	17	52.9	14
Netherlands	16	35.1	13	58	78.4	3
Czechoslovakia	77	30.9	14	35	66.5	9
Italy	23	29.4	15	168	42.6	15
Mexico	11	20.4	16	51	34.5	17
Africa	20	10.1	17	140	38.4	16
Totals	1,453			2,341		

The data presented in table 3 also give information about the relative degree of psychological assimilation among ethnic groups. The most assimilated groups in both samples are those with national origins in northern and western Europe. The Soviet Union, or Russia, is the one outstanding exception to this general finding. There are several explanations for the apparently high degree of psychological assimilation among persons tracing their origins to that eastern European nation. First, the Soviet Union includes a number of countries that once had separate national identities. Second, some immigrants from Russia, such as the Jews, had a separate cultural identity; others, who are especially important for Nebraska, were the descendants of Germans who settled for a century along the Volga River before emigrating after 1873. Third, at least since World War II the Soviet Union has been perceived by many Americans as an enemy of the United States, and people who named Russia as the country of their national origin may have wished to avoid identification with an enemy. In both samples, persons of Mexican, African, and Italian descent are the least assimilated. Czechoslovakians rank fourteenth in Nebraska, whereas American Indians rank fourteenth nationally.

Table 4 shows the percentages for the Nebraska and United States samples who mentioned two or more countries of origin. The larger the percentage, the more a group has intermarried with other groups. While intermarriage is clearly not the only path to social and cultural assimilation, we believe that ethnic exogamy is an important indicator of the crossing of social boundaries and the merging of group cultures. The findings presented in table 4 indicate that thirteen of the seventeen nationality groups in Nebraska are less likely to have a mixed ethnic background than are these groups

TABLE 4

Percentage Who Mentioned Two or More Countries
among Those Who Named a Nation of Origin
Nebraska, 1977, and United States, 1973

Country	Nebraska			United States		
	Number	Percent	Rank	Number	Percent	Rank
Ireland	170	**50.2**	1	387	46.1	4
Switzerland	17	48.8	2	14	44.5	5
England and Wales	208	46.0	3	497	47.4	3
Italy	23	44.2	4	181	17.3	15
Scotland	33	41.9	5	119	50.7	1
France	13	38.6	6	79	41.7	7
American Indian	15	36.4	7	22	36.7	10
Sweden	101	34.7	8	54	48.1	2
Netherlands	16	30.7	9	60	37.9	9
Denmark	59	27.8	10	17	33.9	11
Norway	24	21.2	11	42	33.3	13
Poland	33	20.5	12	115	33.4	12
Germany	600	19.9	13	578	40.1	8
Czechoslovakia	79	19.7	14	41	44.3	6
Mexico	11	16.9	15	56	7.0	17
Africa	20	5.0	16	156	9.3	16
Russia (USSR)	22	3.9	17	82	30.7	14

nationally. If mixed ancestry is an index of sociocultural assimilation, it is apparent that the most assimilated groups in both samples tend to consist of persons whose ancestors came from northern and western European nations. The two exceptions to this generalization among Nebraskans are the Italians and American Indians. A partial explanation for this phenomenon among Indians is that all of those in the state sample live off the reservations. Hence, they generally represent the most assimilated segment of American Indians in Nebraska. In the case of the Italians, it will be recalled that they form a proportionally much smaller group in Nebraska than in the United States as a whole. Generally, the smaller the group in relation to the total population, the greater the outmarriage.[8] This also may explain why persons of Czechoslovak and German origin are more likely to have mixed ancestry in the national sample than in the Nebraska sample. Proportionally they form much smaller groups in the nation as a whole than in Nebraska. The least assimilated groups by this measure in the state are those who report having ancestors from Russia, Africa, Mexico, and Czechoslovakia. The least assimilated in the United States sample are those reporting national origins in Mexico, Africa, Italy, and Russia.

Factors Associated with Ethnic Assimilation: The Independent Variables

Studies of assimilation can be approached at both the group and individual levels. The two are obviously interrelated, but different analytic questions and procedures are involved. For this paper we have chosen to compare groups. We have already seen that some of Nebraska's ethnic groups are more assimilated than others. Our next research task was to discover why that was true.

Social and Economic Variables

Primacy of Arrival. It seems reasonable to propose that, all else being equal, the longer a group has been in an area, the more assimilated it will be. (Of course all else is rarely, if ever, equal.) Statistics on immigration into the United States from 1820 to the present show that the number of persons coming from northern and western Europe peaked in the latter half of the nineteenth century while immigration from southern and eastern Europe was at its highest between 1900 and 1930.[9] Since persons in the so-called new immigration tended to differ more dramatically from those in the United

States with respect to their social and cultural patterns, especially in religion, than did the earlier immigrants, this difference, rather than their more recent arrival, could account for their less rapid assimilation. However, it is possible to isolate these effects at least partially by comparing groups with similar cultures who entered the country at different times.

To measure primacy of arrival in Nebraska, we examined the flow of immigration into each of Nebraska's ninety-three counties from 1870 through 1950 for each of the seventeen nationality groups.[10] This allowed us to find the peak year of immigration for each group into each county. Then, by comparing across counties, we were able to determine an approximate date of arrival. For example, in sixty of the ninety-three counties, the number of persons born in England or Wales peaked in 1880. This means that the largest contingency of the English and Welsh came into the state sometime between 1870 and 1880—placing them among the earliest arrivers. On the other hand, the largest influx of persons born in the Netherlands was in 1920. Each ethnic group was given a score for date of arrival, starting with 1870 and ending with 1950.[11]

Social Distance. The nearer a group's members are to being perceived as the social equals of the dominant population, the greater the likelihood of assimilation.[12] In other words, discrimination against an ethnic group can hinder or prevent social interaction across group boundaries. Furthermore, discrimination can enhance feelings of in-group solidarity and reinforce psychological identification with the group and its origins rather than with the people of the larger society. A social distance scale developed by Emory Bogardus has been administered to national samples of Americans since 1926.[13] A respondent is given a list of thirty ethnic groups and for each is asked such questions as whether a member of that group should be admitted to his club as a personal chum, to close kinship by marriage, and to his street as a neighbor. People from English-speaking nations have consistently been given the most favorable scores, followed by persons from other northern and western European nations. People from southern and eastern European nations receive lower rankings, and the least acceptable are nonwhites or persons from nations with predominantly nonwhite populations.[14] A social distance score was developed for each of the ethnic groups in the present study by averaging the social distance scores for the group obtained in 1926, 1946, 1956, and 1966. We believe that an average of the scores over a forty-year period better reflects the historical experience of the group than would a score obtained at one point in time.

Socioeconomic Status. The higher the socioeconomic status of a group, the greater the assimilation. Participation in America's educational system typically brings people into contact with individuals and cultures beyond a single ethnic group.[15] Higher-status occupations are more likely to expose people to a variety of experiences, both social and cultural, than are those of lower status. Money is a resource that may be used to facilitate contact. A measure of socioeconomic status was developed for each group in the present study by combining average income, educational attainment, and occupational status, after standardizing them to a common base (Z-scores).[16] As might be expected, minorities such as black and Mexican Americans scored relatively low on this index, while persons who trace their ancestry to such nations as England, Wales, or Scotland scored high.

Ecological Variables

Residential Heterogeneity. Settlement patterns varied considerably among ethnic groups as they came into Nebraska. The majority of Czechs, for example, entered the state between 1910 and 1920 and, for the most part, settled in five counties. Most Scots, on the other hand, arrived in Nebraska between 1880 and 1900 and tended to settle in small groups or as individual families throughout the state. We expected higher residential heterogeneity to be associated with greater assimilation. To the extent that a group is scattered, the more difficult it is to maintain group identification and integration and to preserve cultural traditions. To measure this variable, a residential heterogeneity index was constructed that gives a high value if a group is distributed in exactly the same manner as Nebraskans in general— in other words, when ethnicity has no relationship to place of residence.[17] Thus, the lower the score, the less the dispersion, or, to put it another way, the greater the concentration of the group in a specific geographical location in the state.

Population Density. The lower the population density, the greater the assimilation. In the areas of Nebraska with low population density, the great distances between neighbors reduces the size of the social community. Thus, unless an ethnic group represents a very large proportion of the total population in an area, its ability to support ethnic organizations and institutions is quite limited. The result is that the people who do interact with one another must shape organizations consistent with their common needs, which, we suggest, will represent a blending of their diverse ethnic backgrounds. In a high-density area, even when a group is a small proportion of the total population, the number of group members within a certain geographical radius will often be large enough to support and reinforce ethnic traditions through, for example, a church, lodge, recreational activities, or a grocery store. Population density was measured by computing the average community size of the respondents' place of residence for each ethnic group. By this measure some groups were found to be living in areas of much higher density than others. Black and Italian Americans, for example, are concentrated in Omaha, whereas many persons of German and Scandinavian descent live in the farming areas with much lower population density.

Population Size. We expected, all else being equal, small population size relative to the size of other groups to be associated with a greater degree of assimilation. As mentioned, apart from pariah groups (those with very high social distance), the proportionally smaller the group, the higher the incidence of marital exogamy. Furthermore, a small group typically has fewer resources to sustain a particular social system and culture. The proportion of each group to the total population of the state provided a measure of this variable.

Causes of Group Assimilation: Findings

We have seen from our sample of Nebraskans that 8.7 percent could not name a country of origin and that another 10.0 percent named two or more countries, but could not choose one they felt closest to. These respondents could be retained in an analysis of factors associated with assimilation of individuals, but since they cannot be classified in any nationality group, they cannot be included in an examination of factors accounting for the difference in degree of assimilation among ethnic groups. Thus, the findings presented below are based on the 81.3 percent of the Nebraska sample who indicated a national origin.

As can be seen from table 5, with the exception of population size, all of the hypotheses are supported, that is, each of the independent variables is correlated with both psychological and sociocultural assimilation and in the predicted direction.[18]

TABLE 5

Product-Moment Correlations
with Psychological and Sociocultural Assimilation,
Nebraska, 1977

Independent Variables and Hypotheses	Psychological Assimilation	Sociocultural Assimilation
Primacy of Arrival: The higher the primacy the greater the assimilation.	.58	.59
Social Distance: The lower the social distance, the greater the assimilation.	-.68	-.68
Socioeconomic Status: The higher the socioeconomic status, the greater the assimilation.	.40	.60
Residential Heterogeneity: The greater the heterogeneity, the greater the assimilation.	.32	.38
Population Density: The lower the density, the greater the assimilation.	-.65	-.13
Population Size: The smaller the size, the greater the assimilation.	.22	.00

Further examination of the data shows that the relationship between population size and sociocultural assimilation was obscured by residential heterogeneity. When we statistically eliminate the effect of the latter, the correlation between population size and this dependent variable is -.45. The suppression of the relationship was due primarily to the German ethnic group. On the one hand, persons of German origin have very high residential heterogeneity, leading to a prediction of high assimilation. On the other hand, this group is proportionally the largest in the state and thus has a relatively low rate of outmarriage.

The relationship between population size and psychological assimilation is rather complex. Four of the smaller groups in the sample are also groups with very high social distance scores: American Indians and persons tracing their ancestry to Africa, Mexico, or Russia. Because of this, these groups (with the exception of the Russian group) have very low psychological assimilation. If these groups are eliminated from the analysis, and we control for the

effects of the other independent variables, the correlation (beta) is
-.27. This suggests that there may be a relationship between population size and psychological assimilation. However, if there is an
association between these two variables, it apparently applies only
under conditions of relatively low social distance.

The six independent variables together explain 69.7 percent of
the variation among ethnic groups in degree of psychological assimilation and 56.4 percent of the variation in sociocultural assimilation.
Table 6 shows the observed assimilation scores of each ethnic group
and, using multiple regression analysis, the expected scores based
on the six independent variables. Overall, knowledge of these variables adds considerably to our understanding of the forces facili-
tating and hindering assimilation. With respect to psychological
assimilation, predicted scores are within seven percentage points of
the observed scores for thirteen of the seventeen nationality groups.
Sociocultural assimilation is not predicted quite as well, but the
difference between observed and expected scores is ten or fewer
percentage points for thirteen of the groups.

We can only speculate why several of the groups are either much
more or much less assimilated than would be expected on the basis
of their social, economic, and ecological characteristics. However,
some discussion may be useful in developing a better understanding
through future research.

Since some nationality groups make up a very small proportion
of Nebraska's population, these groups are represented by small
numbers of respondents in the sample. And, all else being equal,
the smaller the number of cases, the greater the sampling error.
Thus, some of the deviations from predicted scores may simply
reflect the lack of representativeness of a particular sample. With
this caveat in mind, there are some possible substantive explanations
that can be explored.

With respect to psychological assimilation, persons of Norwegian and Swedish origins are less assimilated than expected. We believe that our measure of residential heterogeneity, based on the
twenty-six state planning and development regions, indicated that
these groups are more heterogeneous than they actually are. That
is, people in these groups are distributed among several planning
areas, but they tend to live in smaller, more concentrated communities within those larger regions. This living pattern is quite different
from that of groups such as the English, who are scattered individu-
ally throughout the state. Persons naming Russia or Scotland as their
nation of origin are more psychologically assimilated than predicted.

TABLE 6

Actual and Predicted Assimilation Scores
for Nationality Groups, Nebraska, 1977

Country	Psychological Assimilation			Sociocultural Assimilation		
	Actual	Predicted	d*	Actual	Predicted	d*
Africa	10	10	0	5	12	-7
Czechoslovakia	32	36	-4	20	25	-5
Denmark	63	56	7	28	36	-8
England and Wales	58	56	2	46	43	3
Germany	56	55	1	20	22	-2
Ireland	46	46	0	50	40	10
Italy	29	27	2	44	34	10
Netherlands	35	42	-7	31	33	-2
Norway	37	48	-11	21	40	-19
Poland	40	38	2	21	24	-3
Russia (USSR)	67	52	15	4	16	-12
Scotland	72	52	20	42	42	0
Sweden	37	58	-21	35	36	-1
Switzerland	64	57	7	49	39	10
France	56	63	-7	38	36	2
Mexico	20	22	-2	17	12	5
American Indian	41	47	-6	36	16	20

*d = difference between actual and predicted score.

We have already mentioned that in Nebraska the majority of the members of the Russian group are in fact German Russians and thus have no allegiance to or feel no sense of identity with the Russian nation. This, along with the other factors discussed above, may account for this finding. If the Scots were as highly assimilated nationally as they are in Nebraska, we could suggest that their greater-than-expected assimilation represents an overcompensation for the increasingly high social distance that has occurred since 1926. Interestingly, Scots have dropped from fourth to ninth in that measurement and by 1966 had greater social distance than such groups as the Italians and Irish. However, since the Scots rank tenth in assimilation nationally, and since we have no reason to believe that persons of Scottish origin in Nebraska are more sensitive to social distance than their counterparts nationally, we have no substantive explanation for this anomalous finding.

Persons of Norwegian or Russian origin are less socioculturally assimilated than expected. The Norwegian group in Nebraska is quite small, about 1.6 percent of the ethnically identified sample. This led to a prediction of relatively high outmarriage. However, many persons in this group live along the northeastern border of the state and thus are residentially close to the much larger Norwegian community in South Dakota. It is possible that the state line used for drawing our sample of Nebraskans imposed an artificial boundary separating a small segment of what is really a larger social community containing eligible marriage partners with Norwegian ancestry. Furthermore, there is some evidence that in Europe the greater isolation of Norwegians led to a stronger sense of group identity than among the people of Sweden and Denmark and that this has led to a stronger motivation to retain their social and cultural characteristics among Norwegian immigrants and their descendants. With reference to persons of Russian origin, it has been pointed out that the characteristics of this group led to a prediction of low marital exogamy. In fact, as can be seen from table 6, the degree of sociocultural assimilation is predicted to be comparable to that of American Indians and not much greater than that of black and Mexican Americans. However, the observed rate is even lower than expected. We return to the point that the large majority of those in our sample are German Russians. The ancestors of the respondents in our sample settled in Russia and maintained a sociocultural system and identity apart from other Russians and our respondents have maintained this tradition in Nebraska. American Indians are more socioculturally assimilated than predicted. As mentioned, the Indians in our sample do not live on reservations. Thus, at least with respect to marital exogamy, we suspect they are among the most assimilated Indians and are not representative of this ethnic group as a whole.

Summary and Conclusion

Between 1820 and 1960 over forty-one million persons immigrated into the United States, and the great majority of these people, more than 80 percent, were born in the nations of Europe. By 1900 the foreign-born and persons having at least one foreign-born parent made up 38 percent of the total population. That these people have had a demographic effect on American society is well documented. For example, immigration accounted for 28 percent of the population growth between 1890 and 1900. Although the number of immigrants entering the nation declined after 1930, the birth rate in recent years has reached an all-time low. The result is that 20 percent of the growth in the American population between 1970 and 1975 was due to immigration. One would imagine that immigration also has had a significant impact on America's social organization and cultural institutions. However, that effect is less well documented. Few empirical, comparative studies of ethnic assimilation and pluralism have been conducted and those that have been done are typically restricted either to a single group, primarily racial minorities, or to a small geographical area. Consequently, we know very little about the extent to which various nationality groups are maintaining their ethnic identities and sociocultural systems. Some scholars have suggested that ethnicity remains strong and that we continue to have a "nation of nations." Others have indicated that at least those of European origin have either assimilated completely or are on the verge of doing so.

The present study, the first in a series, has examined ethnic assimilation in Nebraska. We set out to discover how extensive assimilation has been, whether some groups are more assimilated than others, and if they are, we wanted to find out why.

Overall, the study has provided tentative answers to our questions. Assimilation has been extensive, but is far from complete. Some nationality groups, especially those from northern and western European nations, are more assimilated than others. A number of social, economic, and ecological variables account for group differences in assimilation. Among these are primacy of arrival, social distance, socioeconomic status, residential heterogeneity, population density, and population size.

Notes

The authors express their appreciation to Rumaldo Lovato for his help in carrying out the research reported in this paper, and to the Bureau of Sociological Research, University of Nebraska–Lincoln, for use of the data collected through the Nebraska Annual Social Indicators Survey (NASIS).

1. W. I. Thomas and Florian Znaniecki, *The Polish Peasant in Europe and America*, 5 vols. (Boston: Gorham Press, 1918–20) and Louis Wirth, *The Ghetto* (Chicago: University of Chicago Press, 1928).

Some of the more important early studies of black Americans are John Dollard, *Caste and Class in a Southern Town* (New York: Harper, 1937); Allison Davis, B. G. Gardner, and M. R. Gardner, *Deep South* (Chicago: University of Chicago Press, 1941); St. Clair Drake and H. R. Cayton, *Black Metropolis* (New York: Harcourt, Brace, 1945); and E. Franklin Frazier, *The Negro in the United*

States (New York: Macmillan, 1949). The forced relocation of Japanese Americans led to some research. For example, see Leonard Bloom and Ruth Riemer, *Removal and Return* (Berkeley: University of California Press, 1949). It also should be mentioned that anthropologists collected extensive ethnographic data from American Indians during these years. Representative works are in Ralph Linton, ed., *Acculturation in Seven American Indian Tribes* (New York: Appleton-Century-Crofts, 1940). Works concerned primarily with the origins of prejudice and discrimination include Gunnar Myrdal, *An American Dilemma* (New York: Harper and Row, 1944); T. W. Adorno, Else Frenkel-Brunswik, D. J. Levinson, and R. N. Sanford, *The Authoritarian Personality* (New York: Harper and Row, 1950); and Gordon W. Allport, *The Nature of Prejudice* (Reading, Mass.: Addison-Wesley, 1954).

With respect to studies of Jewish Americans, see, for example, Marshall Sklare, ed., *The Jews: Social Patterns of an American Group* (Glencoe, Ill.: Free Press, 1958). The "Yankee City" volume is W. Lloyd Warner and Leo Srole, *The Social Systems of American Ethnic Groups* (New Haven, Conn.: Yale University Press, 1945). Examples of studies of specific ethnic groups include Irvin L. Child, *Italian or American?* (New Haven, Conn.: Yale University Press, 1943), and Ruth Tuck, *Not with the Fist* (New York: Harcourt, Brace, 1946).

Nathan Glazer and Daniel P. Moynihan, *Beyond the Melting Pot* (Cambridge, Mass.: MIT Press, 1963) and Ruby Jo Reeves Kennedy, "Single or Triple Melting Pot? Intermarriage Trends in New Haven, 1870-1940," *American Journal of Sociology* 49 (January 1944): 331-39. Also see Ruby Jo Reeves Kennedy, "Single or Triple Melting Pot? Intermarriage Trends in New Haven, 1870-1950," *American Journal of Sociology* 58 (July 1952): 56-59. With the exception of some work done in Canada, the Great Plains region has not received the attention given to ethnic groups in other sections of North America. See Frederick C. Luebke, "Ethnic Group Settlement on the Great Plains," *Western Historical Quarterly* 8 (October 1977): 405-30. A recent comparative study in Canada is Leo Driedger, "Ethnic Self-Identity: A Comparison of Ingroup Evaluations," *Sociometry* 39 (June 1976): 131-41.

2. Robin M. Williams, Jr., *American Society: A Sociological Interpretation* (New York: Alfred A. Knopf, 1970), p. 13; Milton M. Gordon, *Assimilation in American Life* (New York: Oxford University Press, 1964), pp. 24-25; Leonard Dinnerstein and David M. Reimers, *Ethnic Americans* (New York: Dodd, Mead, 1975), pp. 139-40.

3. Conducted by the Bureau of Sociological Research, Department of Sociology, University of Nebraska-Lincoln, in the spring of 1977, this phase of a long-term study of quality of life in Nebraska consisted of an interview survey of a representative sample of Nebraskans eighteen years of age or older living in households. Two-thirds of the 1,867 respondents to the survey were interviewed on the telephone and the remainder were interviewed in person. Telephone respondents were drawn from a simple random sample of all households in the state with a telephone. Respondents to the personal interview were selected in a

multistage stratified area probability sample of all households in the state. For additional information, see *Nebraska Annual Social Indicators Survey*, Report No. 5, "Designs, Procedures, Instruments and Forms for the 1977 NASIS" (Lincoln, Nebr.: Bureau of Sociological Research, University of Nebraska-Lincoln, 1977).

4. Gordon has suggested that there are at least seven types or stages of assimilation. In our opinion, some of these are more usefully viewed as independent variables, factors promoting or hindering assimilation. Others appear to be parts or subprocesses of other, broader, types. Our operational measure of psychological assimilation comes closest to Gordon's "identificational assimilation" and our measure of sociocultural assimilation most closely approximates his "marital assimilation." See Milton Gordon, *Assimilation in American Life*, p. 71.

5. The term *Americanization* was introduced by William C. Smith, *Americans in the Making* (New York: Appleton-Century, 1939), and the term *Anglo-conformity* comes from Stewart C. Cole and Mildred W. Cole, *Minorities and the American Promise* (New York: Harper, 1954). *Ethnic federation* also appears in Smith's book.

6. The national data presented in tables 1 and 2 were collected by the National Opinion Research Center, *National Data Program for the Social Sciences* (Chicago: National Opinion Research Center, University of Chicago, 1977).

7. The national data presented in tables 3 and 4 were collected by Response Analysis of Princeton, New Jersey, for Clyde Z. Nunn, Harry J. Crockett, Jr., and J. Allen Williams, Jr. The study was supported by National Science Foundation Grant GS-36754X. The cases were drawn using probability sampling techniques. Details on the sampling procedure and sample characteristics can be found in Clyde Z. Nunn, Harry J. Crockett, Jr., and J. Allen Williams, Jr., *Tolerance for Nonconformity* (San Francisco: Jossey-Bass, 1978). The authors would like to thank Drs. Nunn and Crockett for their permission to use the data in this paper.

8. This does not apply in the very exceptional case of a physically isolated community, for example, the Amish, but has been rather thoroughly substantiated for more common situations. For example, see Lee Burchinal, "The Premarital Dyad and Love Involvement," *Handbook of Marriage and the Family*, ed. Harold Christensen (Chicago: Rand McNally, 1964), pp. 623-74.

9. Irene Taeuber and Conrad Taeuber, *People of the United States in the Twentieth Century* (Washington, D.C.: U.S. Bureau of the Census, 1971), and 1966-74 *Annual Reports*, U.S. Immigration and Naturalization Service (Washington, D.C.: U.S. Department of Labor).

10. The data were compiled from Wayne Wheeler, *An Almanac of Nebraska: Nationality, Ethnic, and Racial Groups* (Omaha, Nebr.: Park Bromwell, 1975).

11. American Indians and persons of African descent presented a special problem in classification. The majority of blacks arrived in Nebraska after 1900,

but through internal migration. Many American Indians were in Nebraska before 1870. Thus, in one sense, both of these groups could be seen as early arrivers. On the other hand, these peoples were prevented from participating in many aspects of the larger society. Despite government efforts to speed up the assimilation of Indians by outlawing "pagan" religious practices (1884) and allotting land to households and individuals rather than preserving tribal ownership (1887), most of the Indians were nevertheless confined to reservations. Much earlier, African cultural patterns were almost entirely destroyed or lost through the separation of group members and families and forced resocialization. However, segregation laws and other cultural norms restricted black Americans from many forms of social, if not cultural, participation. Both blacks and Indians, for example, were prevented from marrying outside their groups. The antimiscegenation law in Nebraska remained in force until struck down by the U.S. Supreme Court in 1967. Given the legal and other barriers to full participation, we decided that it made more sense theoretically to classify these groups as having arrived late, even though they were physically present in the United States at an early date. Hence, American Indians and blacks were given a low score, placing them with other more recent arrivers such as Czechs and Poles.

Realizing that our decision was somewhat arbitrary, we also analyzed the data classifying black and Indian groups as early arrivers. The findings remain quite similar and would not change our conclusions. The major difference is that our ability to explain psychological assimilation is slightly reduced in the second procedure and we explain slightly more of the variation in sociocultural or marital assimilation.

12. Gordon, *Assimilation in American Life*, specifies the absence of prejudice and the absence of discrimination as separate subprocesses or conditions associated with assimilation. Although we agree with this analytical distinction, our data do not provide sufficient information to separate these processes. However, as will be discussed below, the scale used in this study to measure prejudice or social distance asked people about their feelings regarding types of contact with various ethnic groups—a close correlate of discrimination.

13. Emory S. Bogardus, *A Forty-Year Racial Distance Study* (Los Angeles: University of Southern California, 1967). The samples used for his research were drawn from college student populations, a generally more racially and ethnically tolerant segment of the population. However, there is no reason to believe that the ordering of nationality groups would differ between students and the general population.

14. It should be mentioned that Russians ranked thirteenth out of thirty groups in 1926 and 1946. By 1956, Russians had dropped to a rank of twenty-fourth and they remained in that rank in 1966. This adds support to the suggestion made above that Russia has become a negative reference group for some Americans of Russian descent.

15. For a discussion of the research related to this point, see J. Allen Williams, Jr., Clyde Z. Nunn, and Louis St. Peter, "Origins of Tolerance," *Social Forces* 55 (December 1976): 394–408.

16. See ibid. and Melvin L. Kohn, *Class and Conformity* (Homewood, Ill.: Dorsey Press, 1969). The three components of socioeconomic status were total household income in the preceding year, the number of years of schooling completed, and occupational status. The scoring system used to classify occupational status, Duncan's SEI, is discussed in Albert J. Reiss, *Occupations and Social Status* (Glencoe, Ill.: Free Press, 1961).

17. The specific measure used was the asymmetric uncertainty coefficient. For a discussion of this measure, see Norman Nie, C. H. Hull, J. G. Jenkins, Karin Steinbrenner, and D. H. Bent, *Statistical Package for the Social Sciences* (New York: McGraw-Hill, 1975). The measure was computed for each nationality group from a contingency table, with the twenty-six planning and development regions in Nebraska as the independent variable and whether the respondent named the group being analyzed (e.g., saying Ireland if Ireland was the group being analyzed) as the dependent variable. Unfortunately, the sample size is too small to compute reliable coefficients at the county, city, and neighborhood levels. We hope to be able to measure residential heterogeneity at these levels as more data are collected, since they more accurately portray the diverse living experiences of different ethnic groups.

18. Several of the independent variables are highly correlated, causing their standardized regression coefficients (betas) to be highly susceptible to the multicollinearity problem. Therefore, with one exception as discussed below, betas are not presented. For a discussion of the general problem with data of this sort, see Hubert M. Blalock, Jr., "Correlated Independent Variables, the Problem of Multicollinearity," *Social Forces* 42 (December 1963): 233-37. It should be pointed out that the presence of multicollinearity does not have a substantial effect on the total explained variance and the comparison of predicted and actual scores introduced in table 6, below.

The Contributors

Bradley H. Baltensperger is an associate professor of geography at Michigan Technological University. He has published several articles in historical geography.

Josef J. Barton is an associate professor of history and urban affairs at Northwestern University. He is the author of *Peasants and Strangers: Italians, Rumanians, and Slovaks in an American City, 1890–1950* (1975), a study of immigrant society in Cleveland, Ohio.

Miguel A. Carranza is an assistant professor of sociology at the University of Nebraska–Lincoln. He is the coauthor of several articles on ethnic minority relations in sociological journals.

Kathleen Neils Conzen is an associate professor of history at the University of Chicago. She is the author of *Immigrant Milwaukee, 1836–1860: Accommodation and Community in a Frontier City* (1976).

Linda Dégh is a professor of folklore at Indiana University. Born and educated in Hungary, she has taught at Indiana since 1964. Her publications include *Folktales of Hungary* (1965), *Folktales and Society* (1969), and *People in the Tobacco Belt: Four Lives* (1975). She is currently president of the Fellows of the American Folklore Society.

Raymond J. DeMallie is an associate professor of anthropology at Indiana University. He has published several articles on the Sioux and other Great Plains tribes in historical and anthropological journals.

Bruce M. Garver is an associate professor of history at the University of Nebraska at Omaha. He is the author of *The Young Czech Party, 1874–1901: The Emergence of a Multi-Party System* (1978).

Arrell Morgan Gibson is George Lynn Cross Research professor of history at the University of Oklahoma. Among his books are *The*

232   *Contributors*

Kickapoos: Lords of the Middle Border (1963) and *The Chicka-saws* (1971).

John A. Hostetler is a professor of anthropology at Temple University. Among his many publications are *Amish Society* (rev. ed. 1968) and *Hutterite Society* (1974).

David R. Johnson is an associate professor of sociology at the University of Nebraska–Lincoln. He is the author of several studies in ethnicity and demography in the *American Sociological Review* and the *Social Science Quarterly*.

Terry G. Jordan is a professor of geography at North Texas State University. His publications include *German Seed in Texas Soil: Immigrant Farmers in Nineteenth-Century Texas* (1966).

Timothy J. Kloberdanz is an instructor in anthropology at North Dakota State University. He is author of several articles on the culture of German Russians in both Europe and America.

Frederick C. Luebke is a professor of history and holds a courtesy appointment as professor of geography at the University of Nebraska–Lincoln. He is the author of *Immigrants and Politics: The Germans of Nebraska, 1880–1900* (1969) and *Bonds of Loyalty: German Americans in World War I* (1974).

Robert C. Ostergren is an assistant professor of geography at the University of Wisconsin–Madison. He is the author of several articles on Swedish immigration and settlement.

J. Allen Williams, Jr., is a professor of sociology at the University of Nebraska–Lincoln. His publications include *Tolerance for Non-conformity* (1978), monographs on low-income housing, and articles on ethnic minority relations.

Index

Aboriginals. *See* American Indians

Acculturation, 54, 171, 211; of American Indians, 27–29, 47; in burial practices, 121–24, 127; of Czech immigrants, 163–64, 165; of Czech and Mexican immigrants in Texas, 198, 201–2; of Volga Germans, xxii, xxiv, 54–69; among Hungarian Lowlanders in Canada, 140; in Nebraska immigrants' agricultural practices, 170–88; religious, 109–27; resistance to, 124–25; rural, 3–5. *See also* Assimilation

Agricultural practices: of Old Order Amish, 93, 97, 98, 101–2, 104; of Czech freethinkers, 151, 153; of Czech and Mexican immigrants in Texas, 192–202; of Volga Germans, 65–66, 67; of immigrants compared, xxvii; of immigrants in Nebraska, 170–88

Alexander II, 60

American Indians, xiv–xv, xxix; abuses of, 33–34; acculturation of, 27–29, 47; assimilation of, 21, 22, 27, 217, 224; cultural strength of, 19, 21; diplomatic tactics of, 48–51; ethnic migrations of, 19, 21; parallels with European immigrants, 21; and federal government, 21–36; and Indian Territory, 25–27, 30–31, 34–36; removal of, xv, 22–23, 25–26, 29–31; at treaty councils, xv–xvi, 38–51

American Society: A Sociological Interpretation (Williams), 210–11

Amish. *See* Old Order Amish

Arapahoes, 36, 41, 43–44

Arikaras, 41

Arkansas Territory, 24, 26

Assimilation, xxvii–xxviii, 211–12; of American Indians, 22, 27–29, 47; of Old Order Amish in Great Plains, 101–2, 103, 104, 105; Amish response to, 92, 93; factors contributing to, 217–20; of immigrants in Nebraska, 212–25; of rural immigrants, 3–4; statistical findings on, 220–24. *See also* Acculturation

Assimilation in American Life (Gordon), 211

Assiniboins, 41

Authon-ish-ah, 43

Barbour, James, 22, 27

Battle of Horseshoe Bend, 28

Bear Rib, 50

Benton, Thomas, 32

Beyond the Melting Pot (Glazer and Moynihan), 210

Big Yancton, 45

Bittner, Bartoš, 151

Blackfeet, 19

Black Hawk, 44–45

Black Hawk War, 23

Blacks, xxii, xxix

Blue Earth, 44

Bogardus, Emory, 218

Bontreger, Eli J., 95, 103–4

Brown, Robert H., 6

Brož, Jan Štěpán, 151

Brunner, Edmund deS., 1, 2

233

Calhoun, John C., 25–26
Canada: Volga Germans in, 64–65; Hungarian immigrants in, 130–44
Čapek, Tomáš, 151, 155, 162
Cass, Lewis, 32–33
Cather, Willa, xi, xiii
Catherine the Great, 55
Cherokees, 23, 24, 26, 27–28
Cheyennes, 19, 36, 41
Chicanos, xxix. *See also* Hispanos; Mexican immigrants
Chickasaws, 28
Choctaws, 23, 24, 26, 28
Christner, Samuel, 104
Clark, William, 22–23, 29
Colorado: immigrants in, xxi; Old Order Amish in, 96–99
Comanches, 19, 36
Communal activity: among Old Order Amish, 93; among Czech freethinkers, 153, 155–63; and ethnic identity, 11–12; among Hungarian immigrants, 131; among Mexican and Czech immigrants in Texas, 199–200, 201
Conflict: in clustered settlements, 11, 17 n. 28; intercultural, 38–40
Creeks, 28
Crows, 41
Cultural maintenance, xii, xiv; in immigrants' agricultural practices, 187–88; among Old Order Amish, 92, 93, 105; among Czech freethinkers, 155–63, 165; of Czech immigrants in Texas, 197, 199; among Texas Germans, 124–25; among Volga Germans, 59, 67, 68; among Hungarian immigrants, 131–44
Curti, Merle, 4
Cut Nose, 43
Czech immigrants, 191–202; as freethinkers, xxvi, 147–65

Delawares, 23
DeSmet, P. J., 42
Dinnerstein, Leonard, 211
Dutch Reformed groups, 5–6

Eagle Drinking, 51
Engel, Emmanuel, 162
English immigrants, 6–7
Erickson, Charlotte, 6–7
Ethnicity: academic interest in, xi–xii, 210–11, 225; in clustered settlements, 11–13; among Lowlander and Highlander Hungarian Canadians, 134–42, 143–44; identifying and measuring, 212; as expressed in occupation choices of Czech and Mexican immigrants in Texas, 192, 202. *See also* Religious ethnicity; Rural ethnicity
Extinction: of Old Order Amish communities, 94–100

Family: contributing to assimilation, 216–17; as Czech immigrant labor reserve, 196–98; in rural life, 9–11
Five Civilized Tribes, 27–32
Foxes, 23
Freethinkers: Czech, xxvi, 147–65; German, 113–14, 116
Frightening Bear, 44
Frog, 47

General Allotment Act, 36
Geringer, August, 150, 162
German immigrants: agricultural practices of, 173–88; assimilation of, 221; clustering of, 7, 11; in Texas, xxv, 109–27; religious acculturation among, 109–27; stability of, 5
Ghetto, The (Wirth), 210
Glazer, Nathan, 210
Gordon, Milton, 211
Great Plains: aboriginal colonization of, 19–36; Old Order Amish environmental problems with, 95, 96, 97, 98, 99–100, 104; boundaries of, xiii; and Czech freethinkers, 151; Czech immigrants' distribution in, 151–52; ethnoreligion in, xxv–xxvi; environment's effect on ethnicity in, xxix; as Great American Desert, xv, 21, 26; promotion of, 21; Volga Germans' adaptations to, 60–65

Great Plains, The (Webb), xi
Great Plains in Transition (Kraenzel), xi–xii
Gros Ventres (Hidatsas), 41

Handlin, Oscar, 3
Hansen, Marcus Lee: on assimilation, 4; on chain migration, 7–9
Harney, W. S., 50–51
Harrison, William Henry, 22
Havlíček, Karel, 149
Hispanos, xxi–xxii. *See also* Chicanos; Mexican immigrants
Hitchcock, Ethan Allen, 33–34
Hudson, John, 8, 74
Hungarian immigrants: regional ethnicity among, 134–42, 143–44; religious ethnicity among, 130–44; religious life of, xxv–xxvi
Hus, John, 149
Hutterites, 93–94

Immigrant Farmers and Their Children (Brunner), 2
Immigrants: in agriculture, 2; distribution of, xvii, xix, xxx–xxxi; nineteenth-century, xvi–xxi; and population growth, 224–25
Indian removal, xv, 22–23, 25–26, 29–31
Indians. *See* American Indians
Indian Territory, 25–27, 30–31, 34–36
Iron Nation, 47
Iseo, 47
Iška, František, 164

Jackson, Andrew, 28; and Indian removal, 29–31
Janák, Jan, 162
Jefferson, Thomas, 22
Jelen, František, 157–58
John, Henry J., 165
Johnson, Hildegard Binder, 7
Johnson, Robert W., 35
Jonáš, Karel, 161
Jumper, 31
Jung, Václav Alois, 151, 155

Kansas: Old Order Amish in, 99–

103; blacks in, xxii; Czech immigrants in, 152; immigrants in, xx; Volga Germans in, 61–63
Kansas Indians, 29
Kansas-Nebraska Act, 35
Kansas Territory, 26
Kennedy, R.J.R., 210
Kickapoos, 23, 26, 34
Kiowas, 19, 36, 48–50
Klácel, Ladimir, 149
Kohl, J. G., 58
Kovandová, Anna, 161
Kraenzel, Carl, xi–xii
Kral, J. J., 162
Kvíták, F. J., 160

Lame Deer, 47
Latitude pull, 61
Little Owl, 43–44
Lone Horn, 47, 50
Lone Wolf, 48–49, 51
Luebke, Frederick, 4

McQuillan, D. Aiden, 6
Mandans, 41
Manypenny, George W., 35
Masaryk, T. G., 162, 164–65
Mast, Daniel E., 101
Meinig, Donald W., 109
Mexican immigrants, 191–202. *See also* Chicanos; Hispanos
Micanopy, 31
Michigan: rural family life in, 11
Migration: chains, 7–9; explained by information flow, 81; to South Dakota, 73–90
Mík, Josef, 157–58
Minnesota: clustering in, 6–7; ethnic fading in, 9–10
Mintz, Sidney, 198
Missouris, 19
Missouri Territory, 24
Mitchell, D. D., 41–42, 43, 44
Monroe, James, 25
Montana: Old Order Amish in, 96; immigrants in, xxi
Moynihan, Daniel, 210

Náprstek, Vojta, 149
Nebraska: immigrants' agricultural practices in, 170–88; Old Order Amish in, 94–95; assimilation in, xxvii–xxviii, 212–25; Czech immigrants in, 150–52, 154–55; immigrants in, xx; rural family life in, 11; Volga Germans in, 61
New Mexico: immigrants in, xxi
North Dakota: Old Order Amish in, 95; Czech immigrants in, 152–53; immigrants in, xi, xviii, xxix, xxxii; migration chains in, 8; migration to, 74

Oklahoma: blacks in, xxii; Czech immigrants in, 153; immigrants in, xx–xxi
Oklahoma Territory, 36
Old Crow, 47
Old Order Amish: and agriculture, 93; and assimilation, 92, 93, 101–2, 103, 104, 105; cultural maintenance of, 105; early extinct Great Plains settlements of, 94–100; surviving Great Plains settlements of, 100–103; vulnerability of, xxiv–xv
One That Killed the White Buffalo Cow, 47
Osages, 19, 23, 29
Osceola, 31
Ostergren, Robert, 6
Otos, 19

Painted Bear, 45
Palda, Lev J., 161
Park, Robert, 4
Peterson, Albert J., Jr., 62–63
Polish immigrants, 9
Polish Peasant in Europe and America, The (Thomas and Znaniecki), 210
Poncas, 19
Potawatomis, 23, 34
Price, Richard, 198

Quapaws, 23, 29

Racial groups: distribution of, xxiii

Reimers, David, 211
Religion: and clustering, 7, 90; among Mexican and Czech immigrants in Texas; 199–201; and settlement patterns, 114–19; in South Dakota Swedish settlement, 76, 78, 90
Religious acculturation: among German immigrants, 109–27
Religious ethnicity, xxiv–xxvi; in church architecture, 119–21; among Texas Germans, 109–27; impact of Great Plains on, xxvi; among Hungarian immigrants in Canada, 130–44
Rice, John, 6
Rising Sun, 51
Rokůsek, Šimon, 157–58
Rolle, Andrew, 3–4
Rölvaag, Ole, xi, xiii
Rosewater, Edward, 150
Rosický, Jan, 150, 151, 155, 160, 161, 162
Rural ethnicity, xiv; assimilationist interpretation of, 3–4; clustered settlement patterns and, 5–8; communal activity and, 11–12; family life and, 10–11; migration chains and, 7–9; overlooked, 1–2; distinguished from urban ethnicity, 5
Russian-German immigrants: agricultural practices of, 173–88
Russian immigrants: assimilation of, 215–16, 223, 224

Sacs, 23
Sandoz, Mari, xi
Scandinavian immigrants: assimilation of, 222, 224; settlement of, 11. *See also* Swedish immigrants
Schafer, Joseph, 3, 4
Seminoles, 28, 31
Šerpán, Stanislav, 151, 160–62
Settlement patterns, 5–6; and assimilation, 219; and chain migration, 7–9; of Czech and Mexican immigrants in Texas, 192–98; explained by geographic origin, 88; and land availability, 7, 8–9; by sect, 114–

16; of Swedes in South Dakota; village-church, 116–19
Shoshones, 41
Sioux, 19; and 1851 treaty council, 41, 43, 44–45
South Dakota: Czech immigrants in, 152–53; immigrants in, xviii, xx; Swedish migration to, 73–90
Speek, Peter, 2, 4
Spotted Horse, 47
Stake in the Land, A (Speek), 2
Stokes Commission, 33
Swanton, John R., 33, 34
Swedish immigrants: agricultural practices of, 173–88; in South Dakota, xxiv, 73–90; cultural heterogeneity of, 78, 80. *See also* Scandinavian immigrants

Tecumseh, 22, 28
Ten Bears, 51
Tenskwatawa, 22
Texas: agriculture and immigrants in, 190–202; German immigrants in, 109–27; immigrants in, xxi
Texas Germans, 109–27; settlement patterns of, 5–6

Thomas, W. I., 210
"Trail of Tears," 31
Treaty councils, xv–xvi; intercultural conflict at, 38–40
Turner, Frederick Jackson, 3

Vojan, Jaroslav E. S., 162, 163, 164
Volga Germans: acculturation of, xxii, xxiv, 56–59, 62–63, 66–69; in the Russian steppes, 55–60; on North American Great Plains, 60–65; in South American pampas, 65–68

War of 1812, 22–23
Webb, Walter Prescott, xi, xiii
White Bird, 48–49
Wildcat, 31
Williams, Robin, 210–11
Winnebagos, 23
Wirth, Louis, 210
Wolf, Eric R., 59
Wyandots, 23, 34
Wyoming: immigrants in, xxi

Yoder, Jacob M., 96

Zdrůbek, František, 150, 155
Znaniecki, Florian, 210